EXPLORING

REVELATION

A Verse by Verse Exposition
Of the Book of Revelation

DR. BILL SHADE

EXPLORING REVELATION
By: Dr. Bill Shade

ISBN- 9781099457678

Printed in the United States of America

Visit our website at: BillShade.org

GLOBE
PUBLISHERS

Dedication

*To my grandchildren
and my great grandchildren –
may they come to love the Book
and the Author as much as I do.*

*And to those faithful students
who permitted me to be their
teacher and who patiently studied
with us through the greatest
prophetic book of all time –
The Book of Revelation*

CONTENTS

INTRODUCTION:

The book of Revelation is, without a doubt, the most important and strategic book we could possibly study as we rapidly approach the final days of this age. This book is God's precious revelation to His own dear children of the things that are taking shape all around us. It is His way of illuminating our future and encouraging our present. What could possibly be more important that that?

After a lifetime of studying and teaching the book of Revelation in colleges and classrooms, I made a proposition to my Sunday School class. It was, that we would work our way through the book of Revelation, without being limited by time or class schedules. We called our study, *Exploring Revelation*.

Webster defines "Explore" as follows: "to stretch or reach, as with prying curiosity. To view with care; to examine closely. To scrutinize; to inquire; to examine with a view to discovering truth." That is exactly what we did as we pursued this study.

We studied the text word for word, phrase by phrase, and thought by thought. We attempted to leave no textual question unaddressed, no problem ignored, no passage passed over. To fulfill our stated goal of exploring this book, we attempted to scrutinize every corner of it carefully and prayerfully with a view to discovering the truth that is here for us.

Of course, we inquired as to what those before us have said about the text, but our primary area of search was the Sacred Text itself. We wanted to allow the Text to speak clearly and to teach us, so we searched and examined closely, scrutinized, inquired with care and examined closely with a view to discovering truth.

We attempted to "mine the text" so that we could discover the precious gems of truth contained therein. What resulted was the most satisfying, thorough exploration of the book of Revelation that I have ever done, and our students would all agree.

As I sat down to share our study with you, the reader, I will follow the same path taken in our class study. Our main source of information will continue to be the Text, the Text and the Text. We will only examine the various theological opinions about this book as they relate to the interpretation of a given passage. Our interest is not in what other schools of interpretation thought or taught, but in what the Text says, taken in its usual sense as we would examine any other writing. While we recognize that the book of Revelation is filled with symbols, we believe that each symbol represents something that is literal and we will rely on other Scripture to interpret that reality for us, as Paul exhorted, "comparing spiritual things with spiritual" (1 Corinthians 2:13).

Our approach will be based on our complete confidence in the inspired, inerrant, preserved Word of God, and we shall apply that respect to the text and be willing to hear what it says and believe it. We shall therefore approach it in a literal-grammatical/historic manner. In other words, we will assume literal interpretation unless some other approach is clearly indicated.

We will examine the grammar carefully and try to ascertain, as best we can, the intent of the writer. And we will attempt to place what we read in its historic context so that we do not force our own cultural concepts into a foreign setting. All this we will attempt to do as God enables us.

My prayer for you the reader is that you will find here, not only help for difficult passages and questions found in this book, but encouragement, strength and a deep sense of joy as you study with us this final book of the New Testament canon, the book of Revelation.

BACKGROUND

The text itself sets the background for the book. The human author is the beloved Apostle John, also the writer of the Gospel which bears his name and the three epistles called 1, 2 and 3 John. Although John's authorship of Revelation has been denied by skeptics, it was fully accepted and embraced by the early church fathers and unquestioned until the third century.

John identifies himself in the very first verse, but does not tell us anything about his situation until verse 9 where he writes, *I John, who also am your brother, and companion in tribulation, and in the kingdom and patience of Jesus Christ, was in the isle that is called Patmos, for the word of God, and for the testimony of Jesus Christ.*

We know therefore, from the text itself, where John was and why he was there. He was on the isle called Patmos. Smith Bible Dictionary describes Patmos as follows; "A rugged and bare island in the Aegean Sea, 20 miles south of Samos, and 24 miles west of Asia Minor. Patmos is divided into two nearly equal parts, a northern and a southern, by a very narrow isthmus where, on the east side, are the harbor and the town."

Because of its rocky, barren and desolate nature the Roman government used the island as a place of banishment for criminals who were compelled to work the mines of the island. Further, John tells us that he was there *for the word of God, and for the testimony of Jesus Christ.* In other words, he had been banished to that location because of his faithful witness.

Historic sources tell us that John had served as pastor to the church at Ephesus, and was well known to the other churches of western Asia, but was placed under arrest and exiled to the

Island of Patmos by the Emperor Domitian (pro. duh-**mish**-uh n) in 95 AD. Domitian died by assassination the following year (96 AD), and tradition says that John was eventually released and returned to his pastorate in Ephesus where he died. A traditional gravesite is marked among the ruins to this day. He was apparently the only one of the original "twelve" that was not martyred.

Some overall observations may be helpful. It has been observed that the writer (John), is writing from several vantage points.

1. From Revelation 1:1 – 20 (Chapter one) John is on the earth, looking at a vision of Christ.

2. From Revelation 2:1 – 3:22, he remains on the earth and is delivering a message to the seven Churches of Asia among which he had worked.

3. From Revelation 4:1 – 22:21, he is "in the Spirit"(4:2); and able to behold things which are future, both on earth and in heaven.

Chapter 1   The Recorder, The Revelator, & the Recipients

Revelation 1:1-11

Rev 1:1 *The Revelation of Jesus Christ, which God gave unto him, to shew unto his servants things which must shortly come to pass; and he sent and signified it by his angel unto his servant John:*

The book of Revelation opens differently than most other Epistles of the New Testament. The Salutation does not come until verse four. Instead, the writer explains what this book is all about. It is a Revelation, literally a "revealing" of things, both present and future, as God sees them, and that revelation is given by Christ to the churches, through the Apostle John.

Those opening words ought to thrill every true believer. God has not left us in the dark concerning our present or our future. The Apostle Paul once wrote, *But ye, brethren, are not in darkness, that that day should overtake you as a thief* (1 Thessalonians 5:4). Rather, it has pleased God to allow us who are His own to see it all – and that is what this book is all about.

The first verse indicates, not that Jesus Christ is being revealed (although He is revealed throughout the book), but that God has given to Jesus Christ a revelation to give to the Church through His prophet and servant John.

This revelation is of **things which must _shortly_ come to pass.** The word "shortly" is (Gr. τάχος tachos; a *brief* space (of time), that is, in *haste:* - + quickly, + speedily.

It implies not that it will happen soon, but that, when it happens, it will happen with great rapidity.

he sent and <u>signified it</u> by his angel; The word translated "signified," is (Gr. **sēmainō** from sēmeion; an *indication*, especially supernaturally: - miracle, sign, token, wonder). So John is alerting us to the fact that the book of Revelation will be filled with signs and symbols. This does not in any way imply that the things seen are not real, but that the reality will be couched in symbols.

The encouraging fact about Biblical symbolism is that the interpreter is not left to his own imagination to try to identify the meaning. In almost all cases, the symbol or sign, or wonder is interpreted for us somewhere, either in the immediate context, or in some previous Biblical vision. Just as Christ carefully interpreted His parables to His disciples, God has given us the clues necessary to interpret most every sign we will meet.

Rev 1:2 *Who bare record of the word of God, and of the testimony of Jesus Christ, and of all things that he saw.*

John testifies that he faithfully recorded what he heard (the word of God), what he received (the testimony of Jesus Christ), and what he saw (the visions of things to come). So we should be looking then for <u>three types of revelation</u> as we pursue our study: (1) what he heard, (2) what he received or was taught about the revelation, and (3) what he saw.

Rev 1:3 *Blessed is he that readeth, and they that hear the words of this prophecy, and keep those things which are written therein:*

Kenneth Wuest has a most interesting translation of the "Blessing" in this verse; vis. "*Spiritually prosperous is he who reads in the worship assembly of the local church and spiritually prosperous are those who hear the words of this prophecy and observe the things which in it have been written.*"

If nothing else, this Blessing indicates that the Revelation is not just for the seven churches that will initially receive it, but for all of the Church throughout the age.

*for the time is **at hand***. (Gr. ἐγγύς; eggus): From a primary verb to *squeeze* or *throttle*; near, nigh (at hand, unto), ready. Wuest translates this; *for the strategic, epochal season is imminent.* The central idea of imminence is not so much immediacy, but that it can occur at any moment. That is what is declared here, and it is in harmony with all other New Testament statements concerning the last days. The things that are written may occur at any moment. No wonder we are warned to *watch therefore, for you know not what hour your Lord will come* (Matthew 24:42).

The Salutation & Introduction 1:4 – 6

Rev. 1:4-6 *John, to the seven churches which are in Asia: Grace be unto you, and peace, from him which is, and which was, and which is to come; and from the seven Spirits which are before his throne; And from Jesus Christ, who is the faithful witness, and the first begotten of the dead, and the prince of the kings of the earth. Unto him that loved us, and washed us from our sins in his own blood, And hath made us kings and priests unto God and his Father; to him be glory and dominion for ever and ever. Amen.*

We come to the salutation which encompasses the next three verses: Note as we have already observed that this revelatory epistle was intended first to the seven churches in the region of western Asia with which John had ministry contact. As viewed on a map, the seven churches form a sort of half-circle, beginning with Ephesus, then northeast to Smyrna, south to Pergamos and ending with Laodicea (see map pp. 18).

Grace be unto you, and peace,

This blessing, which is common throughout the New Testament writings, is always in that order - first grace and then peace. It is the order of Christian experience – you cannot have the peace of God until you know the grace of God.

from him which is, and which was, and which is to come; and from the seven Spirits which are before his throne; And from Jesus Christ,
In this phrase it should be noted that the Triune nature of God is clearly set forth. The One who *is and was and is to come,* describes God in His essential essence and would, in this context refer to the Father. *The seven Spirits,* is a reference to the seven-fold fullness of the Holy Spirit as revealed in Isaiah 11:2, *and from Jesus Christ,* obviously references the Son. Hence the source of all Grace and all Peace is none other than the Triune God in His fullness. Now John goes on and has some further things to say about the Son:

who is the faithful witness,
Jesus Christ was always and in everything He said and did, *the faithful witness.* His testimony of God, of man, of spiritual realities, of the earth, of the Old Testament Scriptures, was always and absolutely true.

Furthermore, when brought before Pilate, Paul says of Him, *who before Pontius Pilate witnessed a good confession;* (1 Timothy 6:13). His word was always reliable because He is Himself *the Truth.*   To Nicodemus He said; *Truly, truly I say unto thee, We speak that we do know, and testify that we have seen; and ye receive not our witness. If I have told you earthly things, and ye believe not, how shall ye believe, if I tell you of heavenly things* (John 3:11, 12)?

and the first begotten of the dead, The phrase, *First begotten of the dead*, has a deeper meaning than might be at first assumed when reading it. Not only was He the first to experience resurrection to the fullest extent, having a body of flesh and bone (Luke 24:39), but with a new source of life, i.e., the spirit rather than blood, but He became as such the Head, or Firstborn, of a new creation. Paul develops this idea in the following passage.

> It is sown a natural body; it is raised a spiritual body. There is a natural body, and there is a spiritual body.
>
> And so it is written, The first man Adam was made a living soul; the last Adam (Christ) was made a quickening spirit. Howbeit that was not first which is spiritual, but that which is natural; and afterward that which is spiritual. The first man is of the earth, earthy: the second man is the Lord from heaven. As is the earthy, such are they also that are earthy: and as is the heavenly, such are they also that are heavenly. And as we have borne the image of the earthy, we shall also bear the image of the heavenly (1 Corinthians 15:44-49).

This passage sets forth not only the distinction between the body we now have and that which we shall one day have, but the distinction between what we now are and what we shall be. We are "living souls," "earthy," but when we are saved we become new creations in Christ Jesus, we become "spiritual" and "heavenly." And while that will not be fully expressed until our own resurrection, we are part of a distinct generation of which Jesus Christ Himself is the Federal Head.

As naturally born we are all children of Adam who is the Federal Head of the old creation, condemned and under the curse of sin. But when we are born again, we are children of a new Father, we have the life of God, and Jesus Christ is the Head of that new creation. *The Firstborn from the dead*, means that Christ is the Elder brother, the one with all the rights of inheritance in a completely new family. He holds the place of honor.

and the <u>prince</u> of the kings of the earth.

The word translated "prince" is (Gr. ἄρχων archōn; *first* (in rank or power): - chief ruler). Hence Christ is not only head over a new creation, but He is the chief Ruler, the One who holds the right of complete sovereignty over the earth.

Unto him that loved us,
It is wonderfully significant that His first impulse toward us was love. It was love that brought Him to earth for us, that put Him on a cross for us and that compels Him now to seek for us and intercede for us, and minister to us through His Spirit.

and washed us from our sins in his own blood,
There is nothing that can give confidence to the saints of God like the blood of Jesus Christ. His blood answers to every charge a Holy God, a righteous Law, or a vicious adversary could bring against us. The saints rejoice in the absolute assurance that *the blood of Jesus Christ God's Son cleanses us from all sin* (1 John 1:7).

And hath made us <u>kings and priests</u> unto God and his Father;
The passage actually says (lit. <u>made us a kingdom of priests</u>). In Exodus God had declared to Moses:

> *Now therefore, if ye will obey my voice indeed, and keep my covenant, then ye shall be a peculiar treasure unto me above all people: for all the earth is mine: And ye shall be unto me a kingdom of priests, and an holy nation. These are the words which thou shalt speak unto the children of Israel* (Exodus 19:5, 6).

Israel failed to achieve this high and lofty position, because they failed the one condition, "*if ye will obey my voice indeed, and keep my covenant.*" Having failed almost as soon as the law was enacted (Exodus 32), the Priesthood was shut up to the tribe of Levi and the family of Aaron. In contrast, Peter writes:

But ye are a chosen generation, a royal priesthood, an holy nation, a peculiar people; that ye should shew forth the praises of him who hath called you out of darkness into his marvelous light (1 Peter 2:9).

What was impossible under the conditional covenant of the Law, has been accomplished and feely bestowed on us who have partaken of His Grace. But think of John's condition as he wrote this – he was a prisoner on a desolate island, yet his faith laid hold of his exalted position in Christ.

to him be glory and dominion for ever and ever. Amen.
John ascribes glory and dominion to the Lord Jesus Christ, "to the ages of the ages!" (Young's translation) This book opens with the same declaration which it will affirm as it closes, all glory and all dominion belong to the Divine Man, the Lord Jesus Christ.

The Announcement 1:7 (The Theme of the Book)

Rev 1:7 *Behold, he cometh <u>with clouds</u>; and every eye shall see him, and they also which pierced him: and all kindreds of the earth <u>shall wail</u> because of him. Even so, Amen*.

The theme of Christ's coming is central to the entire book. Here He is said to "come with clouds." That is not without significance. Daniel had first seen this event in chapter seven of his book.

> *I saw in the night visions, and, behold, one like the Son of man came with the clouds of heaven, and came to the Ancient of days, and they brought him near before him. And there was given him dominion, and glory, and a kingdom, that all people, nations, and languages, should serve him: his dominion is an everlasting dominion, which shall not pass away, and his kingdom that which shall not be destroyed* (Daniel 7:13, 14).

The idea of clouds being associated with Deity was well established in the Old Testament Scriptures. The Psalmist had written; *Clouds and darkness are round about him: righteousness and judgment are the habitation of his throne* (Psalm 97:2). It was Christ's own reference to the clouds that infuriated the High Priest and brought him to cry, "blasphemy!."

> *Jesus saith unto him, Thou hast said: nevertheless I say unto you, Hereafter shall ye see the Son of man sitting on the right hand of power, and coming in the <u>clouds</u> of heaven* (Matthew 26:64).

And when He ascended into glory, we read; *And when he had spoken these things, while they beheld, he was taken up; and a cloud received him out of their sight* (Acts 1:9), and the angels testified that, *this same Jesus, which is taken up from you into heaven, shall so come in like manner as ye have seen him go into heaven* (Acts 1:11). The declaration, *Behold, he cometh with clouds,* therefore, is not only stating a fact, but declaring in the strongest terms His deity. Some other passages where clouds are associated with His coming are:

> **Matthew 24:30** *And then shall appear the sign of the Son of man in heaven: and then shall all the tribes of the earth mourn, and they shall see the Son of man coming in the <u>clouds</u> of heaven with power and great glory.*

> **Mark 13:26** *And then shall they see the Son of man coming in the <u>clouds</u> with great power and glory.*

> **Mark 14:62** *And Jesus said, I am: and ye shall see the Son of man sitting on the right hand of power, and coming in the <u>clouds</u> of heaven.*

The text says that when the world shall see Him, they *shall wail*, literally, beat their breasts, demonstrating extreme anguish because they recognize He is coming as Lord and Judge.

The Testimony of Jesus Christ 1:8

Rev 1:8 *I am Alpha and Omega, the beginning and the ending, saith the Lord, which is, and which was, and which is to come, the Almighty*.

Complete disclosure! Everything God has to say to us is said in Him. He was not only *in the beginning*, He was the beginning! I AM (*is, and was, and is to come*)." Alpha is the first letter of the Greek alphabet as Omega is the last. Between these two letters is contained all that can be written, all that can be said, all that can be revealed.

The word translated *the Almighty;* is (Gr. παντοκράτωρ; pantokratōr; the *all ruling*, that is, *God* (as absolute and universal *sovereign*): - Almighty, Omnipotent. That sums up the matter – He has total and universal authority. Before this book is ended, He will exercise that authority as, *the kingdoms of this world are become the kingdoms of our Lord, and of his Christ; and he shall reign for ever and ever* (Revelation 11:15).

John's Introduction: Rev. 1:9-11 *I John, who also am your brother, and companion in tribulation, and in the kingdom and patience of Jesus Christ, was in the isle that is called Patmos, for the word of God, and for the testimony of Jesus Christ. I was in the Spirit on the Lord's day, and heard behind me a great voice, as of a trumpet, Saying, I am Alpha and Omega, the first and the last: and, What thou seest, write in a book, and send it unto the seven churches which are in Asia; unto Ephesus, and unto Smyrna, and unto Pergamos, and unto Thyatira, and unto Sardis, and unto Philadelphia, and* *unto Laodicea.*

I John, Although a common name he is well recognized. The youngest of the Disciples of Jesus, he is now the oldest and the only surviving Apostle.

He is recognized as the writer of the fourth Gospel, and of the three Epistles of John. He has served as Pastor in Ephesus and the surrounding area (as we have previously noted), and therefore no further identification is needed. This book is initially addressed to the seven churches of that region and all were intimately familiar with the Apostle John.

Henry Chadwick, writing for Encyclopedia Brittanica has the following to say about the Apostle:

"John was the son of Zebedee, a Galilean fisherman, and Salome. John and his brother James were among the first disciples called by Jesus. In The Gospel According to Mark he is always mentioned after James and was no doubt the younger brother. His mother was among those women who ministered to the circle of disciples.

James and John were called Boanerges, or "sons of thunder," by Jesus, perhaps because of some character trait such as the zeal exemplified in Mark 9:38 and Luke 9:54, when John and James wanted to call down fire from heaven to punish the Samaritan towns that did not accept Jesus.

John and his brother, together with St. Peter, formed an inner nucleus of intimate disciples. John's authoritative position in the church after the Resurrection is shown by his visit with St. Peter to Samaria to lay hands on the new converts there. It is to Peter, James (not the brother of John but "the brother of Jesus"), and John that St. Paul subsequently recited his conversion and mission for their recognition.

John's subsequent history is obscure and passes into the uncertain mists of legend. At the end of the 2nd century, Polycrates, bishop of Ephesus, claims that John's tomb is at Ephesus. That John died in Ephesus is also stated by St. Irenaeus bishop of Lyon 180 CE, who says John wrote his Gospel and letters at Ephesus and Revelation from the Isle at Patmos. During the 3rd century the church of Ephesus claimed to possess the original autograph of the Fourth Gospel." **(Encyclopedia Brittanica)**

The next phrase, **who also am your brother, and companion in tribulation,** implies that most of those to whom he was writing would have, or were at that time going through some form of persecution. *For unto you it is given in the behalf of Christ, not only to believe on him, but also to suffer for his sake* (Philippians 1:29).

But the next phrase was the antidote for despair: **and in the kingdom;** the early Church always looked forward to the Kingdom. They were assured that even as they had suffered they would most certainly "rule and reign with Jesus Christ." It was not only heaven that they looked for, but the final triumph of their once crucified Savior over the earth.

The next phrase is most illuminating; **the patience of Jesus Christ.** Just as we must wait, so He is waiting. The writer to Hebrews tells us; *But this man, after he had offered one sacrifice for sins for ever, sat down on the right hand of God; From henceforth expecting till his enemies be made his footstool* (Hebrews 10:12, 13). If we are sometimes impatient for the Kingdom, let us remember that He too is waiting, and He has promised us, *Fear not little flock, it is your Father's good pleasure to give you the Kingdom* (Luke 12:32).

was in the isle that is called Patmos, As we have seen, John was exiled to Patmos as a result of anti-Christian persecution under the Roman emperor Domitian.

Patmos a small, rocky and barren area where many criminals of Rome were sent to serve out their prison terms in harsh conditions. There were mines on the island that the prisoners were forced to work.

John tells us the reason for his imprisonment, it was **for the word of God, and for the testimony of Jesus Christ.**

John's persecution was because of his ministry of the Word of God and his testimony concerning the Lord Jesus Christ. Peter writes; *Yet if any man suffer as a Christian, let him not be ashamed; but let him glorify God on this behalf.* (1 Peter 4:16).

Now we need to examine this next phrase very carefully. *I was in the Spirit on the Lord's day.*

The International Standard Version **(ISV).** translates this phrase; *I came to be in the Spirit on the Day of the Lord.* The phrase *the Lord's Day,* using the defining word as an adjective, is never found anywhere else in Scripture and is a faulty translation of this passage.

The passage should be rendered, *I was transported in the Spirit, into the Day of the Lord,* a phrase used many times in Scripture and always referring to a time when God intervenes directly in the affairs of men. It was a Day of the Lord when He sent His judgments in past time, and that entire future period which begins with the Rapture of the Church and culminates with the Millennial Kingdom is called *The Day of the Lord.*

John next hears a loud and startling sound: **and heard behind me a great voice, as of a trumpet.** Think for a moment – a trumpet is the instrument of command for the military. This was not a trumpet, but a voice like a trumpet – a loud and startling declaration full of authority. And the words of the trumpet voice were clearly discernable, **I am Alpha and Omega, the first and the last:**

We've already looked at the significance of these words, but here they are given to authenticate the authority of the One who is speaking. He is Sovereign and He is both the cause and the goal of history. He is not only the beginning, He is the ending, and what He started, He will finish!

What comes next is the Divine authority for the Scriptures;

What thou seest, write in a book.
God has ordained that what He desires us to know of Himself and of His purposes, be written down. The command occurs over and over in Scripture:

> **Exodus 34:27** *And the LORD said unto Moses, Write thou these words: for after the tenor of these words I have made a covenant with thee and with Israel.*

> **Isaiah 30:8** *Now go, write it before them in a table, and note it in a book, that it may be for the time to come for ever and ever:*

> **Jeremiah 30:2** *Thus speaketh the LORD God of Israel, saying, Write thee all the words that I have spoken unto thee in a book.*

> **Jeremiah 36:28** *Take thee again another roll, and write in it all the former words that were in the first roll, which Jehoiakim the king of Judah hath burned.*

> **Habakkuk 2:2** *And the LORD answered me, Write the vision, and make it plain upon tables.*

> **1Corinthians 14:37** *If any man think himself to be a prophet, or spiritual, let him acknowledge that the things that I write unto you are the commandments of the Lord.*

The command to John to "write" is found 14 times in the book of Revelation!

Not only is John commanded to write, but those to whom he is to write are clearly stated **and send it unto the seven churches which are in Asia.**

We have already seen that John was well known to these churches and that he had ministered among them. Is it possible that a delegation of "messengers" actually visited him while he was in Patmos? We cannot know, nor are we sure how the finished writing eventually reached the intended churches, but we hold it in our hands today because it did.

There were many churches in Asia. Our Lord choose these seven for a specific reason. Dr. Lehman Strauss observes, "The number seven is used more frequently throughout the book (Revelation) than any other. It speaks of completeness or perfection. God completes His work in cycles of seven. Seven colors make a perfect spectrum. Seven musical notes make up the scale. Seven days constitute one week. At the fall of Jericho there were seven priests, seven trumpets, and the seventh day the people marched around the wall seven times. There are seven set feasts of Jehovah (Leviticus 23); seven secrets in the kingdom parables (Matthew 13) and seven saying of the Savior from the cross. In Revelation the number seven appears forty-nine times, or seven times seven." And so Revelation is initially sent to these seven churches, but is meant for the whole church during this Church Age.

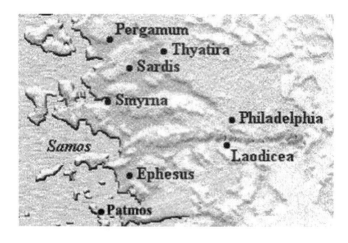

CHAPTER 2   JOHN'S FIRST VISION

Revelation 1:12 – 20

Rev 1:12 *And I turned to see the voice that spake with me.* Remember that the "trumpet voice" he heard was "behind him."

And being turned, I saw <u>seven golden candlesticks</u>; Unlike the seven-branched lampstand in the Tabernacle, these were seven separate and distinct lampstands that made something of a circle. We already learned that they represent the seven churches that are to be addressed in the letter. How significant it is the Lord sees His churches as "light bearers."

Rev 1:13 *And in the midst of the seven candlesticks.* That is His position during this age. He is in the midst of the churches and in the midst of His people (Matthew 18:20).

Rev 1:14 – 16 *One like unto the <u>Son of man</u>, clothed with a garment down to the foot, and girt about the paps with a golden girdle. His head and his hairs were white like wool, as white as snow; and his eyes were as a flame of fire; And his feet like unto fine brass, as if they burned in a furnace; and his voice as the sound of many waters. And he had in his right hand seven stars: and out of his mouth went a sharp two edged sword: and his countenance was as the sun shineth in his strength.*

We can compare this description to the one in Daniel 7:9-14. In Daniel the description is of the "Ancient of Days" before whom "One like a Son of Man" appears, obviously referring to the Son of God. Here, it is the Son Himself. He is the "brightness of the Father's glory and the express image of His person" (Hebrews 1:3).

The Son of Man Described:

one like unto the Son of man, the phrase *Son of man* is used 108 times in the Old Testament, most referring to man in his weakness, but occasionally used to refer to Deity as in the passage in Daniel. It was used by our Lord to refer to Himself 30 times in Matthew's Gospel, 14 times in Mark's Gospel, 26 times in Luke and 11 times by John. It is the name which links Him to us as our Kinsman, it is His human name. He is one of us, He is our Kinsman Redeemer.

Remember, under the Law, one could only redeem another if he were related as a kinsman. The wonderful story of the redemption of Ruth and Naomi by Boaz is given us to illustrate for all time how such redemption worked. Christ could not redeem us unless he were a Kinsman to us, thus he took on flesh and was made a son of Adam as Luke takes great pains to tells us (Luke 3:23-38). Jesus delighted in that name, as He identified with us as our Kinsman Redeemer.

clothed with a garment down to the foot, and girt about the paps with a golden girdle : (or: *a gold band around his chest* [GNB]).

The length of His garment would remind us of the High Priest's garment. Although we are not told its color, we might assume that it was pure white.

The golden sash around his chest would denote deity since gold was always the symbol of deity in the Old Testament system. It also may suggest regal status, i.e., He is not only our High Priest, but He is also our King.

His head and his hairs were white like wool, as white as snow; the whiteness of His hair denotes His age – He is *from old even from everlasting* (Micah 5:2).

and his eyes were as a flame of fire; piercing, penetrating, devouring, it is His eyes which see through every pretense and that will consume the "wood, hay and stubble" of our deeds done in the flesh on the day of judgment (1 Corinthians 3:12 -15).

And his feet like unto fine brass, as if they burned in a furnace; Brass in the Old Testament typology was always associated with Judgment. It was found in the courtyard of the Tabernacle and formed the foundation of the posts, the framework of the altar of burnt offering that spoke of God's judgment upon sin, and the basin and foot of the Laver which spoke of our self-judgment on our personal sin. Here it is "fine brass" absolutely pure that will bring Judgment to all creation.

and his voice as the sound of many waters. It is as if John were standing by a great waterfall – the roar of the water is deafening. This voice will overpower every other sound. The restless waves of human rebellion will be silenced before the roar of His voice.

And he had in his right hand seven stars: Notice they are *in His hand*, which means that He holds control over them. That will become significant as He explains the vision. Note, they are in His "right hand" always the hand of power.

and out of his mouth went a sharp two edged sword: This is not the first time the Word of God has been described in this fashion. Remember, this is a vision of "signs" (Gr. *Σημαίν*; sēmeion a *mark*; of uncertain derivation; a sign).

> **Ephesians 6:17** *And take the helmet of salvation, and the <u>sword</u> of the Spirit, which is the word of God:*
>
> **Hebrews 4:12** For the Word of God *is* quick, and powerful, and sharper than any two-edged <u>sword</u>.

Luther picked up on this idea when writing of the final defeat of Satan, he wrote, "one little word shall fell him." Then he concluded, "That Word above all earthly powers, no thanks to them, abideth. . ."

The symbolism is all too clear, in the judgment of His enemies, He merely speaks a word, and they are destroyed. The One who brought the worlds into being and created all things by the "word of His power" will destroy all His foes and all who would oppose Him with a single word.

and his countenance was as the sun shineth in his strength. How bright is that? Hear the word of God:

> **Matthew 17:2** *And was transfigured before them: and his face did shine as the sun, and his raiment was white as the light.*
>
> **Mark 9:2, 3** *And after six days Jesus taketh with him Peter, and James, and John, and leadeth them up into an high mountain apart by themselves: and he was transfigured before them. And his raiment became shining, exceeding white as snow; so as no fuller on earth can white them.*
>
> **Luke 9:29** *And as he prayed, the fashion of his countenance was altered, and his raiment was white and glistering.*

That experience on the Mount of Transfiguration, was, according to Peter (2 Peter 1:16-18) a preview of the Kingdom, when He shall come in His glory.

John's Response to the Vision.

Rev 1:17 *And when I saw him, I fell at his feet as dead.*
During His time on earth, John leaned upon His breast at the Passover supper, he had the most intimate of fellowship and relationship with Him. Now, seeing Christ in His glory, he fell on his face in worship.

Words of Strength

Rev 1:18 *And he laid his right hand upon me,.* The "right hand" is always the hand of strength. With it He raised John from the earth.

saying unto me, Fear not; I am the first and the last: I am he that liveth, and was dead; and, behold, I am alive for evermore, Amen; and have the keys of hell and of death. Note: he is the same Jesus that died, but He lives and has the "keys", that is, He is the Conqueror of death and hell. Keys always denote authority over something. (What is the first thing demanded of an employee when separated from his company?)

Words of Instruction

Rev 1:19 *Write the things which thou hast seen, and the things which are, and the things which shall be hereafter;*

This verse is the key to understanding the entire book of Revelation, for in it Christ has outlined the contents of the book for us.

1. *The things which thou hast seen,* covers all that we have looked at in Chapter 1.

2. *The things which are,* covers the present church age and we will see that this is the subject of chapters 2 and 3.

3. *The things which shall be hereafter; (or lit. "after these things" i.e., after the Church age),* covers the period from the end of the Church Age, hence from the Rapture to the culmination, and that will be found in the remainder of the book Chapters 4 – 22.

Rev 1:20 *The mystery of the seven stars which thou sawest in my right hand, and the seven golden candlesticks. The seven stars are the angels of the seven churches: and the seven candlesticks which thou sawest are the seven churches.*

The word "angels" is (Gr. ἄγγελος; aggelos; to *bring tidings*; a *messenger*; especially an *"angel"*; by implication a *pastor:* - messenger). (ISV) translates this; *the seven stars are the messengers of the seven churches.* Interestingly, it is the same word Baptists use for those who are sent to represent their local churches at an Associational meeting or a National Convention.

Dr. C.I. Scofield says, "The natural explanation of the "messengers" is that they were men sent by the seven churches to ascertain the state of the aged apostle, now an exile in Patmos (compare (Philippians 4:18) but they figure any who bear God's messages to a church." Or they may be simply special angelic beings who hold a responsibility over a specific church. If indeed there is an angel assigned to believers as individuals, it is not much of a leap to think that one may be assigned to a church. Whatever the case it is the seven Messengers that are addressed and assigned the task of carrying the message to their particular church." **(Scofield Reference Bible; footnote pp. 1331).**

God sees each of His churches as a "candlestick," that is, as a point of light. The purpose of the Church is to reflect the glory of the One who is still, "The Light of the World." As we move to the next two chapters of Revelation, we will get to examine the condition of each of the seven churches represented here.

REVIEW

- Where was John and why was he there?
- For what purpose did Rome use the Island?
- How should the phrase, The Lord's Day be translated?

- Explain the symbol of the 7 golden lampstands.
- Who was in the midst of the lampstands?
- What does that tell us about Christ's present ministry?
- What is the significance of the 7 angels?

CHAPTER 3 Introduction to the Churches

Revelation Chapters 2, 3 (An Overview)

Beginning in Chapter 2 we have the seven letters or messages to the seven churches of Asia.

"The messages to the seven churches have a fourfold application:

(1) **Local**, to the churches actually addressed;

(2) **Admonitory**, to all churches in all time as tests by which they may discern their true spiritual state in the sight of God;

(3) **Personal**, in the exhortations to him "that hath an ear," and in the promise "to him that overcometh"; these are meant to be taken personally by the reader, and

(4) **Historic/Prophetic**, as disclosing seven phases of the spiritual history of the church from, A.D. 96 to the end."
(The Churches; Dr. C. I. Scofield; pp. 1331 Scofield Reference Bible)

This is probably a good place to reflect on the last of these applications, the Historic/Prophetic application. Dr. C. I. Scofield set forth the logic of this approach as follows:

"It is incredible that in a prophecy covering the church period, there should be no such foreview. These messages must contain that foreview if it is to be found at all, for the church does not appear after (Rev. 3:22). Again, these messages by their very terms go beyond the local assemblies mentioned. Most conclusively of all, these messages do present an exact foreview of the spiritual history of the church, and in this precise order.

Ephesus gives the general state of the church at the date of the writing; Smyrna, the period of the great persecutions; Pergamos, the church settled down in the world, "where Satan's throne is," after the conversion of Constantine, circa A.D. 313. Thyatira is the Papacy, developed out of the Pergamos state: Balaamism (worldliness) and Nicolaitanism (priestly assumption) having conquered. As Jezebel brought idolatry into Israel, so Romanism weds Christian doctrine to pagan ceremonies. Sardis is the Protestant Reformation, whose works were not "fulfilled." Philadelphia is whatever bears clear testimony to the Word and the Name in the time of self-satisfied profession represented by Laodicea." **(C. I. Scofield; ibid.)**

Think with me for just a moment. God has unambiguously outlined this entire book of Revelation for us in Chapter 1:19. We saw that chapter one covered the real events that John heard, saw and experienced during his exile on the Isle of Patmos. Chapters 2 and 3 describe "the things which are", that is, as they exist in the life of the churches, and chapters 4 – 22 describe "the things that shall be after these things."

In the later section, there is no reference to the Church or the churches until chapter 22:16 where the risen Christ declares that He sent His angel to declare these messages unto the churches. In other words, the Church is absent from chapter 4 until the concluding words of the book.

How could it be possible for God to revel scores of events, and all the major players in the great earth drama of the last days, and miss any reference to the Church if the Church was still present on the earth? The evidence is clearly that the Church is no longer on the earth from chapter 4 through 19. What God had to say about the Church on earth He concluded in Chapter 3 and then began chapter four with the familiar sound of a trumpet voice saying, "Come up hither."

From Chapter 4 through the remainder of the book there is an ongoing description of things that will most certainly come to pass. But those things have not begun as yet.

The traumatic events recorded even in chapter 6 and onward cannot be described as having happened – they are still future. Yet God thought it important for His Church to know what is coming.

Now, if He took so much time to lay out in sweeping detail the events of the period just ahead of us, the period we call the Tribulation, are we to believe He would give us no clue as to the development of the age in which the Church is born, grows and is finally completed? If there is no shadow of the prophetic history of the Church here, then there is basically none that is in any way complete anywhere else.

Now, I am aware that there are many that object to this approach and I want to examine their objections and see whether they are valid. What follows then are the major objections that are raised against the historic/prophetic interpretation of these messages.

Objections to the Historical/Prophetic View of the Seven Churches (in their own words).

Quote: "It is our view that the historical-prophetical view suffers from numerous problems."

1. **Objection**: There is significant disagreement between different proponents of the view concerning which periods of history are represented, both their characteristics and dates. In this, the historical-prophetical scheme suffers from the same problems as the Historicist Interpretation of Revelation.

- **Answer:** This will likely be true any time someone tries to place a specific date on a broad prophecy. Only in a general sense can the outline of the Church age be traced, with much overlapping. Nevertheless, the general direction and trend of the Church as it developed through seven periods seems clearly to be set forth here in the seven letters.

Dr. Gene Williams, in his book, *From Now To Eternity*, writes, "When I did my academic doctorate in seminary, I was supposed to know everything I needed to know about Church history, in order to be the head of a Church History Department in any university. When I took my written final examination, I had to answer questions about Church History for about forty hours (eight hours a day for five days). When I began studying the book of Revelation, I was astounded that chapters two and three seem to relate to the different phases through which the Christian Church has gone. I do not mean to say that these were not literal historic churches, but they also represent the typical church in particular periods of history." **(Dr. Gene William; *From Now To Eternity*; pp.14, 15)**

2. **Objection:** Church history is far more complex than can be reflected by seven periods sharing global characteristics.

3. **Objection:** The correlation made between the letters and church history is entirely westernized and fails to take into account important movements and activities elsewhere in the world.

• **Answer:** These two objections are really one, they argue that the pattern as set forth in Chapters 2, 3 does not reflect what was happing in the churches in lands like China, Africa, India, etc. This observation may be true, but it does not rule out the validity of the fact that the pattern set forth in the seven letters, clearly reflects the church in the west. However, why should that not be the case since that is where the church was first planted and where the great movements like the Reformation and the missionary movements originated. It was the church in the west that carefully developed the great themes of Theology and everywhere one goes in the world, the other churches look to the west for teaching and help. The question might as well be asked, why did God only choose seven churches in Asia to address? Why not the church in Jerusalem, or Antioch, or Alexandria, or even the St. Thomas Church in India (which existed at this time). God chose seven churches in one general area to reflect the condition and needs of all churches throughout the world and throughout this age.

4. **Objection:** If the churches truly are representative of the course of church history, this fact must have been concealed from the early church or it would have destroyed the concept of imminency.

• **Answer:** True, and why should that not be the case? That is exactly what God told Daniel He would do with prophecies he had given to Daniel: *But thou, O Daniel, shut up the words, and seal the book, even to the time of the end:* (Daniel 12:4). We have a similar situation as regards the prophecies of the OT looking forward to the Savior: *Of which salvation the prophets have enquired and searched diligently, who prophesied of the grace that should come unto you: Searching what, or what manner of time the Spirit of Christ which was in them did signify, when it testified beforehand the sufferings of Christ, and the glory that should follow. Unto whom it was revealed, that not unto themselves, but unto us they did minister the things, which are now reported unto you by them that have preached the gospel unto you with the Holy Ghost sent down from heaven; which things the angels desire to look into* (1 Peter 1:10 – 12). Clearly God sometimes reveals things in a manner that is not clear to those who are contemporary with the prophecy, but will be clear to others coming after.

5. **Objection:** The historical-prophetical interpretation seems to read more into the text than what is intended.

- **Answer:** At best this is a subjective "judgment call" and the answer here is found in Scofield's observation, "these messages by their very terms go beyond the local assemblies mentioned." Let me demonstrate that: (1) It is ironic that the Church at Smyrna would suffer through "tribulation 10 days", and that historically we know that there were ten edicts of persecution against the church by Roman Emperors during that early church period. (2) The Lord threatens the apostates in Thyatira with going into Great (mega) Tribulation. This is the same phraseology that our Lord used for the coming Day of the Lord. While some in Thyatira doubtless faced extreme tribulation as the letter indicates, there seems to be something much larger in view that would correspond to prototype of this church continuing until now and apostates within it going through the coming Day of the Lord. (3) Next note the exhortation to the faithful at Thyatira, "Hold fast till I come." "Till I come? How do you interpret that within the context of only a local church that no longer exists? There are things within these messages that cannot be understood within the narrow context of one church at one time. (4) Finally, for this discussion, there is the promise to the church at Philadelphia, *Because thou hast keep the word of my patience, I also will keep thee from the hour of temptation which shall come upon all the world to try them that dwell upon the earth* (literally; the *earth dwellers*). Nothing of this magnitude can be attributed to the situation in the historic church at Philadelphia. This either goes far beyond a local fulfillment, or God is speaking in unwarranted superlatives.

Having examined the objections, I want to urge that much can be gained in overall perspective by seeing the historic-prophetic nature of these messages and thus getting a sense of the historic stages of development through which the Church has passed, and perhaps a sense of where we are at present.

If we understand the Church Age to be that period of time between Pentecost (when the Church was born), to the Rapture (when the Church leaves the earth), then these chapters help us see a sweeping overview of how the church develops during that period.

I have tried to assign some dates to the various phases of church history that seem to be set forth in these letters. Those dates suggest an over-all representation of the progressive development of things within the church revealing primarily characteristics of particular periods.

For instance, the early first century (up to AD 100), churches were generally young, pure, sound in the faith and could be characterized best by the features presented in the letter to the church at Ephesus. As the church entered the next two hundred years, it entered a period of imperial persecution which paralleled much that was described in the letter to the church at Smyrna.

Once Constantine had made Christianity, not only legal, but "the religion of the Empire," the influences of the pagan world became dominant. Much of the idolatry of Babylon was introduced into the church of Pergamos, corrupting its purity and confusing its message. The corruption of the church metastasized from the corruption of the Imperial State as seen in Pergamos, to the even deeper corruption of an imperial clergy with Papal assumption of both religious and temporal power as seen in Thyatira.

The argument that these various phases were only western and did not reflect Christianity in the rest of the globe is puerile. When Roman Catholicism was in control in the West, it spread its power and influence though out the world. Japan finally rejected Jesuit Christianity in the 1590s, while India had its own reformation in 1653, in the Coonan Cross Oath. The oath was a public avowal by members of the Saint Thomas Christian community that they would not submit to Roman Catholic dominance in ecclesiastical and secular life.

So, in a very real sense, the history of Christianity in the West, has dominated the course of Christianity throughout the world.

Finally, please do not miss the obvious. Chapters 2 and 3 set forth *"the things that are,"* that is they set forth the period we know as the Church Age. Chapter four begins something new, *"the things which shall be after these things."* After what things? After the Church Age. So if there is going to be a Rapture, where would you expect it to be?

It would be at the end of this section, that is, at the end of the Church Age, and that is exactly where we find it: *After this I looked, and, behold, a door was opened in heaven: and the first voice which I heard was as it were of a trumpet talking with me; which said, Come up hither, and I will shew thee things which must be hereafter (*Revelation 4:1) Amazing! We have all the elements of the Rapture event recorded in this one verse.

After the events of the next two chapters, the Scroll is opened and the judgments of God begin to be poured out on the earth. The Day of the Lord begins. Now there are two passages I want to look at briefly.

The first is found in Genesis 19:12-22. In this passage God was about to pour out His wrath upon Sodom and please notice the words spoken to Lot and his family as the angel ushered them out of the city, *Haste thee, escape thither; for I cannot do any thing till thou be come thither.* Do not miss the point here: The beginning of judgment awaited the escape of those who were God's own.

The second is found in 1 Thessalonians 5:4-9. Please notice that the subject is the coming of the Day of the Lord and believers are promised, *For God hath not appointed us to wrath, but to obtain salvation by our Lord Jesus Christ.* As with Lot, the judgment of God, which clearly involves the wrath of God, cannot fall until His Church is taken out.

Finally, note the word given to the Church at Philadelphia (Revelation 3:10). The church is told, *I will keep thee from the hour of* (Gr. **πειρασμός**; peirasmos; trouble), *tribulation, that shall come upon all the world to try them that dwell upon the earth.*

This Church is not only promised deliverance from this period of trouble, but the coming Tribulation is specifically said to be sent to try "earth dwellers:" i.e., those who have no spiritual life but are "*of the earth, earthy*," that is, they are the unsaved who have refused the gospel during this age. All the tenor of Scripture points to a Pre-Tribulation Rapture.

SEVEN STAGES OF CHURCH HISTORY

Church	Church History Typified	Dates (circa)	Verses
Ephesus	The Apostolic Church	A.D. 30-100	Rev. Rev. 2:1-7
Smyrna	The Church of the Roman Persecution	A.D. 100 - 313	Rev. Rev. 2:8-11
Pergamum	The Church of the Age of Constantine	A.D. 313-600	Rev. Rev. 2:12-17
Thyatira	The Church of the Dark Ages	A.D. 600-1517	Rev. Rev. 2:18-29
Sardis	The Church of the Reformation	A.D. 1517-1648*	Rev. Rev. 3:1-6
Philadelphia	The Church of the Great Missionary	A.D. 1649**- present	Rev. Rev. 3:7-13
Laodicea	The Church of the Apostasy	A.D. 1920-present	Rev. Rev. 3:14-22

*With the Treaty of Westphalia in 1648 the power of the Holy Roman Emperor was broken and the German states were again able to determine the religion of their lands.

**1649 - Society for the Propagation of the Gospel In New England formed to reach the Indians of New England[156]

Chart by Dr. Bill Shade

Chapter 4 The Church at Ephesus

Revelation 2:1 – 7

The name Ephesus is thought to mean "desirable" and that is certainly a fitting description of this church. If we are to understand this passage, we must not divorce it from Paul's final message to the Elders of Ephesus as recorded in Acts 20:17–38. In that message, Paul exhorted them to Evangelistic Zeal, Doctrinal Purity and Personal Piety. Our Lord's analysis of this church recorded in these verses is a revelation of how effective Paul's message and ministry to them had been.

Salutation vs. 1
Unto the angel of the church of Ephesus write; These things saith he that holdeth the seven stars in his right hand, who walketh in the midst of the seven golden candlesticks;

The letter is addressed to the church at Ephesus. **Ephesus** was a major city of Asia Minor, a seaport, and the location of the great temple of Artemis (cf. Acts 19:24 – 35), one of the seven wonders of the ancient world.

The Speaker is identified as the One who holds the seven stars (the messengers) in His hand and walks in the midst of the seven candlesticks (churches). The symbolism is obvious, He is the One who is in control and He knows all about everything that each church (and each individual member) is going through. He walks in the midst.

And the message to us is clear. He still holds the messengers in His hand, and requires their performance, and He still knows the heart of every believer, and every church. He also knows, as we will see those who are "tares in the midst of the wheat," and "false brethren," and "wolves among the sheep."

These letters make it clear that in most assemblies (churches), there is <u>a mixture of true believers and those who merely hold a profession of faith,</u> and that the later, will always be a detriment to the church, moving it away from the will and Word of God. The possible exception is Smyrna, the persecuted church. Mere professors are quickly purged when persecution begins. As our Lord Himself noted, *The seeds that fell on rocky ground are the people who gladly hear the message and accept it. But they don't have deep roots, and they believe only for a little while. As soon as life gets hard, they give up* (Luke 8:13 CEV).

Commendation vs. 2, 3
I know thy works, and thy labor, and thy patience, and how thou canst not bear them which are evil: and thou hast tried them which say they are apostles, and are not, and hast found them liars: And hast borne, and hast patience, and for my name's sake hast labored, and hast not fainted.

I know thy works, and thy labor, and thy patience
These words (work and labor) sound like repetition but in the original they are different. Indeed both refer to the act of strenuous effort, but the word "work" is Gr. ἔργον; ergon to *toil* (as <u>an effort or occupation</u>); by implication an *act:* whereas the word "labor" is Gr. κόπος; kopos *toil* so as *reducing* the strength), by implication weariness over time. The thought seems to be, that they were faithfully and continually working, and that they were doing so with much zeal even when they were exhausted.

The Lord in the midst commends their zeal and hard labor and their **_patience._** The word is Gr.*ὑπομονή*; hupomonē - <u>cheerful (or hopeful) _endurance_</u>, _constancy:_ - enduring, patience, patient continuance. Even though their labor was intense to the point of weariness, they were cheerful, enduring, and patient. (Romans 5:3)

My first thought is, "I want to pastor this church." But then I remember that to do so, I have to be ready to work consistently to the point of exhaustion with cheerfulness - that's a tall order. But the Commendation continues:

and how thou canst not bear them which are evil:
<u>The practice of Church Discipline was alive and well at Ephesus.</u> This does not refer to avoiding sinful persons outside the Assembly, but rather to dealing with sin when it appeared in the Assembly. Compare: 1Corinthians 5:1–13; 1Timothy 5:20; Titus 1:9 – 13. A church that will not discipline it members, is on the way to ruin. There are always repercussions from such actions, but when they are done biblically, they should bring the entire Body together.

and thou hast tried them which say they are apostles, and are not, and hast found them liars:
This church was also passionate about sound doctrine. This was <u>not true in every church</u>. Among the many problems found in the church at Corinth, not only was there un-judged immorality, but there were false teachers as Paul writes:

> _However, I am afraid that just as the serpent deceived Eve by its tricks, so your minds may somehow be lured away from sincere and pure devotion to Christ. For if someone comes along and preaches another Jesus than the one we preached, or should you receive a different spirit from the one you received or a different gospel from the one you accepted, you are all too willing to listen._

Such people are false apostles, dishonest workers who are masquerading as apostles of Christ. And no wonder, since Satan himself masquerades as an angel of light. So it is not surprising if his servants also masquerade as servants of righteousness. Their doom will match their deeds! (2 Cor.11:3, 4, 13 – 15 ISV)

And what about the Churches of Galatia?

I marvel that ye are so soon removed from him that called you into the grace of Christ unto another gospel: Which is not another; but there be some that trouble you, and would pervert the gospel of Christ. But though we, or an angel from heaven, preach any other gospel unto you than that which we have preached unto you, let him be accursed. As we said before, so say I now again, If any man preach any other gospel unto you than that ye have received, let him be accursed. (Gal. 1:6 – 9)

It is the sacred responsibility of the leadership of the local church to keep false teaching from getting a foothold within the Assembly. Jesus likened false teaching to leaven, which, once it is introduced would permeate the whole. That is how false teaching works, and it is to the credit of the church in Ephesus that they prevented false teachers from infecting the Body.

The Lord then concludes this commendation with these words; **And hast borne, and hast patience, and for my name's sake hast labored, and hast not fainted.**

We don't know a great deal about the conditions at Ephesus except at the time when the church was founded there (Acts 19). IVPBBC says, "Ephesus had been one of the first Asian centers of the imperial cult of Emperor worship, and Domitian had allowed Ephesus the title of guardian of his temple."

"The city also boasted itself on its notoriety in magic and the worship of Artemis, (or Diana {KJV}). Inscriptions attest that Ephesus also had a sizable Jewish population, of which Christians had originally been a comfortable part, but were separated when Jewish pride began contradicting the Word of Truth (Acts 19:8-10). Hence there was built-in tension between both the Jewish and the Pagan community toward the church and they doubtless had to endure much pressure and many trials. Ephesus was the leading center of Asia Minor in this period." **(Inter-Varsity Press Bible Background Commentary, IVPBBC, 2000).**

In the face of such daily opposition the church at Ephesus had **"borne"** (stood up under stress), and done it with cheerfulness and had done it for the sake of "the Name." That is, they were careful to act in such a way that the Name of the Lord Jesus would not be disgraced or blamed.

This is a great church and one that we might well admire, but not all is well. The One who has eyes like a flame of fire, sees through even the most laudable appearances and goes directly to the heart.

Rebuke:
Rev 2:4 *Nevertheless I have somewhat against thee, because thou hast left thy first love.*

Vincent Word Studies says of this: The word ***Somewhat*** – is not in the text, and unnecessary. The following clause is the object of *I have*. "I have against thee that thou hast left," etc. He then comments, "It is indeed a *somewhat* which threatens to grow to be an *everything*."

For the phrase *I have against*, (see Colossians 3:13 where it is translated "*if any man have a quarrel against any*"). Hence the word conveys that a controversy exists.

Hast left Gr. ἀφῆκας more correctly, rendering the aorist, ***didst leave***. The verb originally means *to send, away or dismiss*. They had already done it! **(Vincent Word Studies)**

So it appears that we might translate, *I have a quarrel against you because you have walked away from your first passion for me.* That is a lover's voice speaking. Only one in deep affection can discern that subtle movement that translates to, "I am too occupied with what I am doing to spend time showing my love to you." The observation is one of a broken heart. It is the first step toward disaster.

So we might ask, as individuals, has there ever been a time when we where more enthralled by our Lord, by His Person, by His Presence, and by His Promises than we are now? Do we still delight to seek Him in the morning?

As a church, do we seek Him? Is the time of prayer, staying in his presence, interceding for His plans, His purposes, and His people, the most precious and valued hour of the week – or is something missing?

It is not a small matter when our loved one no longer wants our attention or values our advances. It is the first sign of the end of love. And there is a terrible price to be paid for such indifference and neglect.

Counsel:
Rev. 2:5 *Remember therefore from whence thou art fallen, and repent, and do the first works; or else I will come unto thee quickly, and will remove thy candlestick out of his place, except thou repent.*

We cannot be sure how this letter changes the church at Ephesus. At the death of Domitian, John was released from Patmos and actually ministered to the church at Ephesus until his death. But in the years that followed, the loss of first love degenerated into the loss of testimony just as the Lord had predicted.

Frederic William Farrar, *Life and Work of Paul* writes, "The candlestick at Ephesus has been for centuries removed out of his place; the squalid Mohammedan village which is nearest to its site does not count one Christian in its insignificant population; its temple is a mass of shapeless ruins; its harbor is a reedy pool; the bittern booms amid its pestilent and stagnant marshes; and malaria and oblivion reign supreme over the place where the wealth of ancient civilization gathered around the scenes of its grossest superstitions and its most degraded sins" **(Farrar, "Life and Work of Paul," ii., 43, 44).**

Farrar's observation reminded me of the Moody Institute of Science presentation, *Empty Cities*, which argues that many tribal societies are not "primitive" but "decadent", having fallen from former greatness (i.e., Maya, and Inca).

You are fallen; Gr. ἐκπίπτω ekpiptō; to *drop away*; specifically *be driven out* of one's course; figuratively to *lose, become inefficient:* - fail.

Notice that in spite of all the good things our Lord has said, (and will say vs. 6), this church has already fallen – it has already failed – it has already lost its passion. How important then is the maintenance of that first fervent love?

Repent and do the first works, i.e., love me as you once loved me. It is the Lover's voice which is calling:

Arise, my love, my fair one, and come away. O my dove, that art in the clefts of the rock, in the secret places of the stairs, let me see thy countenance, let me hear thy voice; for sweet is thy voice, and thy countenance is comely(beautiful). (Song of Solomon 2:13, 14)

Rev 2:6 *But this thou hast, that thou hatest the deeds of the Nicolaitans, which I also hate.*

"Some have equated the Nicolaitans with Balaam. The names, and the ideas behind the two things however, are by no means parallel: *Conqueror of the people* not being the same as *corrupter of the people*. Besides, in Revelation 2:14, the Balaamites are distinguished from the Nicolaitans.

Others believe that this was a branch of Gnostacism. Tertullian speaks of the Nicolaitanes as a branch of the Gnostic family, and as, in his time, extinct. Mosheim (De Rebus Christian Ante. Con. section 69) says that "the questions about the Nicolaitanes have difficulties which cannot be solved." Neander (History of the Christian Religion, as translated by Torrey, vol. i, pp. 452, 453) inclines to an opinion that the name is symbolical, and that it is used in a mystical sense, according to the usual style of the Book of Revelation." **(Robert Barnes)**

The most natural interpretation is to take the word to mean what its literal translation meant. C. I. Scofield writes: "From Greek, "nikao", "to conquer," and Greek, "laos", "the people," or "laity." There is no ancient authority for a sect of the Nicolaitanes. If the word is symbolic, it refers to the earliest form of the notion of a priestly order, or "clergy," which later divided an equal brotherhood (Mat 23:8) into "priests" and "laity." What in Ephesus was "deeds" (Rev 2:6) had become in Pergamos a "doctrine (Rev 2:15)." **(Scofield Ref. Bible Footnote pp. 1332)**

The word nikao is related to the word nike – and means victory.

While the matter cannot be proven, the historic fact is that the development of a "clerical hierarchy" was the foundation upon which all the assumptions of Roman Catholic authority, infallibility and ritualism where built. The NT sets forth a proper Pastoral authority over the local church, but the development of anything like a "priesthood" that would be over the established priesthood of every believer, has no warrant in Scripture and it would not be surprising if our Lord, who knew the future perfectly, would condemn such a tendency at the very beginning of the church.

Rev 2:7 *He that hath an ear, let him hear what the Spirit saith unto the churches;*

This was always the Lord's command (*Who hath ears to hear, let him hear* (Matthew 13:9). It places the responsibility squarely on the hearer. The obvious implication is that to hear is to obey. If we have not obeyed, we have not heard in the biblical sense. So what our Lord is really calling for is our obedience.

To him that overcometh will I give to eat of the tree of life, which is in the midst of the paradise of God. (vs. 7).

This challenge comes at the end of each of these messages and is always accompanied by a promise to those who are "Overcomers." So, who is he that overcometh?

To him that overcometh (from: nikao, to gain the victory)
This is a formula common to all John's letters. It occurs once in the Gospel, 6 times in the First Epistle, 16 times in Revelation, and elsewhere only in Luke 11:22; Romans 3:4; 12:21. (See Romans 8:37 Gr. *hypernikao* more than conquerors. It implies overwhelming victory). **(Vincent's Word Studies)**

The popular Nike sportswear takes its name from this word. Nike was a goddess who personified victory. Her Roman equivalent was Victoria.

> **John 16:33** *These things I have spoken unto you, that in me ye might have peace. In the world ye shall have tribulation: but be of good cheer; I have overcome the world.*
>
> **1John 2:13** *I write unto you, fathers, because ye have known him that is from the beginning. I write unto you, young men, because ye have overcome the wicked one.*
>
> **1John 4:4** *Ye are of God, little children, and have overcome them: because greater is he that is in you, than he that is in the world.*

1John 5:4 *For <u>whatsoever is born of God overcometh</u> the world: and this is the victory that overcometh the world, even our faith.*

Who will partake of the Tree of Life?
Here is the problem, this word implies continuous victory. If the sentence means that only those who perform in continuous victory over the world, and flesh and the devil will receive the promises offered, then who are these "super Christians?" Are these the only ones who will partake of the Tree of Life (i.e., have salvation)? If so, then <u>salvation may be initiated by Christ, but is really obtained by our own efforts, or at least our performance</u>.

An entire theology has been developed from this in recent years, that teaches that only certain super-saints will enjoy the blessings of the Kingdom. Those believing saints that fail will be cast into outer darkness and suffer a kind of purgatory during the Millennial Kingdom.

So, is that what John is teaching or does the Scripture teach that the difference is between those who have genuine faith and those who do not (1 John 5:4)? Is the warning to those who profess but do not possess? Is eternal life only to those who overcome, and who are they?

The answer is clearly set forth by the same author that is speaking here in Revelation. *<u>Whatsoever is born of God overcometh</u> the world* (1John 4:5). <u>That's who it is!</u> It is those who have been born of God and that which overcomes is the life of God within the believer. If this life is resident within him, he is an overcomer.

<u>And what is the overcoming factor</u>? *This is the victory that overcometh the world, even our faith.* If you have it you are an overcomer, because He has overcome the world and He is in you! You have already overcome the dominion of Satan, the decay of the body, the destiny of hell, the doom of the grave, and the decree of destruction. You have already overcome!

Ye are of God, little children, and <u>have overcome</u> them: because greater is he that is in you, than he that is in the world.(1John 4:4).

I am forced to conclude therefore, that overcomers are simply those who possess real spiritual life, and that whatever the temptations, trials or obstacles they face, grace will cause them to overcome in the end. After examining the implications of the former view, I believe it becomes clear that <u>every true believer is an "overcomer."</u>

REVIEW

- Name the fourfold application of the letters to the 7 churches.

- What is the meaning of the name Ephesus?

- What famous Apostles pastored this church at various times?

- Name three things for which this church was commended.

- What was their one failing?

- How do we measure love?

CHAPTER 5 The Church At Smyrna

Revelation 2:8 – 11

Salutation:
And unto the angel of the church in Smyrna write; These things saith the first and the last, which was dead, and is alive;.

The message itself is, in each instance related to the salutation. In each case, Christ presents a phase of His character and Person which will most closely fit the need of the church to which He is speaking. This church is facing persecution and death, but the One who is speaking has already gone through that, so there is nothing to fear.

The word Smyrna itself means "Myrrh." Gr. σμύρνα smurna *myrrh:* - myrrh. Gr. Σμύρνα Smurna *smoor'-nah* The same as; *Smyrna*, a place in Asia Minor. Hence both words are spelled the same.

Notice the salutation: **The first and the last** – *He is before all things and by Him all things consist*, (Col. 1:17) and He will endure forever - *Thou, Lord, in the beginning hast laid the foundation of the earth; and the heavens are the works of thine hands: They shall perish; but thou remainest; and they all shall wax old as doth a garment; And as a vesture shalt thou fold them up, and they shall be changed: but thou art the same, and thy years shall not fail.* (Hebrews 1:10 – 12)

In a situation where life itself hangs in the balance and believers are suffering the loss of all things, how good to remember that the Author and Finisher of our Salvation will be there through our trials and still be there when it is over.

Furthermore, He is the one **which was dead, and is alive.** Even death itself could not destroy Him, nor can it destroy us. It may destroy our body, but we have His Life within us and we live forever.

Commendation:
I know thy works, and tribulation, and poverty, (but thou art rich) and I know the blasphemy of them which say they are Jews, and are not, but are the synagogue of Satan. Vs.9

Notice the first words, *I Know*. What they are going through right now and what they will face tomorrow, isn't escaping His notice, He knows, He feels and He cares.

I know thy works, they were still serving even under the pressure of continuous persecution.

and thy tribulation, as already noted, He knew all that they were going through.

and poverty, this was not a wealthy church, In fact, under the ostracism of their Christian identity, their employment was often terminated, their legal rights were taken away, any form of support was cut out from under them. They were thus, (as believers today under Islamic Sharia are), diminished. The word used by those under Sharia is "dimmies." If we can imagine them living as outcasts we most likely have the picture of their true condition.

But then we hear the words, *(but thou art rich vs.9)* Only those of us who have had the sacred privilege of visiting in lands and places where these conditions are perpetrated, can appreciate the very frequent evidence of the riches of their faith. Often they can pray for miracles and miracles come.

They possess nothing, and have been stripped of barest necessities, yet they have the power of God resting upon them, such as is not seen in places were faith is less costly.

and I know the blasphemy of them which say they are Jews, and are not, but are the synagogue of Satan. Vs.9b

Barnes writes; "The meaning here is plain, that though they worshipped in a synagogue, and professed to be the worshippers of God, yet they were not worthy of the name, and deserved rather to be regarded as in the service of Satan. . . . It may throw some light on the passage, to remark that at a somewhat later period - in the time of the martyrdom of Polycarp - the Jews of Smyrna were among the most bitter of the enemies of Christians, and among the most violent in demanding the death of Polycarp." **(Albert Barnes notes on the Bible).**

The book of Acts records the fact that, after the initial acceptance of the Gospel by Jews and Proselytes, whom Luke calls "devout men, out of every nation under heaven" (Acts 1:5), early opposition began with Jewish authorities. It began at Jerusalem and the record shows that it spread rapidly. As you progress through the book of Acts, it is really a record of Jewish rejection and opposition to the Gospel, not only rejecting the message but stirring up violence against those that proclaimed it. The book closes with these words of Paul;

And when they had appointed him a day, there came many to him into his lodging; to whom he expounded and testified the kingdom of God, persuading them concerning Jesus, both out of the law of Moses, and out of the prophets, from morning till evening. And some believed the things which were spoken, and some believed not. And when they agreed not among themselves, they departed, after that Paul had spoken one word,

Well spake the Holy Ghost by Esaias the prophet unto our fathers, Saying, Go unto this people, and say, Hearing ye shall hear, and shall not understand; and seeing ye shall see, and not perceive: For the heart of this people is waxed gross, and their ears are dull of hearing, and their eyes have they closed; lest they should see with their eyes, and hear with their ears, and understand with their heart, and should be converted, and I should heal them. Be it known therefore unto you, that the salvation of God is sent unto the Gentiles, and that they will hear it. (Acts 28:23 – 28)

Having rejected the Gospel, the Jews became the foremost opponents to the early Church, exceeding even the opposition of the pagans. They opposed and blasphemed both the message and the Lord, and they had indeed become, **the synagogue of Satan.**

Counsel:
Fear none of those things which thou shalt suffer: behold, the devil shall cast some of you into prison, that ye may be tried; and ye shall have tribulation ten days: be thou faithful unto death, and I will give thee a crown of life. He that hath an ear, let him hear what the Spirit saith unto the churches; He that overcometh shall not be hurt of the second death. Vss. 10, 11.

Fear none of those things which thou shalt suffer:
Observe that while this word from the risen Lord encourages them to forsake fear, it nevertheless predicts that there is trouble ahead for them. They are reminded that, *He hath not given us the spirit of fear; but of power, and of love, and of a sound mind* (2 Timothy 1:7).

behold, the devil shall cast some of you into prison, that ye may be tried; and ye shall have tribulation ten days: be thou faithful unto death, and I will give thee a crown of life.

Please observe that this is a spiritual battle we are fighting – *the devil shall cast* some of you into prison. We do not wrestle against mere flesh and blood.

The time of their internment was not to be long, but would be filled with (Gr. θλίψι thlipsis; *pressure,* anguish, persecution, tribulation, and much trouble). This would be a time of extreme suffering that had an end: **be thou faithful unto death.** In other words, not only was the suffering a certainty, but death at the end of the suffering was certain as well. How can a believer bear up under this?

Corrie Ten Boone tells the story of her father's wisdom when she asked a similar question. Corrie feared that she did not have the courage necessary to face imprisonment in a Nazi death camp. Her father reminded her, "When we go somewhere on a train, when do I give you the ticket?" "Just as we are boarding the train father," she replied. "Exactly," he told her, "that is when you need it, and that's when God will give you the courage you need."

Martha Snell Nicholson answers that question in this poem, ***Dying Grace***.

Since death is but the opening of a door
Into a larger, fairer room -- nay, more
It is the welcoming of His voice, the touch
Of His dear hand on ours at last -- if such
is death, why should we ever be afraid
Or doubt that He will keep the promise made?

Then trust Him, frightened child, for He will give
Us grace to die who gives us grace to live!
Await His time -- do we need dying grace
While we are living? But when, face to face
With that last moment, He will take our hand
To lead us home, and we shall understand
And smile at fear, and smiling, enter, for
Our death will be the opening of His door!

Martha Snell Nicholson

"Yea, though I walk through the valley of the shadow of death, I will fear no evil; for thou art with me; thy rod and thy staff they comfort me" (Psalms 23:4)

And there is a reward ahead, *I will give thee a crown of life.* The crown of Life has been called The Martyr's Crown. To win it we must only be faithful unto death. Perhaps you have thought of that crown. Do you covet it? Almeda Pearce did when she wrote:

> When He shall come, resplendent in His glory,
> To take His own from out this vale of night,
> O may I know the joy at His appearing,
> Only at morn to walk with Him in white!
>
> When I shall stand within the court of Heaven,
> Where white-robed pilgrims pass before my sight,
> Earth's martyred saints and blood washed overcomers,
> These then are they who walk with Him in white!
>
> When He shall call, from earth's remotest corners,
> All who have stood triumphant in His might,
> O to be worthy then to stand beside them,
> And in that morn to walk with Him in white!
>
> **Almeda Pearce**

He that hath an ear, let him hear what the Spirit saith unto the churches; He that overcometh shall not be hurt of the second death.

Here again it is so important that we understand who these are who are Overcomers. Are they those who faced death triumphantly and were faithful till the end? Yes, they are Overcomers. But "overcomers" also means the woman who was sure she could not stay faithful under persecution but found that through the Spirit, she could prevail.

Unless "overcomers" means every person in whom dwells the Spirit of the Great Overcomer, then this verse would be teaching that some born again Christians will experience the second death which is the eternal Lake of Fire. Since that would contradict everything we know about our salvation, it seems clear that "Overcomers" are everyone who has been born again and who will escape the penalty of sin through the faith in the finished work of the Redeemer. God's possession of us, and His power in us, will make each of us Overcomers in the end.

REVIEW:

- What did you learn from the letter to the Church in Smyrna?

- How has this passage been a blessing or and encouragement to you?

- Has the message to this church made you think about how you will react when persecution comes to you?

CHAPTER 6 The Church at Pergamum

Revelation 2:12 – 17

Pergamum ("married") - from the Greek word pergamos, which is a combination of two Greek words: Gk. **per** (elevation) and Gk. **Γάμος;** gamos; *nuptials:* - marriage, wedding.

These words combine to mean "elevated by marriage." The church at Pergamus appears to be "married," but to the world, rather than to the LORD. It is obviously an unhealthy marriage and one forbidden by Scripture (2 Corinthians 6:14), and forms the basis for the deep divisions and difficulties within this church and the next.

A.W. Tozer wrote that compromise has been the cancer of the church from the very beginning. He said, "A new Decalogue has been adopted by the neo-Christians of our day, 'Thou shalt not disagree,' and a new set of Beatitudes too, 'Blessed are they that tolerate everything, for they shall not be made accountable for anything,'" **(A. W. Tozer)**

Tozer's words certainly describe the condition of the next two churches. In Smyrna, Satan tried to destroy the church by persecution. In Pergamus, he tries to destroy it by compromise.

Salutation:
And to the angel of the church in Pergamos write; These things saith he which hath the sharp sword with two edges; vs. 12

We anticipate from the opening words of this letter, that there may be some stern admonitions ahead for this church.

We have already learned that the sword comes out of His mouth and is therefore a symbol of the cutting power of His Word. It has the power to slay and to make alive, and He will employ it toward this church.

Commendation:
I know thy works, and where thou dwellest, even where Satan's seat is: and thou holdest fast my name, and hast not denied my faith, even in those days wherein Antipas was my faithful martyr, who was slain among you, where Satan dwelleth. Vs. 13

What made Pergamos, the seat (literally "Throne" Gr. θρόνος; thronos), of Satan? Some background will be helpful. There were elaborate temples to the four great pagan gods in the city of Pergamos. Zeus, Dionysus, Athena and Asklepios (the Egyptian god of healing whose symbol was the snake). To the temple of the latter, invalids from all parts of Asia flocked.

The Temple of Asklepios at Purgamum, became the inspiration for Albert Speer's design for the parade ground at Nuremberg. It was the coliseum for major Nazi events. The Altar of Zeus was reconstructed in the Purgamum Museum in Berlin where it can still be seen to this day.

Historians have said that after the break-up of Alexander's Empire when Babylon, the womb of all idolatry fell, elements of the Babylonian mystery cults where relocated to Pergamos where they perpetuated the ancient pagan rites again.

Pergamos was chiefly the religious center of the province. In addition to Temples to four major deities of the Greek pantheon, three temples had been built to the Roman emperors, in which the emperors were worshipped as gods.

This, at the beginning, had been simply patriotic patronage, but had evolved into a litmus test for loyalty to the Emperor and the Empire. It involved the offering of a small amount of incense on the altar, for which the supplicant received a certificate attesting to his loyalty.

Christians could not perform this act of worship to someone other than God (even the Emperor), and were thereby deemed traitors and dangerous. Is it any wonder that God described Pergamos as, **where Satan's throne is.**

It should be noticed that the crime of the Christians, was turned, from one of loyalty to their God, to a political one of disloyalty to the state. I point that out because in many countries today, especially in totalitarian regimes, the charge against the Christian is always political, so that the state can escape the appearance of persecuting religion (vis. China / DPRK / etc.)

and thou holdest fast my name, and hast not denied my faith, even in those days wherein Antipas was my faithful martyr, who was slain among you, where Satan dwelleth (vs.13).

Twice in this one verse we have reference to Satan (the Adversary), who stands behind all of the dark evil that permeated Pergamos at that time.

The Church at Pergamos had already experienced the martyrdom of one of their own for standing fast against the pressures of paganism all around them. We know nothing of Antipas apart from what we read here in the text, but his testimony had been sufficiently dynamic that it drew the attention of the Roman officials and eventually, unable to break his spirit, they had put him to death.

His name itself begins with **Anti**; "against". The implication is that he stood against the prevailing winds of compromise. Although the details of his death are unknown, the event was significant enough to implant itself upon the memories of those remaining, and to warrant the affirmation of the risen Lord Himself.

Rebuke:

But I have a few things against thee, because thou hast there them that hold the doctrine of Balaam, who taught Balack to cast a stumblingblock before the children of Israel, to eat things sacrificed unto idols, and to commit fornication. Vs.14

few things against thee, not many things, but those that are cited are not small matters.

thou hast there them that hold the doctrine of Balaam, It is obvious that to understand this it must be placed in its historic context. What was it that Balaam "taught Balack" that is perpetuated now at Pergamos? The background is found in Numbers chapters 22 to 25, which you would do well to read in order to understand what is said here.

When Balaam found that God refused to honor his attempts to curse Israel, Balaam realized that his hope for riches was lost. So rather than lose the reward for divination, and knowing the character of Jehovah, that He must judge sin in His people, Balaam suggested a sure way to turn Jehovah's wrath against His people Israel.

He instructed Balack to entice Israel to the celebration of Baal-Peor, one of the most immoral, degrading, ceremonies in the pagan world. Although shrouded in mystery, it is known to involve the grossest forms of sexual activities both with male and female prostitutes and another passage in the Psalms referring to this (Psalm 106:28) seems to imply that there was even cannibalism practiced as part of this dark orgy.

The result was of course God's immediate and severe judgment and a plague broke out among the Israelites which claimed 24,000 lives. In addition, the various tribal leaders were instructed to summarily execute any of their tribe that where involved and by the direct command of God their heads (or bodies) where impaled in public display (Numbers 25:4).

The numbing effect of this kind of pagan idolatry can be seen in the insensitive attitude and action of the Israelite who came into the camp, into the midst of a prayer meeting of repentance in which Moses was presiding, and brought a Moabite temple-prostitute with him in clear view of everyone.

Scripture tells us that; *when Phinehas, the son of Eleazar, the son of Aaron the priest, saw it, he rose up from among the congregation, and took a javelin in his hand; And he went after the man of Israel into the tent, and thrust both of them through, the man of Israel, and the woman through her belly. So the plague was stayed from the children of Israel.* (Numbers 25:7, 8).

This incident was considered such a major transgression that it is referred to again in the books of Deuteronomy, and again in Psalms, Hosea as well as 1 Corinthians, 2 Peter, Jude and Revelation. Balaam's name appears 63 times in the Scripture. With that background, what then does the risen Christ mean when He charges some of them with, **holding the doctrine of Balaam?**

Given what we know about the culture of Pergamos, the answer is fairly simple. There were those who encouraged the believers to "partake of the culture," or in other words "compromise with the world." And because of what the culture was, that is, that it involved participation in ceremonies and events that would include, *eating things sacrificed unto idols, and committing fornication,* God was rightly offended.

The believer is always to remember that in relation to the world (i.e., this world system which is under the dominion of Satan), he is to be "in" the world, but never "of" the world. The intent of this rebuke is obviously that these believers where failing to keep themselves separate from the world.

We already looked at this passage once when we were discussing Church Discipline, but I want to refer to it again.

I wrote unto you in an epistle not to company with fornicators: Yet not altogether with the fornicators of this world, or with the covetous, or extortioners, or with idolaters; for then must ye needs go out of the world. But now I have written unto you not to keep company, if any man that is called a brother be a fornicator, or covetous, or an idolater, or a railer, or a drunkard, or an extortioner; with such an one no not to eat. (1 Corinthians 5:9-11)

It is expected that the world will behave like this, but it is disastrous when a believer does. And there were those in the Assembly at Pergamos, that taught that it was right and proper for a Christian to have this kind of intercourse with the world, and that brought the disfavor of God upon this assembly.

So hast thou also them that hold the doctrine of the Nicolaitans, which thing I hate. (vs.15)

We have already discussed the meaning of the word in our study of the Church at Ephesus. What in Ephesus were "deeds", has now, in Pergamos, become a "doctrine."

Constantine united the empire under the church but he also greatly influenced the church. In the first place, the Emperor wanted all in his realm to be in the church, so he ordered all to be baptized. The obvious result was sudden "church growth" but with unconverted but baptized pagans.

The Emperor also thought that since all the pagan temples had priests with vestal garments, the church should also set apart those in authority with the same. A vestal garment is defined as a chasuble or robe worn by the clergy or choristers during services. The word seems to have come from VESTAL relating to the Roman goddess Vesta or to a VESTAL virgin. Constantine introduced this distinctive dress that would identify the "clergy" and set them apart from the laity, thus, the division was exacerbated between brethren viewed formerly as equals in the church.

Of course the Old Testament priests wore the prescribed robes of the priesthood, but such things were never part of the early church where every believer is considered a "priest" (Revelation 1:6; 5:10).

The Hierarchical structure of church government gradually morphed from a very simple Pastor/teacher over a church or churches, to a Pastor or Bishop that exercised authority over churches within a region.

Originally, this came about because larger churches would plant daughter churches and take oversight and responsibility for them. Ideally, the "daughter church" would come to maturity and take full responsibility for itself, and go on to plant other churches.

The title Bishop was originally and biblically applied to the work of a Pastor in providing oversight to a local church. The word is, Gr. ἐπίσκοπος; episkopos, a *superintendent*, that is, Christian officer in general charge of a church also called a bishop, or overseer.

But with time, the control of the larger churches became permanent, and the office of Bishop took on the meaning of having oversight authority over multiple churches, over a region, and even over entire countries.

Along with the extending the authority of the Bishop, the role of the Pastor was changed as well. His clerical robes made him look like a priest and he began to act as a mediator for his people to God, in spite of the clear teaching that, *there is one God, and one mediator between God and men, the man Christ Jesus* (1 Timothy 2:5).

Acting as a mediator is the role of a Priest and in the New Testament economy, every believer is a priest who has immediate and direct access to God.

But in spite of this clear Apostolic teaching, gradually, and in increasing measure, this division between a laity and a priestly clergy became established. And the source of all of this that is so foreign to the intension of God, was the deeds and doctrines of the Nicolaitans.

Counsel:
Repent; or else I will come unto thee quickly, and will fight against them with the sword of my mouth. Vs. 16

With these words the risen Christ warns that He Himself will enter the battle against these destructive teachings and those who advance them. As always, He will use the weapon of the Word. But there may also be an implied threat that the "Word," might be one of discipline in which He directly deals with those who are involved in the transgression. God can and does discipline His own, and if we have ever felt the sting of His rod, we never want to experience it again.

He that hath an ear, let him hear what the Spirit saith unto the churches vs. 17a

Once again, as in all of these letters, the readers/hearers are responsible to respond. To hear is to obey, and if repentance is called for, as it is here, there must come an active act of obedience in turning from the sin which was rebuked.

To him that overcometh will I give to eat of the hidden manna vs. 17b

Manna is that miraculous bread from heaven. Jesus said of it, *Moses gave you not that bread from heaven; but my Father giveth you the true bread from heaven. For the bread of God is he which cometh down from heaven, and giveth life unto the world.* (John 6:32, 33). It appears that He is offering Himself to them. Some have eaten the "meat sacrificed to idols". Jesus can say; *I am the bread of life: he that cometh to me shall never hunger; and he that believeth on me shall never thirst.* (John 6:35).

and will give him a white stone, and in the stone a new name written, which no man knoweth saving he that receiveth it. **Vs. 17c**

This may be the most difficult portion of this letter to interpret, but there are certain things we know. White and black stones were often used to indicate acceptance or rejection. The mystery religions of paganism used them to determine the worthiness of a new member to join their cult.

Even to this day, certain secret societies use this method to decide whether a novitiate will be accepted or rejected. A white stone or marble symbolizes acceptance, a black stone, rejection. It only takes one black stone to keep the person out. The expression, "black balled" comes from this practice.

The new name may come out of the same ceremony. Once an initiate has been given acceptance, the presiding prelate would pronounce in his ear a secret name that was never to be disclosed.

Some of those at Pergamos had come out of these pagan societies and would be familiar with these rituals. Now, they have been initiated into the fellowship of the saints and the family of God.

The symbol of the white stone is God's assurance that we are accepted. Now add to that the gift of a new name written in the stone and we can be assured that we belong to Him forever.

REVIEW

- What changes took place in the church after Constantine proclaimed Christianity the "State Religion?"

- Did this end persecution?

- What did this do for "church growth?"

- Who were admitted into the church?

- What changes did they bring with them?

- What did "holding the doctrine of Balaam" mean?

- How did the doctrine of the Nicolaitans differ from the pattern set forth in the epistles for church order?

- Who is referred to in the phrase, "the hidden Manna."

CHAPTER 7 The Church at Thyatira

Revelation 2:18 – 29

The Biblical meaning of the name Thyatira is: **A perfume, or fragrant sacrifice.** Scofield suggests a meaning of "continual sacrifice" (i.e., referring to the doctrine of the Mass). This meaning of "sacrifice offering" was suggested by "Hitchcock's New and Complete Analysis of the Holy Bible" and by Dr. Arnold Fruchtenbaum in his book *Footsteps of the Messiah*.

If, indeed, the name suggests sacrifice, it is most significant that from this period forward, the Roman Catholic Church boasted that Christ is continuously "sacrificed" again upon its altars every day in the celebration of the Mass (Read Hebrews 10:11-13).

Salutation:
And unto the angel of the church in Thyatira write; These things saith the Son of God, who hath his eyes like unto a flame of fire, and his feet are like fine brass; vs. 18

Thyatira has been mentioned in Acts, chapter 16 as the home of Lydia, who was converted at Philippi. It is likely that the church began when she and her household returned to her native home. So a godly woman was influential in the planting of the church and at the time of this letter one of a very different character was destroying it. Today the church of Thyatira is no more. Thyatira was southeast of Pergamos, and northeast of Smyrna. Its present population is 15,000 to 20,000. There are nine Muslim mosques.

For some people today tolerance is the only real virtue and intolerance the only vice.

<u>The message to Thyatira goes against the grain of our modern mindset by setting limits to tolerance.</u>

The main criticism of the *angel* or Bishop (Overseer/Pastor) of Thyatira is that he is tolerating something--and someone--that should not be tolerated (v. 20).

And unto the angel (messenger/pastor) of the church in Thyatira write. While all of the seven letters were addressed similarly, this takes on added significance in this letter because of the possible translation of verse 20, which we will discuss later.

These things saith the Son of God, who hath his eyes like unto a flame of fire, and his feet are like fine brass; This description of the risen Christ is <u>unique to this letter</u>. In the others, He is the Son of Man. Here He introduces Himself as the <u>Son of God</u>, perhaps to emphasize His authority and power in a church that is compromised by false teaching and practice.

He refers again to the ***eyes like unto a flame of fire,*** reminding his hearers that nothing escapes His gaze or His knowledge. Again we see ***his feet are like fine brass,*** indicating that He is walking in judgment, and that He will judge (in the sense of take action against wrong doing). This is a very part of His nature. He <u>MUST</u> judge sin where ever it appears. He will do so in our lives as well.

Commendation:
I know thy works, and charity, and service, and faith, and thy patience, and thy works; and the last to be more than the first.

There is a strong word of commendation to this church. They were a working church. The implication is clear that these were activities <u>prompted by love</u>. The word charity is actually agape, that giving kind of love which springs from God's giving. The One who knows the heart can say, I know you do what you do out of a heart of love.

The word service comes from *diakonia*, a word associated with the office of deacon. It implies at its root menial service for the fellowship.

He also sees their faith. He searches the heart. As James so well put it, *a man may say, Thou hast faith, and I have works: shew me thy faith without thy works, and I will shew thee my faith by my works.* (James 2:18). James (and we ourselves), have no other option. We see only what is external. However, God sees the heart. In addition, God commends them for their patience, their steadfast endurance under trial.

Finally, the Lord commends them again for their works, which He says, **and the last to be more than the first.** Instead of growing weary in well doing, as is so often the case, their efforts of love grew greater and more fervent with time. There is certainly much that is praiseworthy here.

Rebuke:
Notwithstanding I have a few things against thee, because thou sufferest that woman Jezebel, which calleth herself a prophetess, to teach and to seduce my servants to commit fornication, and to eat things sacrificed unto idols. And I gave her space to repent of her fornication; and she repented not. Behold, I will cast her into a bed, and them that commit adultery with her into great tribulation, except they repent of their deeds. And I will kill her children with death; and all the churches shall know that I am he which searcheth the reins and hearts: and I will give unto every one of you according to your works. Vss. 20-23

thou sufferest that woman Jezebel,
The rebuke is directed at the church and particularly to the church leadership. It appears that the translation in both the Syriac and Ethoioptic versions reads, *Thou sufferest thy wife Jezebel etc.*

Adam Clark writes, "many excellent MSS., and almost all the ancient versions, read την γυναικα σου Ιεζαβηλ, *Thy Wife Jezebel*; which intimates, indeed asserts, that this bad woman was the wife of the bishop of the Church, and his criminality in suffering her was therefore the greater."

If this is so, then the trouble maker in this church is none other than the wife of the Pastor, who, while he has apparently not joined in her apostasy, neither has he restrained it. If she was indeed the wife of the leadership, it would place the woman in a readily accepted and prominent role.

Furthermore, there is the character of the woman herself that is at issue. Whether her name was actually Jezebel, or whether this was a symbolic name, the implication is clear that she has the character of the woman whose name she bears. It might be well to remind ourselves of just what Jezebel was like.

> **1Kings 16:29 - 31** *And in the thirty and eighth year of Asa king of Judah began Ahab the son of Omri to reign over Israel: and Ahab the son of Omri reigned over Israel in Samaria twenty and two years. And Ahab the son of Omri did evil in the sight of the LORD above all that were before him. And it came to pass, as if it had been a light thing for him to walk in the sins of Jeroboam the son of Nebat, that he took to wife Jezebel the daughter of Ethbaal king of the Zidonians, and went and served Baal, and worshipped him.*

> **1Kings 21:25** *But there was none like unto Ahab, which did sell himself to work wickedness in the sight of the LORD, whom Jezebel his wife stirred up.*

The history of Ahab's reign throughout exhibits him as completely governed by his imperious wife.

1Kings 19:1, 2 *And Ahab told Jezebel all that Elijah had done, and withal how he had slain all the prophets with the sword. Then Jezebel sent a messenger unto Elijah saying, the gods do so to me, and more also, if I make not thy life as the life of one of them by tomorrow about this time.*

1Kings 21:15 *And it came to pass, when Jezebel heard that Naboth was stoned, and was dead, that Jezebel said to Ahab, Arise, take possession of the vineyard of Naboth the Jezreelite, which he refused to give thee for money: for Naboth is not alive, but dead.*

This is the character of the original Jezebel, and the inference seems to be that the woman in this church was just like her.

which calleth herself a prophetess, to teach and to seduce my servants to commit fornication, and to eat things sacrificed unto idols. Vs.20b

Please note the words carefully, *calleth herself a prophetess.* It is always problematic when someone ordains himself (or in this case herself), without the appointment of God. Even Jesus Himself was careful about this. As regards His appointment as our Great High Priest, the writer to Hebrews says, *And no man taketh this honour upon himself, but he that is called of God as was Aaron So also Christ glorified not himself to be made an high priest; but he that said unto him, Thou art my Son, to day have I begotten thee. As he saith also in another place, Thou art a priest for ever after the order of Melchisedec* (Hebrew 5:4-6).

So, she had apparently appointed herself to be a prophetess, and while there does seem to be evidence that some women were given the gift of prophecy in the early church, it was always a gift not an office. So even apart from the many character issues we see here, there is the evident usurpation of unauthorized authority over the people.

There is certainly enough here to indicate that something very wrong was going on in the Church of Thyatira and it was being permitted if not condoned. In the first place, the woman in question was not only acting in the role of a prophetess, but she was apparently acting in a teaching capacity. Once again the words of the Apostle Paul are relevant here, *But I suffer not a woman to teach or to usurp authority over a man, but to be in silence* (1 Timothy 2:12).

Where that rule has been ignored (today we have major denominations actually ordaining women), sound doctrine has almost always suffered. Much of the excesses of the early Pentecostal Movement were brought about by women and the current push to accept transgender and homosexual marriage in the older denominations has been largely championed by women.

The problem is not new. God warned through Ezekiel, *Likewise, thou son of man, set thy face against the daughters of thy people, which prophesy out of their own heart; and prophesy thou against them.* (Ezekiel 13:17).

While the woman at Thyatira had at least the character (if not the name) of Jezebel, she also, like Jezebel, was involved in idolatry and fornication. Whether that "fornication" was actually sexual in nature, or spiritual we are not specifically told.

The twenty third chapter of the book of Ezekiel is one of the most explicit and difficult in the Bible. In it Ezekiel explores the sordid career of both Judah and Israel whom he likens to two promiscuous sisters. In the context, the two committed fornication by making paramours and courtesans of the pagan nations around them, rather than looking to God for their provision and protection. Fornication is often used as a symbol of spiritual unfaithfulness, and it is possible that that is the way it is used here.

On the other hand, literal fornication and all kind of sexual deviation are invariably carried on wherever there is idolatry. Pagan worship nearly always leads to degenerate behavior, orgies and perversion. So, it is very possible that just as was the case at Corinth (1 Corinthians 5:1), there was actual fornication of a sexual nature going on here.

And I gave her space to repent of her fornication; and she repented not. Vs. 21

We do not know from whence the warning came, or from whom, but we know that this woman, who was suffered to do what she was doing by church leadership, had nevertheless been warned. And we further know that she had rejected the warning. I can only wonder what happened to those who delivered the warning. Were they the ones who were disciplined? Excommunicated? Castigated? Rejected? That is what happens when wrong leadership is in the place of power.

Behold, I will cast her into a bed, and them that commit adultery with her into great tribulation, except they repent of their deeds. And I will kill her children with death; vss. 22, 23a

Having rejected the counsel of God, God Himself will now take on the offense and the offender. God pronounces His judgment and it is three-fold: (1) *I will cast her into a bed* (the inference is, of sickness, as contrasted with the bed of adultery), (2) *I will cast* (the action verb is implied) *them* (her cohorts in sin) *into Great Tribulation* (i.e., in this context, into great trouble, anguish, pain) – sin always brings a terrible pay-day, and (3) *I will kill her children with death* – a terrible price to pay for her sin. If we will not repent, we must encounter God's discipline, and any who have experienced it fear it indeed.

and all the churches shall know that I am he which searcheth the reins and hearts: and I will give unto every one of you according to your works.vs.23b

The result of the judgment of God upon Jezebel and all who followed her, would be so clear that all the churches would see it and know that God is alive and well amidst the churches and will bring judgment upon those who reject His Word and counsel.

I remember a pastor we had when I was a boy. He was caught in an adulterous relationship with a woman in the church. He was confronted and warned by the trustees, but he refused to break off the relationship. Within a year, he was in a coffin and his son was in a hospital with a mental breakdown.

But unto you I say, and unto the rest in Thyatira, as many as have not this doctrine, and which have not known the depths of Satan, as they speak; I will put upon you none other burden. But that which ye have already hold fast till I come. Vs.24, 25

It is evident from these verses that the sin in Thyatira had not permeated the entire body. There were then, as there nearly always are, even in the worst of situations, those who love God, are true to his Word, reject the excesses and sins of bad leadership and quietly go on serving as best they can. On them, the Lord lays no additional burden. They are not responsible for the judgment that will come nor where they part of the reason it would come.

Notice, the exact terms: (1) *they have not known this doctrine.* That is, either this corrupt teaching and behavior was done secretly (as many of the false pagan practices of the day were), or it means that if it was done openly, they simply did not ascribe to or accept the teaching in any way.

(2) They *have not known the "depth of Satan".* It is evident that there is something quite sinister in that statement. Something terribly dark was happening in the church at Thyatira and this remnant of the faithful were simply not a part of it. The exhortation to them was simply to **Hold fast till I come.**

This is another of those instances where the wording goes beyond the local and immediate setting and shows that the church portrayed in the picture we have of Thyratira historically, will continue to exist until the end of the age.

And he that overcometh, and keepeth my works unto the end, to him will I give power over the nations: And he shall rule them with a rod of iron; as the vessels of a potter shall they be broken to shivers: even as I received of my Father. Vs. 27

The promise here, that the saints will reign with Christ during the Kingdom and on into eternity, is given to every faithful believer throughout the age. But in these letters, certain blessings are highlighted within given messages which seem to have a particular application to the church being addressed.

This letter has a lot to say about wanton power in the hands of the wrong people. To the faithful God says, I will remove those corrupting influences from the places of power and someday, in the Kingdom, I will place you in position to lead.

In its historic/prophetic interpretation, it is instructive that Thyatira represents the church that developed under the Papacy with all of its corruptions and usurpations of power.

Roman Catholicism has ever tried to rule over both religious and secular spheres and at one time held total power over Emperors and Kings. Her false and corrupting power will be brought to nothing (compare Revelation 17, 18), and in the end, the true saints, which she persecuted and killed, will rule with their victorious Lord.

There is, in this letter, a shadow of not only the period of the Papacy itself but the central teaching of Rome, the Doctrine of the Mass. There are two factors that lead to that conclusion. First, the name Thyatira, as we have seen, suggests sacrifice, and Rome teaches that in the sacrament of the Mass, there is a true and actual sacrifice again being made each time the Mass is celebrated. When the Priest pronounces the "magic formula" which transforms the wafer into the literal body of Christ, then that wafer becomes the actual body of Christ and a true offering for sin.

The second thing that suggests this, is the phrase, *to eat things sacrificed unto idols.* During this time the church multiplied the images of saints, and particularly the worship of the Virgin and the Child. Worship was taken from God and His Living, Victorious, Christ, and given to relics, images and icons. But that is not all.

The very central object of idolatry in Rome is the elevation of the "Host". The Host is Rome's term for the small wafer taken during the Mass. It is also called, "the Blessed Sacrament." One such "Host" is placed in a Monstrance (a sacred liturgical vessel used in Catholic worship for display of the "Blessed Sacrament"), and held up by the priest for the people to worship.

Since the entire fiction that a small cracker can be transformed into the actual body of Christ by the incantations of a Romish priest is puerile, to worship that object is the very zenith of idolatry. It is, as one has said, to make a wafer into God and worship a cracker.

And I gave her space to repent of her fornication; and she repented not. Vs.21

If the church at Thyatira truly reflects in mystery the Roman Catholic Church of the Dark Ages, then these words take on added significance.

Rome was warned by her truest sons through the centuries and especially by men like John Hus, Savonarola, John Wycliffe, William Tyndale, Martin Luther, and John Knox and her response was to attempt to kill the messengers.

As we have already seen, there is an exhortation to those within this church who are faithful to **hold fast till I come** (Revelation 2:25). There is a clear implication in these words that the form of the church in history which this church represents, will continue and that those who are faithful will be delivered (Raptured).

There is another phrase in this letter that is sobering. It is the warning, **I will cast . . . them that commit adultery with her into great tribulation** (Revelation 2:22). The implication seems clear that the apostate part of this church will exist until the end of the Church Age and go into the Tribulation. Perhaps those who commit adultery with her may refer to those elements within the Protestant Denominations that wish to go back under Rome's dominion and that seek reunion with her.

And I will give him the morning star.vs.28
Here again the wording seems to reach beyond the mere local and immediate situation. Yes, Christ is the true "Morning Star" (Revelation 22:16), but the black night of error and corruption that fell during the Roman Catholic dominance (which reached even into the eastern churches [China, Japan, India]), was broken historically by the work of the early reformers, especially the work of John Wycliffe in translating the Scriptures into the common vernacular.

It is significant that Wycliffe was known historically as "The Morning Star of the Reformation." Wycliffe wrote a pamphlet which he called, *The Last Age of the Church*, in which he followed the prophetic teachings of Joachim of Fiore and taught that these letters do indeed form a prophetic picture of the direction the Church was going.

If indeed, the Thyatira Church prefigures that period when Papal domination of the Church had reached its fullest manifestation, then Sardis certainly gives us a glimpse of the Reformation Period as we shall see. In that sense, the Lord gave the weary church a true "Morningstar of Reformation" beginning with men like Wycliffe.

He that hath an ear, let him hear what the Spirit saith unto the churches. (Revelation 2:24 – 29)

The letter thus concludes once again with the admonition, that the responsibility to hear and obey is that of the listener. If we read, study and understand these things, yet fail to apply them to our own behavior, we have not "heard" in the biblical sense.

REVIEW

- Remember the acrostic **LAPP** (Literal / Admonitory / Personal / Prophetic)

- What do we mean when we speak of the Historic/Prophetic application?

- What period of church history do the conditions in the church at Thyatira reflect?

- In what ways does Thyatira reflect this period?

- What was the general time period when Rome completely dominated?

CHAPTER 8 The Church at Sardis

Revelation 3:1 – 6

The meaning of the word Sardis is uncertain. It may be related to *σάρδιος*; sardios (as noun) the gem called: - the sardius stone: deep orange-red to brownish-red variety of chalcedony. Also known as Carnelian.

Salutation:

And unto the angel of the church in Sardis write; These things saith he that hath the seven Spirits of God, and the seven stars; vs. 1

As always, it is instructive to observe the way in which the Sovereign Lord introduces Himself to each church. Here, He reminds them that He has the fullness of the Spirit of God (seven spirits here implies the fullness of the Spirit of God see Revelation 1:4), something that this church seriously lacked, and He holds control over all those who are the appointed messengers/leaders/pastors, of the churches.

I know thy works, that thou hast a name that thou livest, and art dead. Vs.1b

"A name" indicates that this is a church that has a reputation, and from all indications, a very good reputation. Those who know it esteem it highly as being genuine and worthy of commendation.

But the One who knows all and sees all knows that whatever goodness and spiritual power this church may once have possessed has left it, and it is now little more than an empty shell of its former self.

There is no word of commendation to this church as a body, only to those who have escaped the condition which characterizes the greater part (see vs. 4).

One does not have to look far so see "Sardis Churches" in our time, as there have been throughout the Church Age. Churches that were great soul-winning, Bible preaching, centers that impacted their community and their entire area, that are today languishing and little more than monuments of past accomplishments and glory. Like Israel, when the ark of God had been captured by the Philistines, no more profound caption could be written than, *Ichabod, for the glory is departed from Israel* (1 Samuel 4:21). This then had become the true condition of this once spiritually productive church.

It is not clear exactly what produced the sorry condition of the church in Sardis, but one commentator noted that there is no evidence that there was any form of persecution against the Christians in Sardis and that the church was generally well thought of. Might we infer that churches that exist in an environment of acceptance and face little opposition, are highly subject to the same deadness as that which characterized this once great church?

Counsel:
Be watchful, and strengthen the things which remain, that are ready to die: for I have not found thy works perfect before God. Remember therefore how thou hast received and heard, and hold fast, and repent. vs.2, 3a

Watchfulness is always the appropriate and necessary posture of the believer, for we are engaged in a cosmic conflict between the forces of evil and good, God and the Devil.

We are under constant surveillance and subversion. And over what should they watch? *"Remember therefore how thou hast received and heard, and hold fast"* (i.e., remember what you have been taught).

This church had evidently been a bulwark of sound doctrine and practice – they had heard, but they were no longer hearing. How subtly error and lax living slip in where sound teaching and righteous conduct once prevailed.

So here the Lord counsels them to *"remember,"* and to *"strengthen the things that remain."* Obviously, something from the glory years of this church still remained, and while it may have been little, in relation to what had been, God places value upon it and calls upon His people to give attention to strengthening it.

This warning should have been of special significance to the church at Sardis. The city was built on a high precipice that was only accessible from a single entrance which should have rendered it impenetrable. However, history tells us that it was successfully invaded on two occasions, and in each case, the watchmen had fallen asleep. Sardis should certainly have understood the need to "watch."

So the message is to "Remember" and to return (the word repent implies a turning around from one opinion and direction to another), to where and what they had been. They are also to "hold fast", an exhortation that is repeated often in the epistles. *Therefore we ought to give the more earnest heed to the things which we have heard, lest at any time we should let them slip* (or lit. "slip away from them." Hebrews 2:1).

Paul's exhortation to young Timothy is relevant here, *But continue thou in the things which thou hast learned and hast been assured of, knowing of whom thou hast learned them; And that from a child thou hast known the holy scriptures, which are able to make thee wise unto salvation through faith which is in Christ Jesus* (2 Timothy 3:14, 15).

I have been reminded in my own life that God gave me excellent teachers in my early Christian experience – I need to remember, hold fast, and continue.

If therefore thou shalt not watch, I will come on thee as a thief, and thou shalt not know what hour I will come upon thee. Vs. 3b

This is a simple warning, that the Lord will act in judgment if repentance is not forthcoming. Sardis is dwelling in that "*space to repent*" that God's grace always provides, but absent true repentance, judgment will come.

Please note, how it will come, *as a thief*, that is, when he is least expected and they are least prepared. While the comparison to coming as a thief may only refer to the unexpected nature of His coming, the implication is also clear that if He comes in this manner, it will be to bring judgment and judgment involves loss. There will certainly be loss of blessing and likely of reward.

Commendation:
Thou hast a few names even in Sardis which have not defiled their garments; and they shall walk with me in white: for they are worthy. Vs. 4.

As we have observed before, in each of the churches there is a faithful remnant, those who have "not bowed their knees to Baal," or allowed the influences of a pagan culture to dilute their clear witness to Christ and to his holiness. Thus, the promise, *They shall walk with me in white, for they are worthy*.

He that overcometh, the same shall be clothed in white raiment; and I will not blot out his name out of the book of life, but I will confess his name before my Father, and before his angels. He that hath an ear, let him hear what the Spirit saith unto the churches vss. 5, 6.

He that overcometh - Is it necessary to reiterate who these are? They are the true wheat among the tares, the good fish among the bad (Matthew 13). They are those who are truly saved, for their names will not be blotted out of the book of life.

If it be argued, as some still do, that these are some group of super Christians that have excelled above others (others who may be saved, but not so victorious), then one has to explain how true believers, who struggle with defeats in their lives, have their names blotted out of the book of life.

I would find it impossible to square that kind of teaching with the words of Jesus Christ, *My sheep hear my voice, and I know them, and they follow me: And I give unto them eternal life; and they shall never perish, neither shall any man pluck them out of my hand. My Father, which gave them me, is greater than all; and no man is able to pluck them out of my Father's hand. I and my Father are one* (John 10:27 – 30). If I understand anything from that passage it is, that the sheep are the responsibility of the shepherd, and this Shepherd will not loose any of His sheep.

He that has confessed His name, will have his name confessed in heaven. Perhaps it is that very act of confession that sets one off as "an overcomer," a victor!

Historic/Prophetic Perspective:
Now, looking at the church for a moment in the historic/prophetic perspective, you will recall that we said that Thyatira represents the church of the middle ages when Rome was dominate. If that is so, then Sardis represents the Reformation period.

Now, if indeed Sardis represents the Reformation period, isn't it rather surprising that so little is said in a positive way about this church? I believe a clear case can be made of why the letter to Sardis, accurately describes what the Reformation Church became.

The Reformation had its roots in the strong return of the reform leaders to the Scriptures. The study of the Scriptures led to what is known as the 5 Solas of the Reformation.

The five "Solas' were: **(1) SOLA SCRIPTURA** ("Scripture alone"): The Bible alone as the final authority, not the Bible plus tradition, or the Bible plus the Magisterium, or the Pope, **(2) SOLA FIDE** ("faith alone"): We are saved through faith alone in Jesus Christ apart from works, **(3) SOLA GRATIA** ("grace alone"): We are saved by the grace of God alone (once again apart from works or human effort, **(4) SOLUS CHRISTUS** ("Christ alone"): Jesus Christ alone is our Lord, Savior, and King and He is the sole source of salvation, not saints or Mary or the church, or the sacraments and **(5) SOLI DEO GLORIA** ("to the glory of God alone"): We are saved for the glory of God alone – for His pleasure. I can hardly think of a stronger position. The Reformers had indeed a worthy name, and a solid beginning.

But the weakness of the system became exposed because of the relationship which the church then held to the state and interestingly enough it focused on the seemingly insignificant issue of baptism. The Roman Catholic Church had held dominance over the countries where it resided and insisted that every infant be baptized (sprinkled), thus making them a member both of the church and a citizen of the country.

The concept was that the nation, or province was "Christian," and thus every person within the nation or province was united by that common bond. These countries were called Catholic because there was no other religion practiced or allowed by penalty of death. Loyalty to the church and loyalty to the king were one and the same and the initiating act for both was baptism. A kingdom that was bound by both religious and political bonds was considered a secure kingdom.

When the Reformation swept Europe, the reformers continued to hold to the old form of infant baptism (even though several questioned it in their earlier writings). The reason was more political than theological.

Now the country or providence was Protestant, or Lutheran, or whatever reformed system the country adopted. Your status as a citizen depended upon the act of infant baptism making you a member of the church and a citizen at the same time. The unity of the country depended upon everyone being considered Christian.

It goes without saying that while the great Gospel truths of the Reformers were rediscovered and proclaimed, and while many did understand and turn in faith to Christ, the fact that the church and the state where so closely tied, meant that whole areas would become "Protestant" overnight, leaving the spiritual state of many (even sometimes the pastoral leadership) unchanged. These multitudes were considered "Protestant Christians", when in fact most had no work of grace in their lives.

The passion of the churches, both Reformed Protestant and Roman Catholic to hold onto this equation of baptized Citizen/Christian could produce nothing less than a host of baptized pagans, which eventually showed itself in the violence that followed in the Peasant Rebellion and the 30 Year War. Reformation Protestantism had begun well, and had a great name, but had a weakness at its core.

This difference became clear when the Ana-Baptist movement began to flourish. These were true believers who held to the same 5 great solas of reformation doctrine, but taught that baptism was an ordinance to be obeyed by those who had believed and confessed Christ, not a sacrament that actually conveyed the grace of salvation. Hence, when many heard and understood the gospel of saving grace, they were re-baptized (immersed), as a testimony of their faith.

This action did two things. First, it considered infant baptism a pagan rite (historically they were correct, like many other practices Rome had adopted this one from paganism), and thus Ana-Baptists rejected its validity.

Ana-Baptists held that they were not re-baptizing people, they claimed that they had never been actually baptized in the first place. This position of course raised a serious theological difference between Baptists and the other Reformers.

But the second effect was even more dangerous for the Baptists. If infant baptism was not valid, then that took away the act of loyalty to and unity with the state, and meant that a particular state could never be considered truly Christian, but only those within it that had made a true confession of faith could be called Christians.

This struck at the cohesion the state had and its ability to be a completely "united" people. If only those who had a personal conversion experience were Christians and others were not, then the double bond of religion and statehood would be broken and that would create a division among the people that would be dangerous in any time of crisis.

Let me quote here from Dr. Erwin Lutzer's recent book, *Rescuing the Gospel*.

> "The Anabaptists were a threat to the medieval order that united the church and the state. By baptizing only those who professed faith in Christ, they affirmed that the church was a minority within society; but by no means should the church be identified with the totality of society. Christianity, they affirmed, required a lifestyle that could only be achieved by the redeemed, not by those who believed they were Christians because they were baptized as infants.
>
> The Anabaptists insisted that an infant could not be made a Christian even if an ocean of water were poured on his head. They said the infant baptism was therefore no baptism at all but a "dipping in a Romish bath." Consequently, they objected to being called Anabaptists; they were not re-baptizers, they argued, because when they had water sprinkled on their heads as infants, they weren't really baptized at all.

They believed that God, by the Word and the Spirit worked directly on the heart of those who believed in Christ, giving them the gift of the Holy Spirit and power to live a new life . . . and that there must be a purging (of tares from the wheat) if the true believers were to form God-honoring churches.

They believed that God would make the final separation, but believers are commanded to keep the church as pure as they can through discipline and watchful obedience. The church and the state should therefore separate since the state is concerned with everyone in the community (area/nation) whereas the church consists only of the saints." (*Rescuing the Gospel,* page 156).

But both Roman Catholic and the Reformed churches feared that such would weaken the union and the power of both the State Churches and the State itself, and so they rejected this rather evident truth (I say evident because even Zwingli had come to the conclusion that infant baptism was wrong in his early writings, and then, under pressure, reinstated it).

So, the Reformers, and the Roman Catholics, and the Legates of the nations, all agreed that these Baptists were dangerous and had to be destroyed at all costs. Literally thousands of Baptist believers were drowned, put to the stake, impaled, tortured and decapitated, merely for holding to the inescapable conclusions that the 5 Solas would have brought any honest thinker to. Salvation is not in sacraments, infant baptism is a pagan sacrament, and therefore truth demands that it be rejected and the biblical ordinance of believer's baptism be practiced.

The great doctrinal statements of the Reformation Churches were true, but it meant little to the men and women in the pew. They were virtually rendered irrelevant by the holding onto the one error of infant baptism and a unified "Christian" nation. If all are "Christians" from infancy because they were "baptized" then no one needed conversion, and so it could be rightly said, *They had a name that they lived, but are dead.*

REVIEW

- What was the "reputation" of the church at Sardis?

- Explain why God said this church had a name but was dead?

- What was the church at Sardis told to "remember?"

- The Reformation Church came about because of a return to what?

- Name the 5 Solas of the Reformation

- What was the central weakness of the Reformation movement?

- How did the rise of the Ana-Baptist movement expose this?

- Why did the Baptists reject the name Ana-Baptist?

- How did the rejection of infant baptism weaken the unity of the state?

- What did the state, the Reformers and the Catholics agree on?

- What happened to the Ana-Baptist believers during this period?

CHAPTER 9 The Church at Philadelphia

Revelation 3:7 – 13

The name Philadelphia Gr.*φιλαδελφία*; philadelphia means *fraternal affection:* - brotherly love (kindness), love of the brethren.

Salutation:
And to the angel of the church in Philadelphia write; These things saith he that is holy, he that is true, he that hath the key of David, he that openeth, and no man shutteth; and shutteth, and no man openeth; vs, 3:7

The risen Lord introduces Himself to this church as the One who is Holy. It is this attribute which sets the Triune Godhead apart from every other god, and our Holy God expects this attribute to be reflected in His people. It would appear that perhaps either this church best reflected His Holiness, or that He most challenged this church to reflect the character of holiness in their lives.

The risen Lord then introduces Himself as the One that is True. He indeed is the Truth, and He is most concerned with Truth, because by very definition, Truth is that which conforms to reality, that which is, or was, or shall be. The alternative is a world of illusion, myth, falsehood and fantasy. He has proclaimed, "Thy Word is Truth (John 17:17). He intended that this church be most concerned with Truth as well.

And He is introduced as the One that holds the Key of David. The later expression comes from Isaiah 22:22; and implies full authority to rule over a kingdom. There are several applications of this fact to the church at Philadelphia.

First, the church was severely opposed by the Jewish community in that place. We have already discussed Jewish enmity toward the Gospel as it developed even though it was first readily received by Jews. One commentary suggests, "A third-century inscription from the Jewish synagogue at Philadelphia has been recovered. The church in Philadelphia, like the church in Smyrna, had been expelled from the Jewish community . . . Exclusion from the synagogue could lead to more direct persecution by the Roman authorities, as in Smyrna." **(IVPBBC)**

The book of Acts, Galatians and Hebrews all attest to that opposition. Jewish believers had to separate from the Synagogue worship either by choice, as happened in Corinth (Acts 18:6-8), and in Ephesus (Acts 19:8, 9), or they were forcibly excluded as in Antioch (Acts 13:44-49). This opening statement suggested that though excluded by the Jews, the One who really held the final Keys had welcomed them.

In addition, as becomes clear as we read further, this description of Christ, holding the Keys of David, and having the power to open or close doors, will be used to challenge this church to go through the open doors of opportunity which Christ has set before them. Thus, as always, this opening introduction to the character of our Lord, who is the Lord of all the churches, is commensurate with the need of the specific church to which it is given.

Commendation:
I know thy works: behold, I have set before thee an open door, and no man can shut it: vs. 8a

Philadelphia has often been called, the "Missionary Church." We do not actually know much about the "works" or "deeds" of this church, only that the Lord knew them and commended them. But the phraseology used would allow us to suspect that the church at Philadelphia was a church that aggressively spread the Gospel beyond its own immediate area.

The phrase, *I have set before thee an open door, and no man can shut it:* is reminiscent of Paul's very similar language in the following passages:

1 Corinthians 16:9 *For a great door and effectual is opened unto me, and there are many adversaries.*

2 Corinthians 2:12 *Furthermore, when I came to Troas to preach Christ's gospel, and a door was opened unto me of the Lord,*

Colossians 4:3 *Withal praying also for us, that God would open unto us a door of utterance, to speak the mystery of Christ, for which I am also in bonds:*

In each of these passages, the "open door" refers to an opportunity to do what God has called the church to do, namely take the Gospel to the whole world. It would be odd that the phrase would mean anything else here.

Beside this, the adversary will not be able to shut the door. Amazing statement! We have seen the great lengths to which atheistic and other anti-Christian regimes have gone to keep the Bible and the Gospel from getting in, and over and over again, they have been penetrated and the Gospel prevailed.

In a recent report, those who know tell us that what is happening in Iran today, is similar to what happened in China during the Moa era. Literally thousands are turning to faith in Christ and becoming Christians. When God has opened a door, no amount of human power or ingenuity can close it. The history of Missions is the history of God opening doors for the Gospel.

Commendation:
for thou hast a little strength, and hast kept my word, and hast not denied my name. vs. 8b

There are three observations made here by the Lord, and I want to examine each in order. First, *Thou hast a little strength*. Some commentaries find this a criticism of this church, but I am inclined to believe it was not. It says, in effect, "You have some power, though you are poor in numbers and worldly resources." In fact both Alford, Trench, and Düsterdieck believe that is the sense intended here.

The Philadelphia church was far from a mega-church, they were a small assembly in terms of numbers. Furthermore, they were not endowed by wealthy members nor did they have many material resources. Yet for all that, they were an effective church in their witness for Christ.

Furthermore, they were loyal and obedient to the Word of God. The Lord could say of them, *you have kept my Word*.

Finally, they were unbending in their confession of Christ before an adversarial world. They freely confessed His name regardless of the opposition they might have faced.

No wonder they were commended by the Lord.

Behold, I will make them of the synagogue of Satan, which say they are Jews, and are not, but do lie; behold, I will make them to come and worship before thy feet, and to know that I have loved thee. Vs. 9

Once again, the implication is very strong that much of the opposition against the church and against the gospel, originated with the Jews of the area. Remember that Israel had originally welcomed the gospel and thousands were saved and became followers of Messiah Jesus. The early beginnings of the church were entirely Jewish or Jewish proselytes. Then came the opposition of the High Priest and that of the Sanhedrin. Saul of Tarsus led the attack persecuting the believers, even unto death and, "making havoc of the church."

While Saul was eventually converted and became the Apostle to the Gentiles, Jewish resistance and opposition grew and spread so that, as we have seen, everywhere the Gospel was preached, local Jewish leaders opposed and persecuted believers, especially those who were Jewish by birth and became followers of the Messiah, Jesus. This was the condition already noted in the letter to the church at Smyrna; *I know the blasphemy of them which say they are Jews, and are not, but are the synagogue of Satan* (Revelation 2:9).

Obviously, it was this kind of persecution that the church at Philadelphia must have been experiencing, and God promised that He would so display His blessings upon the church that even their fiercest enemies would have to admit that God was among them.

This is not unlike the promise God once gave through Isaiah concerning the enemies of Israel;

> *The sons also of them that afflicted thee shall come bending unto thee; and all they that despised thee shall bow themselves down at the soles of thy feet; and they shall call thee, The city of the LORD, The Zion of the Holy One of Israel* (Isaiah 60:14).

While we have no biblical record of how this took place, Bishop Richard C. Trench refers to a passage in the Epistle of Ignatius in which he refers to this Philadelphian church. The passage implies the actual presence of converts from Judaism, in the midst of the church, and who preached the faith which they once persecuted. If this record is correct, then we can only assume that God opened the eyes of these Jews, as He had once opened the eyes of Saul of Tarsus, to see and embrace their Messiah and Savior, Jesus Christ.

In whatever way this promise was fulfilled at the time of the writing of this letter, the ultimate fulfillment is still future when;

At the name of Jesus every knee shall bow, of things in heaven, and things in earth, and things under the earth; And that every tongue shall confess that Jesus Christ is Lord, to the glory of God the Father (Philippians 2:10, 11).

Because thou hast kept the word of my patience, I also will keep thee from the hour of temptation, which shall come upon all the world, to try them that dwell upon the earth. Behold, I come quickly: hold that fast which thou hast, that no man take thy crown. Vss. 10, 11

This passage presupposes a Historic / Prophetic interpretation

This is an amazing promise and one, that if taken in its natural, literal sense, demands that the interpretation go far beyond the historic setting, to the very end of the age and the Great Tribulation itself. We should therefore examine it with great care.

First, the promise is given because whatever this church has suffered, it has done so with patient perseverance and has retained its testimony and its integrity through it all. Commentator Matthew Henry writes; "Those who keep the gospel in a time of peace, shall be kept by Christ in an hour of temptation; and the same Divine grace that has made them fruitful in times of peace, will make them faithful in times of persecution." (Matthew Henry Concise Commentary)

The second thing we must grapple with is the phrase, Gr. ὥρα πειρασμός; _the hour of temptation_. Whatever this is, it must be a set period of time that is characterized by extreme testing and trial beyond anything that would normally be expected. The word translated "temptation" carries the force of a putting to _proof_ by _experience_ [of evil], solicitation, or provocation); by implication _adversity_. It comes from a root word meaning "to pierce." Obviously, the word is meant to convey extreme trial and testing of the most intense kind.

Thirdly, we must not miss the intended scope of this period of suffering and extreme anguish, *which shall come upon all the world.* This alone indicates that what this prophecy deals with, must go far beyond the local situation and time of the church to which it is addressed. This period of suffering will be world-wide in scope.

Finally, we must not miss the intended objects of this intense time of suffering, *to try them that dwell upon the earth.* The phrase is used eight times in Revelation (3:10; 6:10; 11:10; 12:12; 13:8; 13:14; 14:16; 17:8), and may be translated as a descriptive title, *the earth dwellers.*

The meaning can be best grasp by recalling the distinction Paul makes between the natural man, that is, the man of the earth that has experienced only physical birth, and the spiritual man, that is, the man who has also experienced the new birth.

> *The first man is of the earth, earthy: the second man is the Lord from heaven. As is the earthy, such are they also that are earthy: and as is the heavenly, such are they also that are heavenly. And as we have borne the image of the earthy, we shall also bear the image of the heavenly (1 Corinthians 15:47 – 49).*

The "earth dwellers" therefore, are not merely those that happen to inhabit this planet, but those whose unregenerate natures tie them to that which is earthy, sensual, and even devilish (James 3:15). It is upon this particular group of people that this promised "hour of temptation," is directed. We must derive from this then that this period of trouble is not intended for those who are redeemed, and we have the promise that this church will be kept from it.

Because of the inescapable universal nature of this promise, we may well remember again Scofield's observation, "these messages by their very terms go beyond the local assemblies mentioned."

Though some have tried to do so, there is no honest way of interpreting these words except to say that they must refer to a time yet future, when a period of great trial will be visited upon the earth, and that this church (and by extension, all believers of this Dispensation) will be spared.

Even IVP, hardly a bastion of Premillennialism, writes, The "hour of testing" is too universal for a local testing and must refer either to the great tribulation or, to the final hour, the day of judgment **(IVPBBC)**.

And once again, note the very precise wording "<u>from</u>" the hour of temptation (not as some teach "<u>through</u>" the hour etc.). In short therefore, this promise assures us that the Church will not go through that period of the outpoured wrath of God known as the Great Tribulation but be saved from it.

Walvood writes, "Though scholars have attempted to avoid this conclusion in order to affirm post-tribulationism, the combination of the verb "<u>keep</u>" (*tērein*) with the preposition "<u>from</u>" (*ek*) is in sharp contrast to the meaning of keeping the church "<u>through</u>" (*dia*), a preposition which is <u>not</u> used here. The expression "the hour of trial" (a time period) makes it clear that they would be kept *out of* that period." **(Bible Knowledge Commentary)**

Behold, I come quickly: hold that fast which thou hast, that no man take thy crown. **Vs. 11**

Almost as if to underscore that fact that the preceding promise goes beyond the local situation and points to the end time, our Lord assures us that He is coming. In fact, the very proximity of this promise to the former promise of being saved "from" the Great Tribulation suggests strongly that it is by this very event that we will be saved from that period.

The phrase, "come quickly," does not imply "come soon" but rather that his coming will be sudden; *in a moment, in the twinkling of an eye at the last trump*, etc. (1 Corinthians 15:52).

This verse, along with a number of other verses, imply that His coming is imminent, that it can happen at any time, and that it will be sudden and unexpected.

In the light of the imminency of his coming therefore, the saints at Philadelphia, as well as we today, are to **hold that fast which thou hast, that no man take thy crown**. The word "hold fast" is *κρατέω*; krateō, to seize by strength. Perhaps they have but a little strength, but with it they are to seize what they have.

And what is it that they have? They have kept His Word, and have not denied His name (Revelation 3:8). The Lord is still looking for those who will hold fast His Word, and remain faithful to Him in the face of opposition.

The implication of the final phrase in verse 11, _that no man take thy crown_ is, that those who hold fast will have earned a crown, those who do not, will lose the crown they might have had. The subject here is not salvation, for that cannot be lost. It is rather rewards for faithful service and there is a consistent warning in Scripture that rewards gained, can be lost.

> Look to yourselves, that we lose not those things which we have wrought, but that we receive a full reward. (2 John 1:8).

Those who run the race must run lawfully, or be ἀδόκιμος; adokimos "disqualified" (1 Corinthians 9:27).

Him that overcometh will I make a pillar in the temple of my God, and he shall go no more out: and I will write upon him the name of my God, and the name of the city of my God, which is new Jerusalem, which cometh down out of heaven from my God: and I will write upon him my new name.Vs.12

The promise this time is that overcomers will become "pillars in the temple of God." The phrase would bring to mind at once the two pillars which stood in Solomon's great temple.

Those two pillars were named Jachin and Boaz (1 Kings 7:21), words which connote "stability" and "strength." As used here the promise seems to imply a place of honor and recognition.

And please note where these "pillars" are. They are not in Solomon's temple, but *in the temple of my God*, that is in the eternal temple. And further, *he shall go no more out* (comp. Psalm 23:6). This, it seems, must be understood in the context of the church to which it was said.

To this church the Lord had entrusted an "open door" of opportunity. This church had taken advantage of that door to spread the Gospel as far as they could. In the prophetic view, this church represents that great period of evangelism and missions which was the prominent characteristic of the Bible believing church from the late 1600s till the middle of the last century.

There are still great missionary efforts being made by the church, but the period when she was most characterized by those efforts has tragically passed. The text itself seems to reflect this. They had "gone out" and paid the price of obeying the command to carry His Gospel to the uttermost part of the earth. Now they *will go no more out* but must rest.

and I will write upon him the name of my God, and the name of the city of my God, which is new Jerusalem, which cometh down out of heaven from my God:

Just as this message looks forward to the imminent coming of Christ, so it also looks forward to things which will be described later in the book of Revelation. Wearing the name of God is also referred to in Revelation 14:1.

> *And I looked, and, lo, a Lamb stood on the mount Zion, and with him an hundred forty and four thousand, having his Father's name written in their foreheads.*

As we will see, these are redeemed souls from the twelve tribes of Israel. They shall have the distinction of having the "name" written upon their foreheads. But so shall we, who are the redeemed of this present Church Age. We shall wear the identification of God's name, as belonging to Him, and as belonging to the eternal city the New Jerusalem, that will descend from heaven some day (Revelation 21:9, 10).

There is no word of rebuke to this church. The church of Philadelphia survives the scrutiny of the One who has eyes as of a flame of fire. If God is pleased with this church, then we should take careful notice what it was that pleased Him and emulate it.

At the heart of everything else was that passion for taking the Gospel to those who had never heard, and I have lived long enough to observe, that the church that will make that passion the centerpiece of their existence, will also love His Word, be loyal to His name and experience His blessing.

He that hath an ear, let him hear what the Spirit saith unto the churches.

The letter closes then with that same exhortation which we have examined before, hear and take heed.

REVIEW

- What set the church in Philadelphia apart from other churches?

- What rebuke did God give to this church?

- What significance is there to the phrase, *I set before you an open door*?

- What period of Church history does this church represent?

- What did the Lord promise He would save this church from?

CHAPTER 10 Church of the Laodiceans

Revelation 3:14 – 22

Rev. 3:14 *And unto the angel of the church of the Laodiceans write; These things saith the Amen, the faithful and true witness, the beginning of the creation of God;*

If you are reading carefully, you will notice that this letter begins differently than any of the former letters. Watch closely the wording; ***And unto the angel of the church <u>of the Laodiceans</u> write.*** Each of the other letters where written to the church at a particular location. This is a letter written to the church of the Laodiceans. What is the difference?

The wording implies from the very beginning that this church is controlled by its members. And indeed the very name suggests the same. Vincent says, Gr.*Λαοδικεύς,* Laodikeus; Laodicea means *justice of the people.* In other words, it is the people's court, or to put it another way, the people are ruling. As a result, the very salutation seems to suggest that the church belongs, not to the Lord Jesus Christ, but to the people themselves. If there were no other information about this church available, that would be sufficient to tell you that this church is in trouble.

These things saith the Amen, the faithful and true witness, the beginning of the creation of God; vs. 14

As in each letter, the Lord identifies Himself in the manner which best declares that He can meet the needs of that church. Here He begins with the name, the Amen.

The word means "surely", "verily", "truly", "it is a fact."

The implication would seem to be that this church was not too sure of what the truth is. In fact, perhaps, as in our present culture, they were even doubting that there was such a thing as truth. Our Lord is the Amen! He is the Truth! To know Him is to know truth and we can rest in that.

In addition, He calls Himself, *the faithful and true witness*. What He says you can rest upon. Any church that has lost confidence in the Scriptures, the written recorded Word of God, is adrift without wheel or rudder. Disaster will be the inevitable and predictable outcome. Further reading of the description of this church indicates it was in need of this very confidence.

Finally, our Lord calls Himself, <u>the beginning of the creation of God</u>. The use of the word "beginning" Gr. ἀρχή; archē to translate here is unfortunate because it has given those who deny Christ's absolute deity ground to claim that the verse teaches that He was the first to be created and therefore not fully God. The word indeed means "first" but here it refers not to the order of creation but to rank. Christ is the first in rank over all creation, therefore He is Lord of creation.

I think it is also significant that creation is referred to here. When a church begins to question whether it can take the Scriptures at face value and believe them, one of the first areas that it begins to doubt is the record of creation. God's Word is unambiguous about that.

Genesis 1:1 *In the beginning God created the heavens and the earth.*

Psalm 33:6 – 9 *By the word of the LORD were the heavens made; and all the host of them by the breath of his mouth. He gathereth the waters of the sea together as an heap: he layeth up the depth in storehouses. Let all the earth fear the LORD: let all the inhabitants of the world stand in awe of him. For he spake, and it was done; he commanded, and it stood fast.*

Isaiah 40:26 *Lift up your eyes on high, and behold who hath created these things, that bringeth out their host by number: he calleth them all by names by the greatness of his might, for that he is strong in power; not one faileth.*

John 1:1 – 3 *In the beginning was the Word, and the Word was with God, and the Word was God. The same was in the beginning with God. All things were made by him; and without him was not any thing made that was made.*

Do you know what one of the benefits of this faith in a Creator God is? It is knowing that He who has all knowledge, and all wisdom, and all care for His creatures, created just enough energy in the earth to sustain it, just the right amount of CO_2 to allow plant growth to prosper. He wants us to be good stewards of it, but I am not wringing my hands and wondering whether the earth is going to make it. I've read the last chapter of the book, I know how the story ends.

Rebuke:
I know thy works, that thou art neither cold nor hot: I would thou wert cold or hot. So then because thou art lukewarm, and neither cold nor hot, I will spue thee out of my mouth. **Vss.15, 16**

Again, though the message begins with the same words as in each of the letters, there is a marked and distinct difference. In other churches the Lord always found something (in some churches many things) that He could commend. In this church there is no commendation. He begins at once to rebuke and express His distress over their condition.

Thou art neither hot nor cold. This statement would have come with significant force to this particular church because of their situation. IVP describes it like this, "Laodicea lacked a natural water supply. Water piped in from hot springs six miles to the south, and any cold water that could have been procured from the mountains, would be lukewarm by the time it reached Laodicea. This condition was a standard complaint of local residents, most of whom had an otherwise comfortable lifestyle." **(IVPBBC)**

It is clear from the text that our Lord played upon this very condition in His condemnation of this church; *I would thou wert cold or hot. So then because thou art lukewarm, and neither cold nor hot, I will spue thee out of my mouth.* The condition of the church was comparable to the condition of the place, like the lukewarm water they had to drink, the church was lukewarm toward the Lord and to all of their duties, and hence they were as nauseating to Christ as the local water supply was to the people.

Love for Christ and His Word and work should be hot and fervent. Solomon describes that kind of love when he says;

> *Love is strong as death; jealousy is cruel as the grave: the coals thereof are coals of fire, which hath a most vehement flame. Many waters cannot quench love, neither can the floods drown it: if a man would give all the substance of his house for love, it would utterly be contemned (Song of Solomon 8:6, 7).*

Love, to be real must be intense, and the attitude of this church toward the Lord was anything but intense. It was nauseating, but there is grace mixed with this warning.

The declaration *"I will"* is not necessarily final. It is the word Gr. μέλλω; mellō and according to Vincent carries the sense that, *"I am about to or have in mind."* Not a declaration of immediate and inexorable doom, but implying a possibility of the determination being changed." **(VWS)** Thus there is hope, and that is why the Lord continues to counsel them to change their present state of heart.

Because thou sayest, I am rich, and increased with goods, and have need of nothing; vs.17

Laodicea was a prosperous banking center; proud of its wealth, it refused Roman disaster relief after the earthquake of A.D. 60, rebuilding from its own resources. It was also known for its textiles (especially wool) and for its medical school and production of ear medicine and undoubtedly the highly reputed Phrygian eye salve. Everything in which Laodicea could have confidence outwardly, its church, which reflected its culture, lacked spiritually. **(IVPBBC)**

What a contrast there is between this church and the church in Smyrna. God could say to Smyrna, *I know thy works, and tribulation, and poverty, (but thou art rich)* (Revelation 2:9). From an earthy standpoint, Smyrna lacked all that Laodicea had, yet in the sight of the risen Lord, Smyrna was the "rich" church and Laodicea poor.

By application, probably none of the other churches in these chapters reflect the present state of the church in the West as much as this church does. There has probably never been a time when there has been so much wealth on display as one finds today especially in many of the mega churches. Operating with budgets that run often into the millions, they compete with the world in glitz and glamour and entertainment. Yet many are spiritually dead.

Worse still, they often deny the inspiration and inerrancy of Scripture and ignore the great doctrines of salvation to preach a "feel-good" message of worldly prosperity and comfort. The entire thing is nauseating to the spiritually minded, how much more to Christ Himself. The Laodiceans were actually boasting of their wealth, possessions, and declared they, "had need of nothing."

The neediest church in the world and the neediest believer in the world is the one that is so deceived that they do not know their own desperate need. And that is exactly the state of things in Laodicea.

and knowest not that thou art wretched, and miserable, and poor, and blind, and naked: vs. 17

The entire description is tragic, but most tragic of all are the opening words, *Thou knowest not.* Think of the danger of such a situation. To be naked, and not know that you are naked. To be blind and not know that you are blind. Could anything be more tragic than this?

Webster defines "wretched" as "Despicable; hatefully vile and contemptible." Not a pretty description. Laodiceans dressed well, perhaps even extravagantly, enjoyed the best of cuisine, lived in expensive homes and had a coterie of servants to do their bidding, yet God describes them as wretched, poor and miserable. I wonder how He would describe the church of our time? Our local church? Us?

I counsel thee to buy of me gold tried in the fire, that thou mayest be rich; and white raiment, that thou mayest be clothed, and that the shame of thy nakedness do not appear; and anoint thine eyes with eyesalve, that thou mayest see. Vss. 17, 18

The first word of counsel is to set their eye on that which is eternal, not temporal. As always, Biblical symbolism must be interpreted by how the same symbol was used and interpreted in another place. There are really two ways in which gold is used symbolically in the New Testament. The first would be in 1 Corinthian chapter three, where gold is used as a symbol of the "faith works" of the believer. Works done in faith and for the glory of God are compared to "gold, silver and precious stones."

> For other foundation can no man lay than that is laid, which is Jesus Christ. Now if any man build upon this foundation gold, silver, precious stones, wood, hay, stubble; Every man's work shall be made manifest: for the day shall declare it, because it shall be revealed by fire; and the fire shall try every man's work of what sort it is. If any man's work abide which he hath built thereupon, he shall receive a reward.

If any man's work shall be burned, he shall suffer loss: but he himself shall be saved; yet so as by fire (1 Corinthians 3:11 – 15).

The "gold" that is tried by fire is that which is done for Christ's sake, out of love for Him, with no thought of personal advantage or glory. That is the kind of work that receives the highest reward. That is the kind of work that should be our passion.

"Buying it" of Him, reminds us that we cannot produce this kind of work on our own. It comes only as we rely completely on Him. When that is produced we are "rich," both in present benefits of joy and power and effectiveness, but in future benefits of great reward beyond our wildest comprehension.

That is why men and women have sold great wealth and position and counted it all but loss to serve Christ. As Peter says, *For so an entrance shall be ministered unto you abundantly into the everlasting kingdom of our Lord and Saviour Jesus Christ* (2 Peter 1:11). It's all a question of whether you want your riches here, or there.

The second way gold is used symbolically is found in 1 Peter chapter one. *That the trial of your faith, being much more precious than of gold that perisheth, though it be tried with fire, might be found unto praise and honour and glory at the appearing of Jesus Christ:*(1 Peter 1:7-9). "Gold tried in the fire," is symbolic of the faith of these believers which was being put through the fires of persecution. It is my sense that this is the way in which gold is used symbolically here. This church needed genuine faith, and they did not have it.

The next word of counsel is this, *and white raiment, that thou mayest be clothed, and that the shame of thy nakedness do not appear.* Again we are dependent upon Scripture for and understanding of what is said.

White raiment has already been mentioned in verses four and five of this same chapter.

Thou hast a few names even in Sardis which have not defiled their garments; and they shall walk with me in white: for they are worthy. He that overcometh, the same shall be clothed in white raiment (Revelation 3:4, 5).

It is also mentioned again in Chapter nineteen.

And to her was granted that she should be arrayed in fine linen, clean and white: for the fine linen is the righteousness of saints (Revelation 19:8).

There are two kinds of righteousness in Scripture; there is the imputed righteousness which is the immediate possession of every believer, and there is the practical righteousness, produced in the believer by the power of the Holy Spirit (2 Corinthians 3:18).

I believe that it is primarily imputed righteousness that is meant in this passage. Why do I say that? Because, while in other places the white garments of righteousness are said to symbolize the righteous deed of the saints, here (1) they are counseled to obtain this raiment from Christ Himself, and (2) it is not a question of their garments being defiled, but of them lacking them altogether and standing naked without any covering at all.

There were those (and evidently not a few), in Laodicea that failed to possess that righteousness which comes by faith in Christ. Hence, like Adam and Eve in the garden, they were standing naked before a Holy God. Remember once again that the passage says, *Thou knowest not that thou art . . . naked.*

Tragic to be naked – thrice tragic to be naked and not even know it. Tragic to be unsaved, sitting every week in the nakedness of your own righteousness, and never realizing your condition. Oh, listen to His counsel.

Buy of me – Come to me. He is always the source.

He can provide the faith that is more precious than gold and He can provide the garments of perfect righteousness. Just come to Him.

So the message is clear, there are many in Laodicea that have not experienced the saving grace of God. They are yet in their sins and desperately need the covering of the imputed Righteousness of Christ. And worse of all, they are ignorant of their true condition. They assume that they are right with God when in truth, they are lost and on their way to hell.

By way of application, this passage should warn many in our churches to *make your calling and election sure* (2 Peter 1:10). Remember, *Many will say to me in that day, Lord, Lord, have we not prophesied in thy name? and in thy name have cast out devils? and in thy name done many wonderful works? And then will I profess unto them, I never knew you: depart from me, ye that work iniquity* (Matthew 7:22, 23)

Finally, the Lord counsels them to *anoint thine eyes with eyesalve, that thou mayest see.* Once again the irony of these statements can be seen in the fact that Laodicea was known for its production of eyesalve. History tells us that a medical school was located in Laodicea at the temple of Asclepius (As klee pee us), which offered a special salve to heal common eye troubles of the Middle East.

This, however was not what they needed, but the eyesalve of "Truth" that would cure their spiritual blindness. The Laodiceans saw only as men see, they perceived the things of time and space but were completely ignorant of eternal realities.

Actually, in the order of importance in which they needed these three things, they needed the pure gold of genuine faith, the spotless robes of the imputed righteousness of God and they needed the eyesalve or the Spirit that would allow them to see the reality of eternal things.

As many as I love, I rebuke and chasten: be zealous therefore, and repent.

This statement is the first clear indication that there were those in Laodicea that truly knew their God. However, even these where evidently not living in any kind of victory. The Lord's message to them is that if they are truly His, He will chasten them. This is a precious promise to all of us. If we are loved, we will be chastened if we act in disobedience. The whole subject of chastening is thoroughly dealt with in Hebrews 12:5 – 11.

Behold, I stand at the door, and knock: if any man hear my voice, and open the door, I will come in to him, and will sup with him, and he with me.

In spite of the total failure of this church, their failure had not changed God's love for them or His willingness to receive any who would receive Him. The picture is really that of the Lord of the church, standing outside the door of His own church and knocking for admittance.

This, I am afraid, is in many cases the true picture of the church in our time. Like Samson of old, who set out to do the work of God and *wist not that the Lord was departed from him* (Judges 16:20), so the Laodicean church of our time is void of the true life and power of God and so operates in the flesh.

But while the picture is that of the Lord at the door of the church, the invitation is specific – it is to "any man". *If any man hear my voice*; that voice that says *come unto me and him that cometh I will in no wise cast out. And open the door*, and this indeed seems to be the door to his individual heart, the promise is, *I will come in to him, and will sup with him, and he with me*.

Jesus is offering a personal relationship to any individual who will receive Him, yet finds himself at the door of a church that has shut Him out. He is always ready to receive any who will receive Him.

If indeed, as I believe, this church is reflective of the general condition of the church in the final days of this age, it is interesting that this closing invitation to any individual who would receive Him. It is strangely parallel to Jesus invitation to the people in Israel at the very time the majority of the nation were rejecting Him. It is found, you will remember, in Matthew chapter 11. *Then began he to upbraid the cities wherein most of his mighty works were done, because they repented not:* (Matthew 11:20). There follows the harshest words of condemnation found anywhere in the Gospel records.

But though the nation as a whole has refused Him, His love for individuals within the nation that will receive Him is felt in the words which follow;

> *Come unto me, all ye that labor and are heavy laden, and I will give you rest. Take my yoke upon you, and learn of me; for I am meek and lowly in heart: and ye shall find rest unto your souls. For my yoke is easy, and my burden is light* (Matthew 11:28 – 30).

Jesus is always ready to receive the individual that will receive Him. Hence even out of the most apostate condition of the end-time church, Jesus is still calling those who will hear His voice.

To him that overcometh will I grant to sit with me in my throne, even as I also overcame, and am set down with my Father in his throne.

Do not overlook this promise. No matter what the general condition of the church has been through the ages, those who belong to Him and are faithful to Him, will rule and reign with him in the coming Kingdom. It is that hope and expectation that makes every suffering and difficulty of the road bearable.

He that hath an ear, let him hear what the Spirit saith unto the churches

And this section finally ends with the same exhortation we have heard again and again. Our Lord implores us to "hear". To hear is to obey, and to obey is to be blessed and to be faithful to the end is to reign with him forever. May God give us – may God give me – ears that hear and a heart that will obey.

REVIEW

- How does the description of this church as "wretched and blind and naked" parallel the condition of much of the church in our time?

- Do you see any similarities in the Laodicean church to the church of the last days as described in 1 Tim. 4:1-3; 2 Tim. 3:1-9; 4:3,4; 2 Pet. 2:1-3; 3:3; 1 John 2:15-22?

- What is the message to those who are blind, and poor and naked?

CHAPTER 11 A Throne, Thrones & Beasts

Revelation 4:1 – 11

Dr. Charles Ryrie, has well said, "Chapters 4, 5 are a unit, since they together describe a scene in heaven that will give John the proper perspective on the terrible judgments that will follow." **(Charles C. Ryrie; *Revelation* pp. 47)**

We come now to the third section of this book, noted in the text in the words, *I will shew thee things which must be hereafter.* We have already noted that the word *hereafter* can best be translated, **"After these things."**

After what things? After the ***things which <u>are</u>*** (Rev. 1:19). In other words, the <u>things which **are** during this present time or age</u>. And what are *the things that are* during this age? Well, we found out in Chapters 2, 3. It is the churches. This is the Church Age, the time in which Jesus Christ's words will be fulfilled**, *I will build my church.***

The Apostles wrestled with that idea at the first Jerusalem Council.   There James, who apparently moderated the Council, summed up the discussion by saying,

> *Simeon hath declared how God at the first* (that is "for the first time"), *did visit the Gentiles, to take out of them a people for his name. And to this agree the words of the prophets;* (Acts 15:14, 15).

It was difficult for these church leaders, all Jewish, to absorb the great plan and purpose of God to raise a people, largely from outside the Jewish nation, that would be separate from that nation and yet bear His name and His testimony.   Still, they agreed in the end that was what God was doing.

But James goes on to say, **After this I will return, and will build again the tabernacle of David, which is fallen down; (Acts 15:16).** In other words, there would be something after this, that is, after the building of the Church. The words clearly expect that after the Church is complete, God **will build again the tabernacle of David.** God will once again take up His unfinished business with David's nation of Israel.

So, what are the things *after these things*? Those are the things after the Church Age, or after Christ has completed His Church. Hence, we submit, that what we are about to see in Chapters 4 – 22, are the things that will happen after the Church Age is complete.

Of course, that brings up the question immediately, when and how will the Church Age be completed. The answer to the first part of that question has clearly been denied us and everyone who has tried to circumvent that fact and set a date for Christ's coming has been duly shamed. The coming of Christ to receive His Bride (the Church), is imminent, that is, it can happen at any moment and no one knows the day nor the hour when that will occur.

But the second part of that question we do know. As early as John 14, Jesus promised, *I go and prepare a place for you, and if I go and prepare a place, I will come again, and receive you unto myself; that where I am, there ye may be also* (John 14:3). Notice the precise wording here. First, ***I go to prepare a place for you***. Just as the Jewish bridegroom, betrothed to his bride, does not receive her until he has prepared a place (a home) for her, so our Divine Bridegroom waits until all that He is preparing is ready before He will return for us.

Now note the next phrase, ***I will come again and receive you unto myself***. There is movement on His part, He comes, but there is also movement on her part, she is received unto Himself.

This is the earliest passage that refers to that event we call the Rapture. In later passages we learn that He will come in the air and we will be transformed and "caught up" (the meaning of the word Rapture) and meet Him in the air.

When His Bride the Church (comprised of every born again person from Pentecost until the Rapture) is complete, He will come and receive that Bride to Himself and **so shall we ever be with the Lord**. (1 Thessalonians 4:17).

When that happens the Church Age is over, and we then turn to *the things which are after these things*.

Rev 4:1 *After this I looked, and, behold, a door was opened in heaven: and the first voice which I heard was as it were of a trumpet talking with me; which said, Come up hither, and I will shew thee things which must be hereafter.*

Someone said to me recently, "if Revelation is a book of prophecy, why isn't the Rapture found in it?" Interesting question! First, I assured him that indeed the Rapture is found in the book of Revelation, but I added, "if you are looking for the word Rapture, you will not find that."

In the same passage we referred to above, (1 Thessalonians 4), we find the statement,

> *For the Lord himself shall descend from heaven with a shout, with the voice of the archangel, and with the trump of God: and the dead in Christ shall rise first: Then we which are alive and remain shall be caught up together with them in the clouds, to meet the Lord in the air: and so shall we ever be with the Lord (1 Thessalonians 4:16, 17).*

The word translated, *caught up*, is the Greek word, ἁρπάζω; harpazō, for which the Latin equivalent is the word **Rapto**, from which we get our English word Rapture. Each of the words mean "caught up.

Please note where we are in the book of Revelation. We have just completed God's revelation of the Church Age, and John (who is part of that redeemed throng) sees heaven open, a trumpet voice speaks, it commands him to **come up hither**, and John is transported in the spirit to heaven.

The Rapture is not taught in the book of Revelation, it is rather staged, and how significant that it occurs just after the last revelation concerning the Church is finished.

Rev 4:2a *And immediately I was in the spirit:* Although at the Rapture our bodies will be changed and "caught up", John seems to be certain that only his spirit was harpazo (caught up). This same word is used here, in the Rapture passage (1 Thessalonians 4:13-18) and in the passage concerning Paul (see below).

Paul, having a similar experience was not so sure;

> *I knew a man in Christ above fourteen years ago, (whether in the body, I cannot tell; or whether out of the body, I cannot tell: God knoweth;) such an one caught up* (harpazo), *to the third heaven. And I knew such a man, (whether in the body, or out of the body, I cannot tell: God knoweth;) How that he was caught up into paradise, and heard unspeakable words, which it is not lawful for a man to utter.* 2 Corinthians 12:2 - 4

It is evident that Paul was not sure, because all of the sensory functions which he would normally experience in his body, he likewise experienced on this occasion. Therefore, he felt no difference and could not discern whether he was in the body or not.

(Just a side note: this event has often been connected to his stoning at Lystra, but that could not be, since Paul tells us that it was 14 years since that experience, and 14 years before the writing of 2 Corinthians would make it earlier than the beginning of his missionary journeys.)

John, on the other hand is affirmative about his state – he was caught up in the spirit - but from Paul's experience, we can be certain that John was fully awake and in full charge of his faculties.

THE THRONE

Rev 4:2b *and, behold, a throne was set in heaven, and one sat on the throne.*

From this point and throughout the forth chapter, the focus is upon the Throne, the Occupant of the Throne, and those that surrounded the Throne. We gaze first at the One who occupies the Throne.

Rev 4:3 *And he that sat was to look upon like a jasper and a sardine stone: and there was a rainbow round about the throne, in sight like unto an emerald.*

BKC says, "This jasper is a clear stone in contrast to the opaque jasper stones known today; it may have resembled a diamond. The carnelian (sardine stone), is also known as the ruby (the NIV translates it "ruby")." **(Bible Knowledge Commentary)**

If this is correct, what John saw was an effusion of light (notice there is no description of a face, or form), as brilliant as a diamond with traces of deep red like a ruby.

The shape of a rainbow was described as such only in that it was an effusion of light that surrounded the Throne. The color was crystal green. And by the way, an emerald is one of the most precious of gems and very expensive.

All this considered, what John saw was that there was someone that occupied the Throne, but His glory was indescribable.

THAT WHICH IS ABOUT THE THRONE

Rev 4:4 *And round about the throne were four and twenty seats: and upon the seats I saw four and twenty elders sitting, clothed in white raiment; and they had on their heads crowns of gold.*

It is extremely crucial that we identify these individuals correctly, because their identity will determine our understanding of much else that we will deal with in this chapter. Are they disembodied spirits like those we find under the altar (6:9), or are they resurrected saints in glorified bodies. I think both the description given and the activities they perform suggest strongly the latter.

But that isn't enough, because "who" they are will aid us in determining the timing of other important events. For instance, if we identify them, as some do, as representative of the totality of both Old and New Testament saints, then we must conclude that the event that got them there, the preceding Rapture, must include both Old and New Testament saints.

In essence then, a great deal of our understanding of what has preceded and what follows will be determined by our identification of these individuals. So, let's begin by examining what John tells us about them.

The first thing we note is the number of these individuals. There are twenty-four. Now that number appears again and again in David's organization of the Kingdom as recorded in 1 Chronicles, 24, 25, 27. The Priests were first organized into twenty-four courses (1 Chronicles 24:1 – 19; Luke 1:8).

Next David organized the singers into twenty-four divisions (1 Chronicles 25). Finally, the captains where organized into twelve divisions, each comprised of twenty-four thousand men. In each case, when the twenty-four heads of these individual groups met, they were representative of the whole body of that group.

Since numbers have significance in Scripture, it is interesting that twenty-four is recognized as the number of representation. So, whoever these persons are, they are representative of a much larger body.

Next, we notice that these persons are seated upon "seats" Gr. θρόνος; (thronos), i.e., thrones. It is the same word used for the Throne of God. Obviously, these are lesser thrones, but the word would indicate that these individuals rule and reign as well.

Next, observe that they are called, "elders" Gr. πρεσβύτερος; presbuteros. Elders is the designation the New Testament gives to the highest rank of leaders in the church. Hence, we would conclude that since there are twenty-four of them, the number of representation, and they are Elders, they must be representative of the whole church.

The twenty-four elders are dressed in white robes always a type of righteousness. We encountered this in two verses in chapter three and they confirm the interpretation:

> Thou hast a few names even in Sardis which have not defiled their garments; and they shall walk with me in white: for they are worthy. He that overcometh, the same shall be clothed in white raiment; and I will not blot out his name out of the book of life, but I will confess his name before my Father, and before his angels (Revelation 3:4, 5).

Thus, these twenty-four elders, are redeemed souls, clothed in the Righteousness of Christ.

Finally, these representatives of the whole Church, have on their heads crowns, Gr.στέφανος; stephanos of gold. These are not Gr.diadēma, "diadem" as worn by a sovereign, but these are similar to the award given in the Greek games. They have been called "victor's wreaths."

It appears then that these are crowns of reward like those promised to believers for certain kinds of service (1 Corinthians 9:24; 1 Thessalonians 2:19; 2 Timothy 4:8; James 1:12; 1 Peter 5:4). If that is the case, then these individuals must already have been judged and received their rewards.

Conclusion: We conclude then that what John saw was a representation of the entire New Testament Church displayed as perfect in righteousness, judged and rewarded and prepared to rule and reign with Christ in His coming Kingdom.

Rev 4:5 *And out of the throne proceeded lightnings and thunderings and voices: and there were seven lamps of fire burning before the throne, which are the seven Spirits of God.*

We now shift our attention back to the primary Throne and are met with peels of thunder and lightning – an admittedly fearsome situation and one which always suggests some kind of impending doom. Thunder and lightning are mentioned eight times in the book of Revelation and in all but two cases they were portends of judgment about to fall. In the remaining two cases, they preceded the outpouring of praise from the redeemed.

As John hears and sees the thunder and lightning and voices, he also observes seven lamps of fire burning before the Throne and he is told the meaning of these. They are *the seven Spirits of God* (vs. 5b). So, someone says, "are there really seven Spirits of God?"

I think the passage is best understood in the light of another passage found in Isaiah chapter eleven.

> *And the spirit of the LORD shall rest upon him, the spirit of wisdom and understanding, the spirit of counsel and might, the spirit of knowledge and of the fear of the LORD; And shall make him of quick understanding in the fear of the LORD: and he shall not judge after the*

sight of his eyes, neither reprove after the hearing of his ears: But with righteousness shall he judge the poor, and reprove with equity for the meek of the earth: and he shall smite the earth with the rod of his mouth, and with the breath of his lips shall he slay the wicked. (Isaiah 11:2 – 4).

This is, of course, a great Messianic passage that describes the way in which Messiah will judge and rule the nations. He shall do so in the seven-fold plenitude of the Spirit of God. Not seven separate Spirits, but seven representative characteristics of the Spirit and seven (the number of completeness and fullness), hence, the fullness of the Spirit.

Rev 4:6a *And before the throne there was a sea of glass like unto crystal:*

It is well to remember, that the Old Testament Tabernacle, and after it the Temple, were laid out according a vision of heavenly things as seen by Moses. It should not surprise us then if we find some familiar objects before the throne.

In the Tabernacle, before the entrance to the Holy Place, stood the brazen laver. It was meant for cleansing and it was essential that the priest always wash at the Laver before and after serving in the sanctuary. Solomon turned the small laver into a "sea" when he built the Temple (2 Chronicles 4:2).

Now looking at the reality of the heavenly things, John sees another sea. Only this sea is no longer liquid. It is a sea of glass, for the saints have already been cleansed, and later in the book (Revelation 15:2), they will stand upon the sea giving praise and honor and glory to God.

It must have been a most beautiful sea, for it would have reflected back all of the glory of the One who sat upon the Throne above it.

Rev 4:6b *and in the midst of the throne, and round about the throne, were four beasts full of eyes before and behind.*

John next sees four "living creatures," Gr.ζῶον; zōon, a living creature. that is, living, animated, moving beings translated by the KJV "Beasts". The fact is, we do not know exactly what these creatures are. They have many similarities to the Cherubim that Ezekiel saw (see Ezekiel 10:20). In Chapter one Ezekiel refers to them as four (Hebrew: חי chay *khah'ee),* translated, "living creatures" (Ezekiel 1:5).

Of Cherubim, Albert Barnes says, "they are designed as symbolic representations of the majesty of God, or of his providential government, showing what sustains his throne; symbols denoting intelligence, vigilance, the rapidity and directness with which the divine commands are executed, and the energy and firmness with which the government of God is administered." **(Albert Barnes; Notes of the Bible)**

These Cherubim may be distinct from the Seraphim. Isaiah saw an uncertain number of (Hebrew שׂרף śârâph; *saw-rawf'),* *burning,* (that is, figuratively), which he called Seraphim. The word is not used anywhere else in Scripture. It denotes purity, holiness, and, indeed, they cease not to ascribe holiness to God. (See Isaiah 6:3).

Webster distinguishes them as, "winged angelic beings described in biblical tradition as attending on God. Cherubim are regarded in traditional Christian angelology as angels of the second highest order of the nine-fold celestial hierarchy of angels ranked from lowest to highest into the following nine orders: angels, archangels, principalities, powers, virtues, dominions, thrones, cherubim, and seraphim." **(Webster's Dictionary; Merriam Webster).**

What we do know is that wherever the Cherubim are seen throughout the Old Testament, they seem to be in a position of guarding the holiness of God from anything approaching that might defile it. Hence, the Cherubim at the gate of the Garden of Eden, Cherubim embroidered into the curtains that hung over both the Holy Place and the Holy of Holies in the Tabernacle, and Cherubim upon the Ark of the Covenant overshadowing the mercy seat.

In Ezekiel 28, the prophet looks beyond the earthly king of Tyre and speaks of the tragic fall of one who had been *the anointed Cherub that covereth* i.e., the now fallen Satan.

Rev 4:7 *And the first beast was like a lion, and the second beast like a calf, and the third beast had a face as a man, and the fourth beast was like a flying eagle.*

The four faces are also not new. Ezekiel sees the identical representation in Ezekiel 1:10. These Cherubim seem to be able to appear in different forms for specific purposes. Whatever else they represent, they seem to mirror the four-fold revelation of the God-man as He is presented by Matthew (the Lion/King), Mark (the servant/sacrificial ox), Luke (the perfect man), and John (the eagle which is *from above and above all* - John 3:31 i.e., God).

Rev 4:8 *And the four beasts had each of them six wings about him; and they were full of eyes within: and they rest not day and night, saying, Holy, holy, holy, Lord God Almighty, which was, and is, and is to come.*

John has already told us that these living creatures have "eyes before and behind." He now adds that they are "full of eyes within." ASV translates that, *full of eyes round about and within.* In other words, there is nothing that escapes their gaze, nothing within or without which can be hidden from them.

We also note that, like the Seraphim seen by Isaiah, they possess six wings. Isaiah tells us that, *with twain he covered his face, and with twain he covered his feet, and with twain he did fly* (Isaiah 6:2). No statement is made here concerning the use of their wings, but only that they have them.

However, like the Seraphim in Isaiah's vision, *they rest not day and night, saying, Holy, holy, holy, Lord God Almighty, which was, and is, and is to come.* They never cease praising *El Olam,* the eternal God, for His holiness. As David said, *Justice and judgment are the habitation of thy throne: mercy and truth shall go before thy face* (Psalm 89:14).

Rev 4:9-11 *And when those beasts give glory and honour and thanks to him that sat on the throne, who liveth for ever and ever, The four and twenty elders fall down before him that sat on the throne, and worship him that liveth for ever and ever, and cast their crowns before the throne, saying, Thou art worthy, O Lord, to receive glory and honour and power: for thou hast created all things, and for thy pleasure they are and were created.*

Our attention is again turned to the Twenty-Four Elders. Heaven is already ringing with the praises of the living creatures, now the Elders (1) fall down before Him who sits on the Throne, (2) and worship Him who lives for ever and ever, (3) and they cast their crowns before the throne and cry, *Thou art worthy*.

This action, of casting their crowns, is one of the most significant acts of worship we are permitted to see. If we are correct that the Elders represent the entire Church Triumphant and Redeemed, and that the *Stephanos* (crowns) they are wearing are the rewards received for service, then the act is full of symbolic significance.

It says nothing less than, "this crown was given to me for what I did, but you Lord, deserve it, for anything I did, you were the doer of it, without You, I would not even be redeemed.

Please accept my crown as the most profound act of gratitude I can give, for Savior, You and You alone are worthy."

Finally, note their praise for the preeminence of God in creation. He created it all, and it was for His pleasure it was all created. In a day when the godless world denies the very fact of creation, how glorious it is to hear His saints ascribe to Him the praise He is due.

If Chapter 4 focused our attention on the Throne, its occupant and what surrounded it, chapter 5 will focus our attention on a scroll and who can open it.

REVIEW

- Now that you have studied this section, and identified some of the things that we saw and some of the symbolism, reread the entire chapter, slowly and thoughtfully, and see if it does not "come alive" for you.

Chapter 12 The Lamb & The Scroll

Revelation 5:1 – 14

Rev 5:1 *And I saw in the right hand of him that sat on the throne a book written within and on the backside, sealed with seven seals.*

Quite obviously this "book" is a scroll as would be the usual vehicle for recording anything in that day. This, however, is not simply a common scroll. It has all the appearance of a chief legal document and it is in the hand of God Himself. Notice that it is specifically the "right hand" which holds the scroll. The right hand is always considered the hand of power and authority.

The scroll's contents cannot be known because it is sealed, and not just with one seal but a series of seven seals.   These would likely be placed in progressive locations so that as one seal was opened, the reader could progress until he would encounter the next seal. That seal would then have to be broken and so forth.

Another important feature of this scroll is that it is written on both sides. That seems to imply that at some point, if we are to read the entire scroll, we will have to turn it over, and that seems to be exactly what happens as we move along in what the scroll reveals to us.

Rev 5:2 *And I saw a strong angel proclaiming with a loud voice, Who is worthy to open the book, and to loose the seals thereof?*

Notice that the "strong angel" makes no attempt to claim the scroll himself, but rather announces a challenge to all (*in heaven, and in earth and under the earth*), that the scroll is there to be taken – however there is a condition. It is not a condition of strength, as in "who is able?" It is rather a condition of character – "who is worthy."

Rev 5:3, 4 *And no man in heaven, nor in earth, neither under the earth, was able to open the book, neither to look thereon. And I wept much, because no man was found worthy to open and to read the book, neither to look thereon.*

The universal challenge has gone forth to any and every man and no one steps forward to accept it. I think it is important to note here that it must be a man (*ha Adam* – a son of Adam). No angel is eligible, and that fact will help us to determine later, the nature and significance of the scroll itself.

Considering the scope of those who John mentions, it appears that there is a search made of heaven and earth and even the realms of the dead to find a single one who can meet the challenge. When it is finished, the report comes back, *no man was found worthy*.

This creates a very dramatic and traumatic moment for John who breaks down in a state of desperate weeping. Some have asked the reason for this or even suggested that John wept out of disappointment that he would not be able to view the contents of the scroll. I think that misses the point completely.

John wept out of a sense of deep shame that he belonged to a race, that of the multiplied millions who have lived, not a single one was worthy to claim the scroll. We are a sinful lot and *every man at his best state is altogether vanity* (Psalm 39:5), and the challenge of the scroll only magnified our depraved, debased, and pathetic condition.

Rev 5:5 *And one of the elders saith unto me, Weep not: behold, the Lion of the tribe of Judah, the Root of David,*

hath prevailed to open the book, and to loose the seven seals thereof.

It is just at the point of John's despair that he hears the welcome announcement: there is a Man that can meet the conditions. Please note again the significance of this one being a man. We shall identify him in a moment, but it is important now that we hone in on the fact of his humanity.

The Dominion Mandate

In Genesis before God ever created man He determined that man should have dominion over all the rest of creation

> *And God said, Let us make man in our image, after our likeness: and let them have dominion over the fish of the sea, and over the fowl of the air, and over the cattle, and over all the earth, and over every creeping thing that creepeth upon the earth* (Genesis 1:26).

The dominion mandate is rehearsed once again in the eighth Psalm. In that context it affirms man as the pinnacle of God's creative order, and reiterates God's intention for man to have dominion over all creation.

> *For thou hast made him a little lower than the angels, and hast crowned him with glory and honour. Thou madest him to have dominion over the works of thy hands; thou hast put all things under his feet:* (Psalm 8:5, 6).

But in the book of Hebrews, the writer quotes from Psalm eight and then adds,

> *Thou hast put all things in subjection under his feet. For in that he put all in subjection under him, he left nothing that is not put under him. But now we see not yet all things put under him* (Hebrews 2:8).

What we have in this statement is the admission of man's failure to fulfill the dominion mandate.

It is interesting and thrilling to read in the next verse these words, *But we see Jesus, who was made a little lower than the angels for the suffering of death, crowned with glory and honor;* (Hebrews 2:9). The solution to man's failure, is the God-Man, Jesus Christ. What man squandered in the fall, Jesus Christ will reclaim when he takes the scroll out of the hand of Father God.

And this helps us to understand and identify the meaning and significance of the scroll itself. Dr. Renald Showers says that the scroll represents the *title deed* to the earth. In other words, God's design that man should have dominion, rests in the title deed to the earth, and will be fulfilled in the Man, Christ Jesus.

So, in chapter 5 we see Jesus receive the title deed to earth's dominion, and in chapter 6 we see Him beginning to implement the authority to take back the earth from the Grande Usurper, Satan, until He has fulfilled the prayer of the saints, *Thy Kingdom come.*

We have looked at the significance of the scroll, now let us turn our attention to the One who claims it.

The Lamb and the Scroll

Rev 5:6 *And I beheld, and, lo, in the midst of the throne and of the four beasts, and in the midst of the elders, stood a Lamb as it had been slain, having seven horns and seven eyes, which are the seven Spirits of God sent forth into all the earth.*

The One who in verse 5 is announced as, *the Lion of the tribe of Judah, the root of David*, now appears to John as a Lamb. John sees Him as One who has been slain, that is, the marks of His sacrifice are still visible. However, though He has been slain, he is not dead, for He is standing in the midst of the elders. I cannot resist a reference here to Psalm 22.

This Psalm is the great song of the Crucified Messiah. The words He spoke from the cross, and the things which were done to Him are all recorded here a thousand years before they occurred. I have often observed that if you want a historic recital of what happened at the crucifixion from eye witnesses, turn to the Gospel accounts. But if you want to know what was going on in the mind and heart of the Savior, turn to Psalm 22.

But the Psalm isn't only about the death of the Savior, but it is also about His resurrection and subsequent victory. In verse 22, death is swallowed up in victory and we see Him emerge alive in the midst of His brethren, and He is singing! The Psalm reads, *I will declare thy name unto my brethren: in the midst of the congregation will I praise thee.*

Hebrews quotes this passage like this, *I will declare thy name unto my brethren, in the midst of the church will I sing praise unto thee* (Hebrews 2:12). What a picture, Jesus Christ singing in the midst of His church.

In similar fashion, here in Revelation, we see the Lamb brought back from death, standing in victorious life in the midst of His brethren (the elders). Though it is not mentioned here, I wonder if He is also singing?

Finally, we notice that this Lamb has seven horns and seven eyes. Horns, wherever they appear symbolically in Scripture, speak of power. Seven is the number of completeness, so His is complete power – we may use the term omnipotence. Likewise, He has seven eyes which speak of His full and complete knowledge of all things, and we call that, omniscience. He is well equipped to take on the task of recovering the dominion of the earth.

Rev 5:7-10 *And he came and took the book out of the right hand of him that sat upon the throne. And when he had taken the book, the four beasts and four and twenty elders fell down before the Lamb, having every one of*

them harps, and golden vials full of odours, which are the prayers of saints. And they sung a new song, saying, Thou art worthy to take the book, and to open the seals thereof: for thou wast slain, and hast redeemed us to God by thy blood out of every kindred, and tongue, and people, and nation; And hast made us unto our God kings and priests: and we shall reign on the earth.

What a thrilling sight this is. The twenty-four elders understand the full significance of His action. He has taken the scroll in order that He might take dominion over the earth by His great power and finally reign. Their reaction is one of immediate worship. They fall before His feet, they praise him with their harps and they emit the fragrance of their prayers.

And they sing a new song. It is a song that recognizes His victory over death and His ultimate triumph over all the forces of evil and the fact that His victory is their victory. Look at the words. They confess and agree that he is *worthy*. Remember, that was the condition of taking the scroll. All agree that it is His by right.

Next, they praise Him for their redemption through the shedding of His blood. Then they praise Him that some from every kindred, tribe, tongue and nation are present, and finally, they declare the assurance of their own destiny to rule and to reign with Him as a kingdom of priests.

It may be worthy to note that there is a variation in the text at this point and the KJV prefers the personal, *hath made us*, while some of the later translations say, *Hath made men* (or *them*, or *people*, etc.).

Part of the choice is, I believe, due to a failure to correctly identify the elders as the redeemed of this age, and therefore they remove the personal nature of the song. If we correctly identify the elders as representing us, the completed, victorious, triumphant church, then the personal pronoun is preferred, *He hath made us kings and priests*! Amen.

After the elders sing, they are joined by the angelic hosts. But please note the song changes.

Rev 5:11, 12 *And I beheld, and I heard the voice of many angels round about the throne and the beasts and the elders: and the number of them was ten thousand times ten thousand, and thousands of thousands; Saying with a loud voice, Worthy is the Lamb that was slain to receive power, and riches, and wisdom, and strength, and honour, and glory, and blessing.*

The song changes because now the heavenly choirs join in and they have never experienced redemption, and so they praise Him because He is worthy to receive *"power and riches, and wisdom, and strength, and honor, and glory, and blessing."* And what a choir it is, *ten thousand times ten thousand and thousands of thousands.*

There is an old song we used to sing that says, "Holy, Holy, is what the angels sing, And I expect to help them make the courts of heaven ring. But when I sing redemption's story, they will fold their wings, for angels never felt the joy that my salvation brings." **Johnson Oatman**

UNIVERSAL ADULATION

Rev 5:13, 14 *And every creature which is in heaven, and on the earth, and under the earth, and such as are in the sea, and all that are in them, heard I saying, Blessing, and honour, and glory, and power, be unto him that sitteth upon the throne, and unto the Lamb for ever and ever. And the four beasts said, Amen. And the four and twenty elders fell down and worshipped him that liveth for ever and ever.*

Finally, John hears voices from throughout the universe, singing the praises of the One on the Throne and the Lamb. It is difficult to fit this universal adoration into the "time-apparent" of the vision since the battle to recover earth's dominion has not yet begun, and, will in fact only begin in the next chapter. But perhaps, as some have suggested, this is anticipatory, and John is allowed to get a glimpse of what will be, *when the kingdoms of this world have become the kingdoms of our Lord and of his Christ.*

In any case when it happens, as it most certainly will, it will fulfill the closing prayer of the Psalms, *Let every thing that hath breath praise the LORD. Praise ye the LORD.* (Psalm 150:6).

REVIEW

- Please identify the things you learned in this section.
- What new truths did you see?
- What makes sense now which perhaps had not done so before?
- What blessed you most about this section?
- How will this help you in the days ahead?

Chapter 13 Six Seals Opened

Revelation 6:1 – 17 Introduction and Background

In chapter six the first of the seals on the scroll is opened, and with it begins the final drama of the battle of the ages. This chapter begins the take-back of the earth and the entire world system.   It might be well for us to consider the condition of this world system at that time just after the Rapture of the Church.   Perhaps we should begin with the acknowledgment made by an old hymn.

> *This is my Father's world*
> *Oh let me ne'r forget*
> *That tho the wrong, seem oft so strong,*
> *God is the Ruler yet!*
> *This is my Father's world,*
> *The battle is not done,*
> *Jesus who died, shall be satisfied,*
> *And earth and heaven be one.*
> **Maltbie D. Babcock**

When God engaged the land of Egypt during the days of Pharaoh He told the proud and haughty monarch that He would display His power, *that thou mayest know, that the earth is the Lord's* (Exodus 9:29). It is obvious that modern man needs to learn the same lesson.

The Old Testament prophets looked down through the ages and caught a glimpse of the shape of things going into this period known as *The Day of the Lord.* Micah laments the spiritual and moral condition that prevailed in another day and which will prevail as the coming Day of the Lord arrives.

The good man is perished out of the earth: and there is none upright among men: they all lie in wait for blood; they hunt every man his brother with a net. That they may do evil with both hands earnestly, the prince asketh, and the judge asketh for a reward (a bribe); *and the great man, he uttereth his mischievous desire: so they wrap it up. The best of them is as a brier: the most upright is sharper than a thorn hedge: the day of thy watchmen and thy visitation cometh; now shall be their perplexity. Trust ye not in a friend, put ye not confidence in a guide: keep the doors of thy mouth from her that lieth in thy bosom. For the son dishonoureth the father, the daughter riseth up against her mother, the daughter in law against her mother in law; a man's enemies are the men of his own house* (Micah 7:2-6).

Remember, the Rapture has occurred, the Church is in heaven, and there is not a redeemed man or woman on earth. So, as we approach this greatest of dramas, the final battle between God and evil, we are able to note <u>five essential purposes</u> behind the judgments of God that are about to fall during this Tribulation period. These Judgments have:

1. A Dispensational Significance (Judgment for Grace rejected).

2. A Consequential Significance (Revelation 16:4 -7; they are direct retribution for evils perpetrated).

3. A Controversial Significance (Jeremiah 25:31-33 – God has a controversy with the nations & the Beast).

4. A Purifying Significance (Zechariah 13:8, 9 – in relation to Israel and all who will be redeemed).

5. A Merciful Significance (2 Peter 3:9, 10 – no earthly judgment is as terrible as Hell- each is meant to lead men to repentance).

Each of these will discussed more in depth later.

Jehovah's Controversy With The Nations

Jeremiah tells us that the LORD has a controversy with the nations that will play out during this period. They have scorned His commandments, rejected His grace and mocked His servants. Now the Lord will speak in judgment.

> *A noise shall come even to the ends of the earth; for the LORD hath a controversy with the nations, he will plead with all flesh; he will give them that are wicked to the sword, saith the LORD. Thus saith the LORD of hosts, Behold, evil shall go forth from nation to nation, and a great whirlwind shall be raised up from the coasts of the earth. And the slain of the LORD shall be at that day from one end of the earth even unto the other end of the earth: they shall not be lamented, neither gathered, nor buried; they shall be dung upon the ground* (Jeremiah 25:31-33).

Isaiah goes into greatest depth and detail about this tumultuous time in a passage that has become known as "Isaiah's Apocalypse." In this passage the prophet reveals that judgment will not only come upon the earth and its rulers, but upon those spiritual powers that stand behind world leaders and move them to greater and greater evil and wickedness.

When God sent His plagues upon Egypt, it was not only upon Pharaoh and his people that the judgments fell but, *against all the gods of Egypt I will execute judgments:* (Exodus 12:12). Every battle is at its core a spiritual battle. Notice, in this extended passage, how Isaiah reveals that the same will characterize the judgments of the Great Tribulation.

Behold, the LORD maketh the earth empty, and maketh it waste, and turneth it upside down, and scattereth abroad the inhabitants thereof. And it shall be, as with the people, so with the priest; as with the servant, so with his master; as with the maid, so with her mistress; as with the buyer, so with the seller; as with the lender, so with the borrower; as with the taker of usury, so with the giver of usury to him. The land shall be utterly emptied, and utterly spoiled: for the LORD hath spoken this word.

The earth mourneth and fadeth away, the world languisheth (stricken with sickness) *and fadeth away, the haughty people of the earth do languish. The earth also is defiled under the inhabitants thereof; because they have transgressed the laws, changed the ordinance, broken the everlasting covenant. Therefore, hath the curse devoured the earth, and they that dwell therein are desolate: therefore, the inhabitants of the earth are burned, and few men left.*

The new wine mourneth, the vine languisheth, all the merry hearted do sigh. The mirth of tabrets ceaseth, the noise of them that rejoice endeth, the joy of the harp ceaseth. They shall not drink wine with a song; strong drink shall be bitter to them that drink it. The city of confusion is broken down: every house is shut up, that no man may come in. There is a crying for wine in the streets; all joy is darkened, the mirth of the land is gone. In the city is left desolation, and the gate is smitten with destruction. . . Fear, and the pit, and the snare, are upon thee, <u>O inhabitant of the earth</u>.

And it shall come to pass, that he who fleeth from the noise of the fear shall fall into the pit; and he that cometh up out of the midst of the pit shall be taken in the snare: for the windows from on high are open, and <u>the foundations of the earth do shake</u>.

The earth is utterly broken down, the earth is clean dissolved, the earth is moved exceedingly. The earth shall reel to and fro like a drunkard, and shall be removed like a cottage; and the transgression thereof shall be heavy upon it; and it shall fall, and not rise again.

And it shall come to pass in that day, that the LORD shall punish the host of the high ones that are on high, and the kings of the earth upon the earth. And they shall be gathered together, as prisoners are gathered in the pit, and shall be shut up in the prison, and after many days shall they be visited. Then the moon shall be confounded, and the sun ashamed, when the LORD of hosts shall reign in mount Zion, and in Jerusalem, and before his ancients gloriously (Isaiah 24:1-23).

So, these passages help us to comprehend the full scope of what is at stake. It is nothing less than retaking the dominion of the entire earth. This is not the first time this has been the issue.

In the temptation, Satan offered Christ dominion over the entire earth, but at the price of Christ's submission to Satan. Our Lord refused, but He did not deny Satan's right to make the offer. Our first father Adam had handed over his dominion to Satan when he obeyed his wicked suggestion to eat of the forbidden fruit, and now the Last Adam, will contest that dominion to take it back.

And the devil, taking him up into an high mountain, shewed unto him all the kingdoms of the world in a moment of time. And the devil said unto him, All this power will I give thee, and the glory of them: for that is delivered unto me; and to whomsoever I will I give it. If thou therefore wilt worship me, all shall be thine. (Luke 4:5-7).

Satan will make the offer of world dominion one more time in the very near future, to a man that will readily agree. We call him, the Anti-Christ.

So, with that background we are ready to begin chapter six and the opening of the first seal.

The First Seal

Rev 6:1, 2 *And I saw when the Lamb opened one of the seals, and I heard, as it were the noise of thunder, one of the four beasts saying, Come and see. And I saw, and behold a white horse: and he that sat on him had a bow; and a crown was given unto him: and he went forth conquering, and to conquer.*

Please notice that it is the Lamb that is opening the seals. Remember that He is the One proclaimed worthy to *take the scroll and to open the seals thereof* (Rev. 5:5).

When the first seal is opened the first thing we hear is the loud roar of thunder. Thunder always implies that a storm is coming, and a sharp clap of thunder threatens that the storm will be violent and that it is near.

The invitation to John to *come and see* and to view the vision which now plays out before his eyes is given by one of the living creatures we saw in chapter four. And since John has been commanded to write a record of what he saw, we are also invited, as it were, to look at what occurs before us.

However, what we see is not the anticipated dark and threatening scene that we might have expected, but rather a seemingly benign picture of a horseman on a white horse riding forth with a bow in his hand. This vision is so disarming that many have identified this rider as Christ Himself, but they have been badly mistaken, just as those in the future will be confused and disappointed by making the same mistake.

Yes, some seven years later Christ will descend riding upon a white horse, but the similar appearance of this rider is purposely deceptive.

Look carefully at the complete description and at what follows.

- This person is wearing a crown (Gr. *stephanos*-victor's wreath)
- We are told specifically that the crown was "given to him". We must then determine as we read further, who might have given it.
- He also rides with a purpose. It is *conquering and to conquer*. (The word is Gr. *nikao* as in *Nicolaitans*). Thus, he is conquering the world to establish a world government.
- He has a bow in his hand but there is no mention of arrows. We conclude therefore, that he rides forth in peace, to accomplish it without warfare.

As we look further at what follows, we see additional indicators that this is not the true Christ.

Since we have established the principle that Scripture interprets Scripture, we will turn to our Lord's own words as recorded in Matthew chapter twenty-four, where a similar sequence is found. Note the opening warning to those who asked about future things that would precede Christ's coming.

> *And Jesus answered and said unto them, Take heed that no man deceive you. For many shall come in my name, saying, I am Christ; and shall deceive many* (Matthew 24:4, 5).

It is evident that this is what we see here. This rider therefore, must be the ultimate Christ pretender, the one John, in another place, called *the Anti-Christ*.

The Second Seal

Rev 6:3, 4 *And when he had opened the second seal, I heard the second beast say, Come and see. And there went out another horse that was red: and power was given to him that sat thereon to take peace from the earth, and that they should kill one another: and there was given unto him a great sword.*

Again, John is invited to observe, and he sees a red horse. The rider, for whom we have no description may be the same as the one upon the white horse. Having established his power, war and destruction now follow. The rider is given the power to take peace from the earth.

Again, this raises the question of who is behind this rider enabling him, giving him all this power. We are not told here, but we do get the answer in chapter 13 where we are told, *and the dragon gave him his power, and his throne, and great authority* (Revelation 13:2). The phrase, *great authority,* is from the word Gr. *exousia* which carries the idea of superhuman power.

Notice to, that there is an inference of anarchy here, *that they should kill one another.* Any who fail to accept the program which this person sets forth will be destroyed, and apparently, they are destroyed often by others who have fully embraced his program, even family members and closest friends. Jesus predicted it in these words, *And then shall many be offended, and shall betray one another, and shall hate one another* (Matthew 24:10).

The great sword he is given symbolizes the ultimate in military power. No wonder we later read, and they worshipped the beast, saying, *Who is like unto the beast? Who is able to make war with him?* (Revelation 13:4)

The Third Seal

Rev 6:5, 6 *And when he had opened the third seal, I heard the third beast say, Come and see. And I beheld, and lo a black horse; and he that sat on him had a pair of balances in his hand. And I heard a voice in the midst of the four beasts say, A measure of wheat for a penny, and three measures of barley for a penny; and see thou hurt not the oil and the wine.*

Another horse, and indeed another rider now appears. The horse is black. The symbolism is unmistakable, it is one of world-wide famine. One of the indicators of serious famine is that the flesh of the victim turns darker.

The rider carries a scale indicating that things are so bad that food is weighed out by measure. One of the four living creatures tells us the cost of basic food per measure. Our problem is that we cannot know exactly what that "measure" is. Some translations take the liberty of using the word "quart," to give the reader some idea, but this is no way certain and, quite possibly a quart may exceed the actual amount intended.

In any case, what one gets is a measure of wheat (one meal for one person) for a denarius, (worth about fifteen cents and representing a day's wages), or three meals of barley for one person for the same price. The final phrase means that nothing would be left to purchase either oil (with which to prepare the grain), or wine (something to drink with your meal).

And what of those who could not find work for a day? What of the children, the mothers, the aged? And this rider rides across the entire earth. This is a world-wide condition brought on, as so often happens, by the global war that preceded it.

Finally, we need to remind ourselves that this occurs at a time when self-interest has completely taken over and there will be little or no compassion left on the earth.

There will be no UNISEF, Red Cross, or Samaritan's Purse to rescue anyone.

Rev 6:7, 8 *And when he had opened the fourth seal, I heard the voice of the fourth beast say, Come and see. And I looked, and behold a pale horse: and his name that sat on him was Death, and Hell followed with him. And power was given unto them over the fourth part of the earth, to kill with sword, and with hunger, and with death, and with the beasts of the earth.*

The coming of the fourth rider is now inevitable. As famine follows war, death follows famine. The rider is fearsome indeed. He wears the colorless face of death and portends the demise of a fourth of the world's population.

To try to get a grasp of what that might mean let us assume a world population of about 7 billion people. Now let us assume that the preceding Rapture (4:1), and war (6:5, 6), have taken a billion away. That would leave about 6 billion as we come to this point. One fourth of 6 billion is 1.5 billion people who have to die for this prophecy to be fulfilled. That number is, frankly, greater than any of us can really grasp.

John is further told how they will die. War, famine, pestilence and wild animals all combine to take their lives. The picture is horribly gruesome, but there is something even worse.

John sees a vision of what follows the rider of death, and it is none other than Hell itself. In other words, these calamities are coming upon an unsaved world and after death is the torment of Hell. It is a fearful and dreadful prospect, but it is the inevitable result of a world that has rejected the Savior.

As terrible as all this is, we find an exact parallel in our Lord's words in Matthew 24:1-8, which concludes with the words, *all these are the beginnings of sorrows.* The picture is that of a woman in travail, the first pangs of birth have come, and now much more serious labor pains will begin.

The Martyred Saints

Rev 6:9-11 *And when he had opened the fifth seal, I saw under the altar the souls of them that were slain for the word of God, and for the testimony which they held: And they cried with a loud voice, saying, How long, O Lord, holy and true, dost thou not judge and avenge our blood on them that dwell on the earth? And white robes were given unto every one of them; and it was said unto them, that they should rest yet for a little season, until their fellow servants also and their brethren, that should be killed as they were, should be fulfilled.*

The next seal deals with something entirely different, those who are slain for their testimony of Christ during the Tribulation period. This, of course, means that there will be multitudes who come to God during this terrible period, and how that happens we will see in the next chapter. They are seen by John, under the altar. What altar?

Although the Altar of Incense, which stands before the Throne is referred to several times in the book of Revelation, it is not the altar spoken of here. No sacrifice, or oblation was ever to be made on the Altar of Incense.

The word translated altar here is Gr. *θυσιαστήριον*; thusiastērion, which specifically means "a place of sacrifice." It would be analogous to the brazen altar in the Tabernacle where blood sacrifices where offered. Thus, these individuals were considered sacrifices, not for the expiation of sin, but simply for the sake of their testimony to God and to His Word.

John heard them crying loudly to the One for whom they had laid down their lives. He is addressed as Lord (absolute Sovereign), He is Holy, and He is the One who is True. Their plea is that He would take His great power and judge those who had slain them.

The plea is not that of vindictiveness, but of vindication, for as is always the case, they had been accused and wrongly maligned to justify their execution. Their vindication is also the vindication of the Lord's Name, and they long for that.

They are each given a white robe, showing that Christ recognizes their innocence and the purity of their lives, and they are exhorted to rest and assured that it will be only a short time. The Tribulation period is a total of only seven years, and there is great likelihood that half or more of that may be already past when they are given this assurance.

Finally, note that they should rest until they are joined by many more that will likewise be slain. These are specifically called their "fellow servants" and "brethren," and there is yet another thing here we should not miss. The phrase, *should be fulfilled*, uses the word Gr. πληρόω; pla ̄roō, meaning, "complete."

There is a specific number, known to God, who will sacrifice their blood for His sake. What happens therefore, will not be random, but under the perfect providential care and control of God. How comforting to know that he is in control.

Summary: what we seem to have in this chapter, to this point is an overview of this entire period. On a timeline, the final world ruler will not be revealed until after the Rapture (2 Thessalonians 2:1, 2). He will come peaceably and take control of the final phase of the old Roman Empire. But when his power is consolidated, he will begin to eliminate any who oppose him and war against any nation which does not submit to his rule.

His promises and policies will be so deceptive that many will enthusiastically support them, and those who do not will be branded traitors. As we have already seen, the result will be many betraying and killing one another.

As war spreads, so the aftermath of war will spread, and famine and death will reign.

This is the general overview of the period and it is difficult to place these pieces on any kind of strict timeline except that according to Matthew 24, these are just the beginning of sorrows, hence all of this takes place during the first three and one-half years of the Tribulation.

In the midst of it all, those who come to faith and serve the God of heaven will be counted (as they are in oppressive countries today) traitors and criminals and be martyred by the thousands (and perhaps by the millions).

Matthew 24:1-14 covers the first half of the seven-year period, then verse 15 marks the beginning of the second with these words, *When ye therefore shall see the abomination of desolation, spoken of by Daniel the prophet, stand in the holy place. . .* While we have seen verses 1- 8 are parallel with the first four seals, verses 9-14 seem to match perfectly with the fifth seal.

Where do all these martyrs come from in verses 9-11? When the Church is raptured, there will be virtually no believers left on earth.

One writer suggests that they will be saved in the days just following the Rapture, but this becomes problematic in the light of the teaching that those who heard the gospel before the Rapture and rejected it, will be blinded as 2 Thessalonians 2:11, 12, clearly teaches; *And for this cause God shall send them strong delusion, that they should believe a lie: That they all might be damned who believed not the truth, but had pleasure in unrighteousness.*

Those who are saved during this period, and there will be an innumerable host, will apparently <u>not</u> be those who have formerly rejected the gospel, so that begs the question, how will this great multitude come to faith. I believe we may find a part of the answer to that question in chapter 7.

That brings us now to the opening of the sixth seal and a great earthquake.

There are at least five earthquakes noted in the book of Revelation. These are found in Revelation 6:12; 8:5; 11:13; 11:19; and 16:18. Two of these are to be noted because they are world-wide in scope.

This one, and the final one in chapter 16 seem to be the most widespread and intense. In fact, let's read the text carefully, for I believe it leaves us no alternative to accepting this event as a world-wide cataclysm.

The Global Earthquake

Rev 6:12-14 *And I beheld when he had opened the sixth seal, and, lo, there was a great earthquake; and the sun became black as sackcloth of hair, and the moon became as blood; And the stars of heaven fell unto the earth, even as a fig tree casteth her untimely figs, when she is shaken of a mighty wind. And the heaven departed as a scroll when it is rolled together; and every mountain and island were moved out of their places.*

We know that there will be a great earthquake near the middle of the seven-year period. Ezekiel predicts just such and event in Ezekiel 38. It will be God's response to the invasion of Israel by the confederate nations (primarily Islamic), led by Russia. Ezekiel tells us how God responds:

> *My fury shall come up in my face. For in my jealousy and in the fire of my wrath have I spoken, Surely in that day there shall be a great shaking in the land of Israel; So that the fishes of the sea, and the fowls of the heaven, and the beasts of the field, and all creeping things that creep upon the earth, and all the men that are upon the face of the earth, shall shake at my presence, and the mountains shall be thrown down, and the steep places shall fall, and every wall shall fall to the ground. (Ezekiel 38:18-20)*

If words have meaning, this is an event of greater magnitude than anything we have known till now. The quake begins in the Levant specifically in Israel. But it expands to the far reaches of the earth.

There are subterranean oceanic movements that effect sea life. There are even atmospheric disturbances that affect the birds of the air. Buildings and structures of all kinds will fall in rubble and mountains will be moved out of their place. I discuss some of the science behind this in my book *The Prophetic Destiny of Israel and the Islamic Nations.*

As we study the event predicted by Ezekiel, we find many parallels to this one in Revelation. We have cause to believe that the Ezekiel event occurs near the mid-way point of the seven-year period. If indeed these two passages are looking at the same event several things should be noted:

This would be the culminating event of that first 3 ½ years of the Tribulation Period. This would be the first direct intervention by God. Ezekiel makes it clear that this is no natural event. This is the hand of God displaying His anger (Ezekiel uses the word "rage"), toward rebellious man beginning with those nations which are invading His Land. This is the first event that triggers a response of fear toward God among men.

The Universal Sense of Doom

Rev 6:15-17 *And the kings of the earth, and the great men, and the rich men, and the chief captains, and the mighty men, and every bondman, and every free man, hid themselves in the dens and in the rocks of the mountains; And said to the mountains and rocks, Fall on us, and hide us from the face of him that sitteth on the throne, and from the wrath of the Lamb: For the great day of his wrath is come; and who shall be able to stand?*

The magnitude of this earthquake is such that it portends doom to the earth dwellers. We are told that from the greatest to the least, men will seek shelter and be filled with a sense of impending destruction. And true to form, they, like Adam before them, will seek to hide themselves from the face of God. Their prayer is not one of repentance but of fear. Furthermore, there seems to be a moment of reality when men realize that what they have just experienced begins the Day of the Wrath of the Lamb.

Finally, it should be stressed that up until this event, the wars, famines, pestilence, death, all were a result of man's doing under the dominance of the Anti-Christ. But now, beginning with this event, God intervenes, and His judgments begin to come. It is no longer just the natural outworking of man's wicked designs, but, just as with Egypt of old, God will now send His judgments to bring a rebellious and evil earth under His Divine Dominion.

REVIEW

- We have discussed the apparent "Timeline" of these events. In which part of the 7-year Tribulation period do these take place.

- According to Matthew 24, what event marks the midway point of the 7-year period?

- The earthquake in chapter 6 seems to be identical to the one in what Old Testament book?

- What did you learn from this specific study?

- What questions does this chapter leave unanswered?

CHAPTER 14 144,000 & A Vast Multitude

Revelation 7:1 – 17

Rev 7:1 *And after these things I saw four angels standing on the four corners of the earth, holding the four winds of the earth, that the wind should not blow on the earth, nor on the sea, nor on any tree.*

Once again, we come upon the phrase, *after these things*. Each time it seems to denote a new phase in the ongoing drama that is unfolding. As we have traveled through the opening of the six seals (in Chapter 6), we would perhaps anticipate next the opening of the last or seventh seal. But we find instead an interruption to the on-going action.

This may be the right place to talk about the chronology of the Revelation account. Obviously, we can see movement forward toward the final culmination from the time that the Lamb takes the "little book" out of the hand of God and goes forth to reclaim His dominion over the earth.

But one of the complexities of the Revelation record is that it does not move forward in any kind of a straight line where one event follows the next in a chronological fashion. Instead, there are interruptions in the action. There are parenthetical portions. There are personalities introduced that act over the entire extended period so that the actual sequence of what we are reading may move back to events preceding the ones we just read about. There is repetition, review and recapitulation, and we will sometimes struggle to place certain events in their exact location on a chronological line.

That is the case with the passage just before us. We have moved through the sixth seal in chapter six and if we have correctly identified the global earthquake as the same event spoken of by Ezekiel and Joel, then we can be sure that we have come to about the middle of the Tribulation week as we close chapter six.

What we will see in this chapter is the effect of those preceding events and the sealing of 144,000 Jews, servants of God, (therefore they are converted Israelites), and the result of their testimony, that is namely an innumerable multitude of redeemed from every kindred, tribe, tongue, and nation. The action of sealing these witnesses occurs about the middle of the week. The scene of the redeemed multitude looks forward to the effects of the 144,000 witness over the final three and one-half years of the Tribulation.

In chapter eight the sequence of events seems to move forward once again, but it is not always clear how far forward. Chapter 11 speaks of two witnesses whose ministry lasts for three and a half years, but there is debate as to whether it is the first or the second three and a half year periods which is in view.

Then in Chapters 12 – 15 there is another interlude where we are introduced to the primary players in the Tribulation drama. The action of these is spread over the whole period and there are events that we cannot say with certainty just at what point they take place.

We will discuss this feature of the book further when we get to some of these crucial areas, but it is significant enough that I felt we needed to be aware of this issue here.

Now, one of the exciting features of the book of Revelation is that it reveals the part the angels play in the events of this earth. Angels are spirit beings and so, because we cannot see them, we seldom think of them. But we are reminded that they *are ministering spirits sent to minister to those who shall be the heirs of salvation* (Hebrews 1:14). Here in this book, we get to see something of that ministry as we view their power and mighty deeds.

As the chapter opens, they are sent to the four "corners" or literally *angles* (Gr. *Gonia*) of the earth. They are sent in the four directions from which the wind blows for the purpose of restraining it for a time. The winds are under the control of **the four angels, to whom it was given to hurt the earth and the sea,** so the theme here is still the pouring out of judgments. The winds are thus symbolic of the storms of judgment that are coming.

Put in the context of the tumultuous global disruptions we have just observed in the final verses of chapter six, where great storms (both literal and figurative), have rocked the entire earth, this provides a welcome reprieve.

As chapter seven opens there is a great calm, an interruption in the ongoing march of the judgments of God. The winds of judgment have begun, but now they are restrained, and a great hush takes over before the outpouring of judgment commences. This period of calm and the events recorded in this chapter are crucial to understanding what God is doing both with Israel and through Israel for the peoples of the earth.

If we are correct in identifying the earthquake and associated phenomena as the same event recorded in Ezekiel 38:18 – 23 and Joel 2:10,11, then we should expect that we might trace the same results. Notice that in both the Ezekiel and the Revelation passage the description of the tectonic movements which effect even the air and the sea are the same. In both accounts, the event is global in scope.

The passage in Joel adds the further description of Israel's reaction (Joel 2:12-17), in which the nation, recognizing their helplessness, cries out in repentance and pleads for God's intervention. When that occurs, God intervenes bringing the traumatic and literally earth-shaking judgments as recorded in all these passages upon the invaders.

In the Ezekiel passage God brings the earthquake to judge the combined armies of Russia and the Islamic nations who have invaded Israel and are about to annihilate her. The outcome of God's intervention, according to Ezekiel will be a cry of repentance and recognition of God on Israel's part.

The earthquake, the shaking, the turmoil among the invading armies, their panic, and terror result in their total destruction of each other,

> *And I will set my glory among the heathen, and all the heathen shall see my judgment that I have executed, and my hand that I have laid upon them. So the house of Israel shall know that I am the LORD their God from that day and forward.* (Ezekiel 39:21, 22).

> And again in verses 28, 29; *Then shall they know that I am the LORD their God, which caused them to be led into captivity among the heathen: but I have gathered them unto their own land, and have left none of them any more there. Neither will I hide my face any more from them: for I have poured out my spirit upon the house of Israel, saith the Lord GOD.*

The end result of this event as recorded by both Ezekiel and Joel will be an outpouring of the Spirit upon Israel, which clearly indicates that the nation (at least a large portion of the nation), will, at this point, come to faith and conversion.

After the earthquake is past in our passage here in Revelation, and the other two passages, leading to a sudden calm, God performs an act which should make every believing heart rejoice, but which has also caused untold controversy among students of the Scriptures. It is the sealing of 144,000 out of the tribes of Israel.

First, let us consider the purpose of this act.

Rev 7:2, 3 *And I saw another angel ascending from the east, having the seal of the living God: and he cried with a loud voice to the four angels, to whom it was given to hurt the earth and the sea, Saying, Hurt not the earth, neither the sea, nor the trees, till we have sealed the servants of our God in their foreheads.*

How shall we interpret this act of "sealing" the servants of God. First, note that they are already God's servants. We will see in the following verses that they are all Israelites. At the beginning of the seven-year period they were unconverted yet now we are introduced to them as "servants of God." How did that happen?

As chapter six closed we saw the global phenomena of the great earthquake, that shook the earth, the sea and even the atmosphere. I suggested that this seems to be the same event recorded in Ezekiel chapters 38, 39, and Joel Chapter 2.

If so, it comes just as the Russian/Islamic alliance is about to destroy Israel as both Ezekiel and Joel tell us. Not only does the earthquake defeat their enemies (the invading armies kill one another in the panic that ensues), but, as both Ezekiel and Joel clearly indicate, the experience drives Israel to their knees and God responds. Not only are they delivered from their enemies, but spiritual conversion comes to many in Israel. The final verse of Ezekiel 39 reads, *Neither will I hide my face any more from them: for I have poured out my spirit upon the house of Israel, saith the Lord GOD* (Ezekiel 39:29).

So, it is out of these newly converted Israelites that God chooses twelve thousand from each of the twelve tribes to seal. Whether that seal is visible we are not told, nor are we specifically told the purpose of the seal in this passage. But this is not the first time God has sealed a group of people and if we compare Scripture with Scripture, we can infer with a degree of certainty the purpose of this action. I refer to another passage in Ezekiel, found in chapter nine.

And Jehovah said unto him, Go through the midst of the city, through the midst of Jerusalem, and set a mark upon the foreheads of the men that sigh and that cry over all the abominations that are done in the midst thereof. And to the others he said in my hearing, Go ye through the city after him, and smite: let not your eye spare, neither have ye pity; slay utterly the old man, the young man and the virgin, and little children and women; but <u>come not near any man upon whom is the mark</u>: and begin at my sanctuary (Ezekiel 9:4 – 6).

Two things are readily observable from this passage. First, those who are sealed are those who have the heart of God toward sin and all that was happening around them that was an affront to God. They sighed, and they cried over the conditions they saw and lived with every day. Like Lot of old, their righteous souls were vexed with the filthy conversation (actions) of the wicked (2 Peter 2:7).

Secondly, we observe that the purpose of sealing these individuals was to protect them from the Divine sentence of death that was about to fall upon the wicked. The judgments of God would fall all around them but would not touch those who were sealed.

While it may be incidental to our present discussion, it is worth noting that the judgments were to begin at the sanctuary of God. God always begins there, with judging the sins of His own people before He extends judgment on the world. Peter repeats this principle when he says, *For the time is come for judgment to begin at the house of God: and if it begin first at us, what shall be the end of them that obey not the gospel of God?* (1 Peter 4:17).

So, we conclude that the purpose of the placing of the seal is to protect them from Judgments, just as God once before protected Israel and the Land of Goshen from His judgments upon Egypt (Exodus 8:22; 9:26).

Rev 7:4 *And I heard the number of them which were sealed: and there were sealed an hundred and forty and four thousand of all the tribes of the children of Israel.*

We come now to the actual record of those that were sealed and we find the very clear affirmation that these 144,000 are from *all the tribes of the children of Israel.*

Consistent with our literal/historical/grammatical method of interpretation therefore, we can conclude nothing else than that these are Jewish men who have come to faith through the experiences discussed above, and that they have committed themselves to fully follow the Lamb, Yeshua Hamashiach.

Those who are sealed are now enumerated by tribe. It is amazing to me how much resistance there is among expositors to accepting this passage at face value. Every possible argument has been put forth to try to avoid the obvious.

One hears arguments like, "Israel has been rejected by God because they rejected Messiah." "God is finished with literal Israel and the Church is now the 'Israel of God.'" "No Jew knows what tribe they are from so it is impossible to interpret this literally." And of course, even some of the cults try to claim the 144,000 as comprising their own group.

There is no textual, grammatical, or historic reason to question this passage. The text says clearly that they are from the all the tribes of the children of Israel, and even goes so far as to name each individual tribe. That should be sufficient for anyone who approaches this with an open mind.

Rev 7:5-8 *Of the tribe of Juda were sealed twelve thousand. Of the tribe of Reuben were sealed twelve thousand. Of the tribe of Gad were sealed twelve thousand. Of the tribe of Aser were sealed twelve thousand. Of the tribe of Nepthalim were sealed twelve thousand. Of the tribe of Manasses were sealed twelve thousand. Of the tribe of Simeon were sealed twelve* *thousand. Of the tribe of Levi were sealed twelve thousand. Of the tribe of Issachar were sealed twelve thousand. Of the tribe of Zabulon were sealed twelve thousand. Of the tribe of Joseph were sealed twelve thousand. Of the tribe of Benjamin were sealed twelve thousand.*

It is significant that God begins with **Judah**. Jacob had prophesied long ago, *Judah, thee shall thy brethren praise: Thy hand shall be on the neck of thine enemies; Thy father's sons shall bow down before thee* (Genesis 49:8). Although born the forth son of Jacob, the first three are disqualified and Jacob names Judah as the one who will have dominion.

Of course, there is great significance in this, because King David was of the tribe of Judah, and our Lord himself came of that tribe. In fact, Jacob goes on to compare Judah to a lion, and indeed, our Lord is called, the Lion from the tribe of Judah. Twelve thousand out of Judah are the first to be sealed.

The **second** tribe to be sealed is **Reuben**. You will note that Reuben is actually the firstborn. Jacob had characterized Reuben as, *Unstable as water, thou shalt not excel;* (Genesis 49:4). Nevertheless, grace prevails and Reuben is counted among this redeemed throng of those who follow the Lamb.

Gad, Asher, and Naphtali are next. Each of them is given due reference in Jacob's blessings, but there is nothing in what Jacob said that seems specific to this present text, although it is significant that these tribes are still in existence and known and recognized by God. Of course, in these days, even though genealogical records may be lost, the science of DNA can establish lineage.

Manasseh is next. He is the eldest son of Joseph. When Reuben was rejected from being given the birthright, Jacob chose Joseph's sons whom he claimed as his own. Thus Manasseh, is counted as one of the twelve tribes, and twelve thousand from Manasseh are sealed.

Simeon and Levi are next. These two are the second and third sons of Jacob. They are often together and not always for good. They massacred the men and women of Shechem out of a spirit of vengeance (Genesis 34:25-29) and Jacob denounced them for it (Genesis 49:5-7), and prophesied that they would be separated in the Land. Simeon was largely lost due to the fact that his territory was in the midst of that of Judah; and Levi, was scattered as the priestly tribe throughout the other tribes (see Joshua 21:1-45). In fact, Levi is seldom named in the lists of the tribes since they were given no inheritance among the tribes, but the service of God was their inheritance.

Twelve thousand from each of **Issachar and Zabulon** are next sealed. Both tribes are mentioned in Judges as being part of the army of Deborah and Barak that defeated the hosts of Midian, though Zabulon seems to have been the dominate fighter (Judges 5:14, 15).

Joseph of course was not the name of a tribe. From Joseph had come two tribes, Manasseh, and **Ephraim**. It seems that sometimes their father's name was used in a generic sense to refer to one of the tribes that sprang from him. For instance, in the list of tribal leaders that were sent to spy out the Land as recorded in Numbers chapter thirteen, the name Joseph appears as a reference to Manasseh. *Of the tribe of Joseph, namely, of the tribe of Manasseh, Gaddi the son of Susi* (Numbers 13:11). So in the list given here in Revelation, Joseph's name is mentioned rather that his son Ephraim, although Ephraim is obviously meant.

Finally, the last tribe mentioned is **Benjamin** (son of my right hand; Genesis 35:18). Benjamin was a youngest of Jacob's sons, whose mother, Rachel died giving him birth. Particularly precious to his father, Benjamin becomes a central figure when Joseph (as ruler in Egypt) demands that his brothers produce him before he would release Simeon (Genesis 42).

Although Saul, Israel's first King was a Benjamite, the sordid story of the men of Gibeon (Benjamites), occupies the final three chapters of the book of Judges and forms a backdrop for the subsequent loss of the Kingdom by Saul and the establishment of Judah as the ruling tribe. Benjamin's lot (territory), as a tribe was between Judah and Ephraim, and he later became connected permanently to Judah when the Kingdom was divided (1 Kings 11:31; 12:21).

On his deathbed Jacob said of Benjamin; *Benjamin shall ravin as a wolf: in the morning he shall devour the prey, and at night he shall divide the spoil* (Genesis 49:27). The prophecy suggests that Benjamin would be a tribe, violent in spirit, which, indeed, history demonstrated to be true.

Which brings us to the fact the since Levi is included in the list one tribe is omitted completely and that is the tribe of **Dan**. A number of conjectures have been advanced as to why Dan's name does not appear. Some believe that it is because Dan was the first tribe to go into idolatry and they remained in idolatry during their entire time until the captivity.

If there is any truth to that idea, it may also explain why Ephraim's name was not mentioned, although the tribe is listed as we have seen under the name of Ephraim's father, Joseph. The idolatrous career of Dan, actually began in the tribe of Ephraim in the very early days of the Judges, when, as we are reminded throughout the book, *"there was no king in Israel and every man did that which was right in his own eyes."*

Judges chapter seventeen opens with the story of Micah, an Ephraimite from Mount Ephraim, who had stolen eleven hundred shekels of silver from his mother. After his mother cursed about the theft, he returned the silver, and she then took it and had a graven image or teraphim (household idol) molded and carved. Then, Micah hired a Levite to act as his priest and to carry on this idolatrous worship in the name of Yaweh.

After all, wasn't every priest supposed to be a Levite? It is obvious that like all false religion and idolatry, Micah was trying his best to make his religion acceptable to God. When we get to the next chapter (Judges 18) we find out who this Levite was.

The next chapter of judges tells the story of a group of spies sent out by the tribe of Dan to find an easier lot for the tribe than the one assigned by Joshua. On their journey north they passed through the tribal territory of Ephraim and came upon Micah, his very expensive teraphim, and his hired, private, family priest who was a Levite.

Upon their return trip north with six hundred armed men to conquer the territory they had spied, they made a visit to Micah, and stole his teraphim and his priest and set up an idolatrous worship in Dan from which they never recovered. Judges records, *And the children of Dan set up the graven image: and Jonathan, the son of Gershom, the son of Manasseh, he and his sons were priests to the tribe of Dan until the day of the captivity of the land* (Judges 18:30).

There is some question concerning the text at this point, for while Manasseh did have a son named Gershom, this Gershom is specifically called a "Levite" and he had not been living in the area of Manasseh, but Judah, vis: *And there was a young man out of Bethlehem-Judah of the family of Judah, who was a Levite, and he sojourned there* (Judges 17:7). This suggests that the Gershom of this story was not a son of Manasseh, but of Moses. If so, the idolatry recorded in this story was perpetuated by Moses' own posterity in the third generation.

So perhaps Dan is omitted because of his history with idolatry. Others believe that the False Prophet who promotes the worship of Anti-Christ will come from Dan. It is possible that one or both of these theories is correct, or perhaps this is just another occasion where the list of the tribes differs. In any case Dan is not among those sealed.

The Purpose for the 144,000

While no specific purpose is stated in the text for the 144,000, their proximity to the great multitude from every kindred, tribe, tongue and nation (Revelation 7:9,10), strongly suggests that there is a causative relationship between these two groups.

What would that be? It would imply that the great multitude of redeemed are a direct result of the testimony of the 144,000. In that case, these men are not only "servants" of God and of the Lamb, but evangelists, proclaiming the coming Kingdom, and calling men and women to repent and turn to Messiah Jesus for salvation.

As I was studying this passage, I referenced a number of sound biblical sites on-line and here is a sample of what I found:

- "What is the Purpose of the 144,000? The context indicates that they will serve the Lord as evangelists. I say this because their description is followed immediately by that of "a great multitude which no one can number, from every nation and tribe and people and tongue" (**Revelation 7:9**). Because they are placed adjacent to the 144,000 believing Jews, the implication is that they are converted by the Jews during the Tribulation."
  http://christinprophecy.org/articles/the-mysterious-144000

- The 144,000 Jews are a sort of "first fruits" (**Revelation 14:4**) of a redeemed Israel previously prophesied (**Zechariah 12:10**; **Romans 11:25–27**), and their mission seems to be to evangelize the post-rapture world and proclaim the gospel during the tribulation period. As a result of their ministry, millions—"a great multitude that no one could count, from every nation, tribe, people and language" (**Revelation 7:9**)—will come to faith in Christ.
  https://www.gotquestions.org/144000.html

- Since we are given a vision of the 144,000 Jewish servants of God, and since that vision is followed by the world's mightiest revival and since according to Old Testament predictions God is going to bless all nations through Abraham and his seed, we naturally come to the conclusion that these 144,000 Jewish servants are like many Jewish "Pauls" who will be honored with the task of conducting the world wide revival in the Tribulation.
  http://www.biblicalresearch.info/page27.html (David Cooper)

I have written at length about the 144,000 both in the WWBI course on Eschatology and in my book, *The Prophetic Destiny of Israel and the Islamic Nations.* Suffice it here to say that through the ministry of evangelism and calling the nations to repentance and faith in Jesus Christ, Israel will, at long last, fulfill the purpose for which God called them. They will be the witness of God and His truth to the nations, just as God destined them to be. (Isaiah 43:10 – 12; 44:8)

The Great Multitude

Rev 7:9, 10 *After this I beheld, and, lo, a great multitude, which no man could number, of all nations, and kindreds, and people, and tongues, stood before the throne, and before the Lamb, clothed with white robes, and palms in their hands; And cried with a loud voice, saying, Salvation to our God which sitteth upon the throne, and unto the Lamb.*

In this next portion of John's vision, he sees one of the most glorious sights ever described in holy writ. This throng of the redeemed is truly the most diversified group ever assembled and they give testimony to the fulfillment of that promise so long sought by so many; *And this gospel of the kingdom shall be preached in all the world for a witness unto all nations; and then shall the end come* (Matthew 24:14).

Notice their appearance; they are clothed in white robes, which we have seen symbolizes righteousness, whether their own righteous lives as martyrs, or the imputed righteousness of Christ. They have palms in their hands.

There are several references to the use of palm branches in Scripture. They are associated with the Feast of Tabernacles (Leviticus 23:40), and used even to this day in Israel to celebrate the Feast. The Feast of Tabernacles rejoices at the end of the harvest, and so they are a symbol of rejoicing.

But they are also associated with victory. Triumphant conquerors were often greeted by happy throngs waving palm branches, so there seems to be a symbol of victory here as well. Finally, they were associated with the act of the coronation of a king (1 Kings 1:38-40). This was the significance they held when Jesus rode upon the ass' colt (John 12:12, 13), presenting Himself as Messiah and King to Israel and the crowds assembled strawed palm branches along the way.

So, we see this blood-washed throng, waving their palm branches as a symbol of rejoicing, victory and the sure coming Kingdom.

Finally, our text says that they cry with a loud voice. The original Gr. *phōnēi megalēi*, suggests "the multitude shouts its praises as with one voice" (Swete). Although from every imaginable tribe, tongue and nation, they harmonize perfectly the praises of God, ascribing salvation to Him and to the Lamb.

Rev 7:11, 12 *And all the angels stood round about the throne, and about the elders and the four beasts, and fell before the throne on their faces, and worshipped God, Saying, Amen: Blessing, and glory, and wisdom, and thanksgiving, and honour, and power, and might, be unto our God for ever and ever. Amen.*

Now they are joined by all of those who surround the Throne. The angels, and the twenty-four elders, along with the living creatures, all fall on their faces in worship. We are so unaccustomed to such displays of ardor, that we would be scandalized were it to occur during our worship services, yet, in the perfect environs of heaven it seems the natural reaction to the glory and grace of God.

The attributes about which they sing are enumerated, "Blessing, and glory, and wisdom, and honor, and power, and might," all of these with thanksgiving. And now we come to the question, "who are these and were did they come from?"

Their Identity

Rev 7:13,14 *And one of the elders answered, saying unto me, What are these which are arrayed in white robes? and whence came they? And I said unto him, Sir, thou knowest. And he said to me, These are they which came out of great tribulation, and have washed their robes, and made them white in the blood of the Lamb.*

The question is raised by one of the elders, and John is at a loss to answer it. He rather defers to the asker and is told, *These are they which came out of Great Tribulation.* The Greek here is emphatic, Gr.ἐκ τῆς θλίψεως τῆς μεγάλης, Literally it reads, *out of the tribulation, the great one*. We can not misinterpret these words. This multitude are not simply those who have come out of the usual tribulations of life. No, they are those who have been redeemed from the Great (mega) Tribulation. We are therefore looking at a throng of innumerable size that will have been saved during the most horrific time of trouble the world will ever see.

Secondly, we are told that they have washed their robes. We have seen this so often and will see it yet again. A robe used symbolically, speaks of character, and these have been cleansed by the blood of the Savior. They are new creatures in Christ Jesus. But do not miss the action on their part.

Salvation is all of God, but it must be received. A person must believe. Apart from that, salvation remains unclaimed.

Their Condition

Rev 7:15-17 *Therefore are they before the throne of God, and serve him day and night in his temple: and he that sitteth on the throne shall dwell among them. They shall hunger no more, neither thirst any more; neither shall the sun light on them, nor any heat. For the Lamb which is in the midst of the throne shall feed them, and shall lead them unto living fountains of waters: and God shall wipe away all tears from their eyes.*

Their blessed condition is contrasted with what they endured and came out of. As we journey further into this terrible time of trouble, we begin to imagine what must have been their lot while on earth.

The writer to the book of Hebrews describes a similar group of persecuted saints. After telling of the victories of some, there follows these words; *and others were tortured, not accepting deliverance; that they might obtain a better resurrection: And others had trial of cruel mockings and scourgings, yea, moreover of bonds and imprisonment: They were stoned, they were sawn asunder, were tempted, were slain with the sword: they wandered about in sheepskins and goatskins; being destitute, afflicted, tormented; (Of whom the world was not worthy:) they wandered in deserts, and in mountains, and in dens and caves of the earth* (Hebrews 11:35 – 38).

The only difference in this *great multitude, which no man could number,* is that all of this came upon them within that short period of the Tribulation with such force and intensity as has never occurred before and will never occur again. Remember, our Lord Himself said, *For then shall be great tribulation, such as was not since the beginning of the world to this time, no, nor ever shall be. And except those days should be shortened, there should no flesh be saved;* (Matthew 24:21, 22)

But now all that has changed! They serve before the Throne and God is among them. How very blessed they are. They shall never again know hunger, or thirst, or be smitten with heat or cold, for they are the direct concern of the Lamb Himself who meets their every need.

They will enjoy those "living fountains of water" or actually, it should read, the fountains of the water of life. They will know and experience the fullness of all that eternal life means, and like a loving father whose child has been injured, God Himself will wipe away all tears from their eyes.

No wonder they sing. No wonder they rejoice. No wonder they praise the Lamb who redeemed them to Himself. *Eye hath not seen, nor ear heard, neither hath it entered into the heart of man, the things that God hath prepared for them who love him* (1 Corinthians 2:9).

REVIEW

- Name one thing you learned from this chapter that was new to you.

- Of what nationality were the 144,000?

- Where did the "Great multitude which no man could number" come from?

- How do we believe they came to hear and respond to the Gospel?

- Describe how their condition has now changed.

Chapter 15 The Final Seal and 4 Trumpets

Revelation 8:1 – 13

Rev 8:1 *And when he had opened the seventh seal, there was silence in heaven about the space of half an hour.*

This interlude of silence is significant in at least two ways. First, it portends drastic and cataclysmic events about to take place.   There was a similar interlude at the beginning of chapter 7, although there, it took place on earth, whereas, this takes place in heaven.

In chapter 7, the four angels held back the four destructive winds while God set a protective seal upon His servants, the 144,000. The chapter ends with a tumultuous sound of praise from the innumerable multitude of the redeemed, along with the vast hosts of heaven itself. Now, suddenly, a prolonged silence, like the proverbial "calm before the storm," and we anticipate something of profound importance is about to take place.

The second, and perhaps even more important reason for the silence, does not become apparent until we read on to verses 3, 4. There the angel offers incense upon the golden altar. This is reminiscent of the temple worship and seems to parallel the description we find in Luke's Gospel.

> There was in the days of Herod, the king of Judaea, a certain priest named Zacharias, of the course of Abia: . . . And it came to pass, that while he executed the priest's office before God in the order of his course, According to the custom of the priest's office, his lot was to burn incense when he went into the temple of the Lord. And the whole multitude of the

people were praying without at the time of incense (Luke 1:5, 8-10).

In the course of Temple worship when the priest went into the Holy Place to offer the incense, the custom was for all the worshipers to remain in silent prayer until he returned. Verses 3, 4 of chapter 8, pictures just such a situation. There is silence in heaven as the Angel-Priest offers incense with the prayers of the saints, and we shall shortly see the effect of those prayers.

How many there were and when those prayers were uttered we are not told. But we are assured that when we pray, God takes notice and sooner or later there is an answer to our prayers. It may not even come during our lifetime, but it will come.

Rev 8:2 *And I saw the seven angels which stood before God; and to them were given seven trumpets.*

Do not miss the connection between the seven trumpets about to sound and the seven seals, the last of which has just been opened (8:1). There is a plethora of sevens found in the book of Revelation. There are seven spirits of God and seven candlesticks and seven angels and seven churches and seven kings and seven mountains. Beside these there are seven seals that have now been broken to open the scroll, and out of the seventh seal now comes seven trumpets, and we will see that after the seventh trumpet will come seven vials (or bowls) of the wrath of God.

Seven is the divine number of completion. God instituted a week of seven days, a Sabbath of seven years (Exodus 23:11), and a seven-times-seven-year period leading to the year of Jubilee where all property reverted to its original owners. Revelation is the completion of God's word to man and it should not surprise us to find the number which reflects completion used frequently in it.

Rev 8:3-5 *And another angel came and stood at the altar, having a golden censer; and there was given unto him much incense, that he should offer it with the prayers of all saints upon the golden altar which was before the throne. And the smoke of the incense, which came with the prayers of the saints, ascended up before God out of the angel's hand. And the angel took the censer, and filled it with fire of the altar, and cast it into the earth: and there were voices, and thunderings, and lightnings, and an earthquake.*

This verse forces us immediately to consider this personage who is acting in the role of a priest. What occurs here is reminiscent of the divine service found throughout the Old Testament Tabernacle and Temple worship. The offering of the incense, with the prayers of the saints is a service reserved exclusively to one who has been ordained a priest. We do not find angels or even kings performing this service (2 Chronicles 26:18).

Therefore, we must conclude that this angel is none other than the One called The Angel of the LORD, in other words the Lord Jesus Christ Himself. He alone is our Great High Priest and He alone bears the prayers of the saints to God. *For there is one God and one mediator between God and men, the man Christ Jesus* (1 Timothy 2:5).

It would appear that this also is an enactment of the protocol on the Day of Atonement. Sir Isaac Newton writes, "It was the custom of the priest to take fire from the great altar in a <u>silver censer</u>, but on the day of expiation the high priest took the fire from the great altar in a <u>golden censer</u>; and when he was come down from the <u>great altar</u>, he took incense from one of the priests, who brought it to him, and went with it to the <u>golden altar</u>; and while he offered the incense the people prayed without in silence." **(Adam Clarke Commentary on the Bible).**

Notice, the similarity to the detail found here in Revelation.

The "Angel/Priest", takes a "golden censor" and carries it to the "golden altar" (which is the Altar of Incense), and offers it, then takes coals from the Altar (this time, the Altar of Burnt Offerings or Brazen Altar from which all fire used in the Tabernacle service had to originate [see Leviticus 10:1, 2]), filled the censor and poured it out upon the earth.

The symbolism here is profound. The Altar of Burnt Offerings was symbolic of Calvary, where our Lord offered Himself for our sins. All worship in the Tabernacle or Temple had to originate here, thus all fire used in Tabernacle worship had to be taken from this altar. And the fire of that altar, sanctified the prayers of the saints and made them a sweet offering to God. But the same fire which sanctified the prayers of the saints, became the fire of judgment upon those on the earth.

To examine this a step further, the fire of the Brazen Altar was always a symbol of the righteous judgment of God upon sin. That fire once fell as judgment upon the Savior, who had become sin for us, although He knew no sin, and now that fiery judgment begins to fall upon those who have rejected our Savior's substitutionary death and have continued in their sin and rebellion, *and there were voices, and thunderings, and lightnings, and an earthquake.*

Rev 8:6 *And the seven angels which had the seven trumpets prepared themselves to sound.*

Note that this team of angelic trumpeters, like the trumpet section in a large orchestra, await the signal of the Divine Conductor, before they begin. All that is about to happen is under the will and direction of the Lamb, who holds the scroll.

Rev 8:7 *The first angel sounded, and there followed hail and fire mingled with blood, and they were cast upon the earth: and the third part of trees was burnt up, and all green grass was burnt up.*

As I studied this passage, I was amazed at the number of commentators, especially older ones, who see this entire section as symbolic. They imagine that the grass stands for people and trees for nations and interpret this as the barbarian conquest of Rome, the French Revolution, or the Bolshevik Revolution in Russia. I see nothing here that would permit such a fanciful interpretation.

It seems plain to me that we are intended to understand that these are judgments which fall upon the ecological systems of the earth and therefore grass means grass and trees mean trees. We must guard against trying to interpret these passages in light of our own experiences. If one thing seems clear it is that these judgments are supernatural and beyond anything we have known or experienced.

While it is true that God Himself in Isaiah chapter 40, used the simile of grass to represent the frailty of man, He made quite evident his meaning in that passage, while there in no indication of such a symbolism being employed here.

> The voice said, Cry. And he said, What shall I cry? All flesh is grass, and all the goodliness thereof is as the flower of the field: The grass withereth, the flower fadeth: because the spirit of the LORD bloweth upon it: surely the people is grass. The grass withereth, the flower fadeth: but the word of our God shall stand for ever (Isaiah 40:6-8).

God has used the forces of nature which he created and which He ultimately controls to do his bidding on numerous occasions in both Biblical and secular history. Consider the following:

> And the Lord sent thunder and hail, and the fire ran along the ground; and the Lord rained hail upon the land of Egypt (Exodus 9:23).

He gave them hail for rain and flaming fire in their land. He smote their vines also and their fig trees; and brake the trees of their coasts (Psalm 105:32, 33).

And it came to pass, as they fled from before Israel, and were in the going down to Bethhoron, that the LORD cast down great stones from heaven upon them unto Azekah, and they died: they were more which died with hailstones than they whom the children of Israel slew with the sword (Joshua 10:11).

The LORD also thundered in the heavens, and the Highest gave his voice; hail stones and coals of fire (Psalm 18:13).

I find, therefore, no justification for trying to spiritualize the events of this chapter, or the next. It appears that quite clearly, literal hail fell, and the storm contained such electrical disturbances that fire accompanied it, even perhaps "running along the ground," as it once had done in Egypt. And while I have no explanation for the mixture of blood in the storm, it might either have occurred as creatures where hurled into the air by the force of the storm, or it is even possible that God, who turned water into blood (and will again), made this storm, by His direct power, a supernatural event.

I have said in the past, and would observe again, that there are two great prerequisites for understanding the book of Revelation. The first is a solid knowledge of Scripture from Genesis to Jude (for everything in former Scripture culminates here), and the second is a willingness to allow God to say what He means and believe Him. Both of those principles come into play in interpreting this and future passages.

The end result of this first of the Trumpet judgments is the loss of a third of the food and shelter resources of the earth. In an earth that has already been impoverished by the war, and famine and death of the earlier "Seal Judgments", what disastrous effects would this have on the remaining peoples of the earth?

Rev 8:8, 9 *And the second angel sounded, and as it were a great mountain burning with fire was cast into the sea: and the third part of the sea became blood; And the third part of the creatures which were in the sea, and had life, died; and the third part of the ships were destroyed.*

As we come to the second Trumpet Judgment, we do indeed have a clear indication as to how we should understand it. The text says, *"as it were a great mountain."* The implication clearly is that while it was not literally a mountain, it was "like a great mountain." The ISV translates it, *something like a huge mountain burning with fire.*

Now there is a similar passage found in Jeremiah concerning Babylon which reads;

> *Behold, I am against thee, O destroying mountain, saith the LORD, which destroyest all the earth: and I will stretch out mine hand upon thee, and roll thee down from the rocks, and will make thee a burnt mountain* (Jeremiah 51:25).

In prophetic symbolism, a mountain always stands for, or is a symbol of a kingdom. The Jeremiah passage, then, is highly symbolic, indicating the fall of the kingdom of Babylon. There is another passage that has similarities to this found in Revelation chapter 18.

> *And a mighty angel took up a stone like a great millstone, and cast it into the sea, saying, Thus, with violence shall that great city Babylon be thrown down, and shall be found no more at all* (Revelation 18:21).

Both of those passages refer to the fall of the literal Babylon, and/or the system of both commerce and false religion promulgated by her.

Our present passage in Revelation, <u>does not seem to have the same connection</u>. There is no mention or even inference of this fiery falling object having any relation to Babylon.

This object seems clearly to be just what is described – a huge flaming sphere, as big as a mountain, which falls violently into the sea. The most likely explanation would be that a meteorite, of large proportion struck the earth and caused the resultant reaction.

The sea is said to be *turned into blood*. Whether this is a direct miraculous act of God in conjunction with the falling "mountain-like" object, or whether this is a resultant chemical reaction from the possible toxins that make up the meteor, we are not told, and it is best not to guess. Suffice it to know that a blood red tide resulted from this and that an unthinkable third of seas creatures died.

The second related result appears to be the destruction of ships. The impact of such an object would, no doubt create a tsunami flowing from the impact site in a 360 degree movement. The wave height, speed and force would be beyond anything ever before experienced and it is not difficult to imagine the destruction of entire fleets.

Thus, this second Trumpet Judgment, removed one more resource from the people of the earth. Even though hosts of people themselves are not touched directly by this judgment, the resultant loss of food supply and means of fishing, shipping, and traveling, will have an unprecedented impact upon the earth population.

Just as with the judgments upon Egypt of old, there is an ever-ascending intensity to each of these judgments and each is designed, not only to punish, but to reflect the glory of God and to lead men to repentance, for God has not changed and, *He is not willing that any should perish, but that all should come to repentance* (2 Peter 3:9).

Rev 8:10, 11 *And the third angel sounded, and there fell a great star from heaven, burning as it were a lamp, and it fell upon the third part of the rivers, and upon the fountains of waters;*

And the name of the star is called Wormwood: and the third part of the waters became wormwood; and many men died of the waters, because they were made bitter.

Once again, we are faced with simply accepting what the Holy Spirit says as we examine this next judgment. Many in the past have attempted to spiritualize this and identified the "great star," as an angelic being. It is true that both the stellar bodies and the angelic hosts are referred to as "stars" in this book (Revelation 1:20; 12:4). However, in this particular passage there seems to be no indication that the word is used symbolically. As Dr. Henry Morris indicates, the word "star" may be used to refer to any heavenly body, either planet, or meteorite, or star fragment.

This burning (perhaps molten), object, affects a third of all the water supplies and rivers of the earth. Some have wondered exactly how that could happen. Let's just think about how it could affect an area as large as our own country.

There are eighteen watershed regions in the continental United States. At least eight of those extend across the northern tier of our country and spill their water from north to south into the rivers that run through the remaining countryside. A cosmic body that entered the atmosphere in an already molten state, could easily disintegrate into fragments that could spread over thousands of miles and pollute the source of rivers over a vast area.

The "star" has a name, it is Wormwood. The word is translated from the Gr. ἄψινθος; ap'sinthos, and carries the sense of extreme bitterness, even poison. It has been thought by some to be equivalent to hemlock.

The English word Wormwood is found nine times in the KJV, all but one of those times in the Old Testament. There it is translated from the Hebrew לענה; la'ănâh, which means to curse, or to regard as poisonous.

Whatever its composition, its poisonous dust is scattered across a vast area where the springs which feed the streams and rivers are located. Hence the entire watershed is polluted with a bitter substance that makes the waters like hemlock and poisons all who drink them.

It is interesting that this is one of the areas of danger that has long been seen as a terrorist target. If those who wanted to destroy us could taint the water sources, immeasurable harm might be done. Here, the dreaded death comes, not from a terrorist, nor on a single reservoir or area, but from a Divine judgment poured out on a third of the waters of the world.

Here, again, God shows His power and His glory, but the intent, as always, is to make men repent of their sin and turn in helpless faith to Him. But just as happened with Pharaoh in Egypt, men hardened their hearts in stubborn rebellion against God.

Rev 8:12 *And the fourth angel sounded, and the third part of the sun was smitten, and the third part of the moon, and the third part of the stars; so as the third part of them was darkened, and the day shone not for a third part of it, and the night likewise.*

Darkness, that is literal darkness, was one of the plagues God sent upon Egypt.

And the LORD said unto Moses, Stretch out thine hand toward heaven, that there may be darkness over the land of Egypt, even darkness which may be felt. And

Moses stretched forth his hand toward heaven; and there was a thick darkness in all the land of Egypt three days: They saw not one another, neither rose any from his place for three days: but all the children of Israel had light in their dwellings (Exodus 10:21 – 23).

In the case of Egypt God does not tell us how He achieved the resultant darkness, only that He did. Here, in Revelation, we are told that a third part of the sun, and moon, and stars were "smitten" Gr. Πλήσσω; plēssō the idea of *flattening* out); to *pound*, that is, (figuratively) to *inflict* with (calamity): - smite.

Frankly, the phenomenon is completely beyond our understanding. Dr. Henry Morris believes that there is a reduction of the sun's energy output for a short period of time, and since the moon and the closest planets all derive reflected light from the sun, they would be affected to the same degree.

Whatever the explanation might be, the effect upon the earth would be a strange anomaly of partial light during the day and total darkness at night. Again, all of this is meant to tell man that the One who rules in the heavens controls it all and must be worshipped and obeyed. But, just as with the former judgments, men plod on in their rebellious path to destruction.

Rev 8:13 *And I beheld, and heard an angel flying through the midst of heaven, saying with a loud voice, Woe, woe, woe, to the inhabiters of the earth by reason of the other voices of the trumpet of the three angels, which are yet to sound!*

Now, as if the former Trumpet Judgments were not destructive enough, a voice comes declaring that the final three Trumpet Judgments will be far worse than all that have preceded them. The voice sounds, not from an "angel," as the KJV translates it, but from an "eagle." Though this may seem strange indeed, we must not forget that it would not be the first time that God enabled one of the animal kingdom to speak (Numbers 22:28).

One of the contemporary translations reads as follows; *Then I looked, and I heard an eagle that was flying high in the air say in a loud voice, "O horror! horror! How horrible it will be for all who live on earth when the sound comes from the trumpets that the other three angels must blow!"* **(Good News Bible)**

Please note again, a variation of the phrase "earth dwellers." Here it is translated, *the inhabiters of the earth*. It is the same phrase we have seen previously and reminds us that these judgments are particularly meant for those persons who are "of the earth", in other words, those who have no spiritual life by reason of a new birth experience.

We come now to a chapter break and we are introduced to the final Trumpet blasts which come with quite elongated descriptions and require our careful attention and analysis.

REVIEW

- What was the significance of the silence at the opening of the chapter?

- Where in Scripture do we find a direct parallel to what happens here?

- Who do we believe offers the incense with the prayer of the saints to God?

- How should we interpret the disasters in this chapter – as spiritual symbols or literal events?

- What warning are we given about the last three Trumpets about to sound?

Chapter 16   Trumpets, Locusts & Horses

Revelation 9:1 – 21

Rev 9:1 *And the fifth angel sounded, and I saw a star fall from heaven unto the earth: and to him was given the key of the bottomless pit.*

We have been careful in our interpretation of each of these judgments to stick closely to the text and attempt to give as literal an interpretation as possible. We will do the same here, only now, something has changed.

We have seen in the former chapter a star, and a mountain-like object fall upon the earth. As this chapter opens we see another "star" falling, but there is a profound difference in this one.   This "star" is described using a personal pronoun and "he" is given a "key to the bottomless pit."   We have noted before that the word "star" is used to describe both heavenly bodies as well as angelic beings (Revelation 1:20). Here, the evidence clearly suggests that this "star" is an angel.

The phrase, "the bottomless pit," is from the Gr. ἄβυσσος; abussos; "*depthless, that is, (specifically), (infernal) "abyss": -* deep, (bottomless) pit." It is a synonym for hell, or the infernal regions of the earth. It is the destiny of fallen spirits and all the lost, until the final resurrection at which time death and hell will be cast into the lake of Fire (Revelation 20:14).

The abyss is always associated with the deepest regions of the earth and pictured as having a shaft which in some way opens it to the world of men.

Now, we must remember that we are dealing exclusively in the realm of the spiritual.

Hence, any "shaft" or entrance into the abyss would also be in a different dimension as well. We need not suppose or postulate some physical shaft, which might be discovered. No, this entire passage is filled with spiritual realities.

Please note next that this "star" is said to have "fallen" from heaven to earth. The word used is Gr. πίπτω, πέτω; piptō petō; "to fall." Hence, this angel does not simply descend from heaven, in which case the word used would be Gr. Καταβαίνω; katabainō; "to descend."

The wording would seem to suggest a fall, not only from a location (heaven), but from a position and would perhaps reflect the words of Isaiah chapter fourteen; *How art thou fallen from heaven, O Lucifer, son of the morning!* (Isaiah 14:12). Once we see what this angel does, it is not difficult to identify him as Lucifer.

He is given the "key" to the bottomless pit. We have already seen that the phrase "bottomless pit" refers to the regions of hell. The key is given to the angel by someone, and we already know who holds the key. Revelation chapter one declares; *I am he that liveth, and was dead; and, behold, I am alive for evermore, Amen; and have the keys of hell and of death* (Revelation 1:18). So, a key is given to this fallen angel to open the shaft of the abyss. That action alone would be enough to cause us to expect something terrible indeed.

Rev 9:2 *And he opened the bottomless pit; and there arose a smoke out of the pit, as the smoke of a great furnace; and the sun and the air were darkened by reason of the smoke of the pit.*

What would you expect to see if the doors of hell were opened? From the descriptions of hell we have, we know it to be a place of fire and brimstone. Would it not be natural then to expect that out of the shaft of the Abyss, the *smoke of a great furnace* would issue?

It would appear that the smoke is literal, and that it literally blots out the light of the heavenly bodies as it blankets the earth. The text particularly mentions the air. Talk about "air pollution," this is another result of this period of judgments.

Rev 9:3, 4 *And there came out of the smoke locusts upon the earth: and unto them was given power, as the scorpions of the earth have power. And it was commanded them that they should not hurt the grass of the earth, neither any green thing, neither any tree; but only those men which have not the seal of God in their foreheads.*

There now emerges from this smoke what the Scripture describes as "locusts", although they are distinct from any locusts we have ever seen. If the description was meant to give us a comparable, anyone who has ever seen an invasion of locusts knows what terror and destruction they bring. Joel describes just such an invasion of locusts in the first chapter of his prophecy and then likens it to the invasion of the "northern armies" in chapter two.

These locusts, however, do not destroy the fruit of the earth, but are sent to bring extreme torment on any, and all who do not have the seal of God in their foreheads. We know at once that this would exclude the 144,000 who are sealed of God, but there may be an implication here that others who have believed were also sealed and spared from such torment.

Rev 9:5, 6 *And to them it was given that they should not kill them, but that they should be tormented five months: and their torment was as the torment of a scorpion, when he striketh a man.*
And in those days shall men seek death, and shall not find it; and shall desire to die, and death shall flee from them.

Several things should be noted from these verses. First of all, this torment, although intense beyond comprehension, had a time limit of five months. Second, the type of pain is described as, "when a scorpion strikes a man." By God's grace I have not had that experience, but those who have, testify that it is a degree of pain beyond anything they ever experienced before. No wonder the eagle cried "woe, woe, woe."

Finally, we read a statement that goes completely beyond our grasp, "men shall seek death and shall not find it. . ." Try to imagine that. Suicide attempted, but life will not end. Just what comes into play here we do not know, but so terrible are their torments that the old enemy death is suddenly seen as a friend, but one they cannot find.

Rev 9:7-11 *And the shapes of the locusts were like unto horses prepared unto battle; and on their heads were as it were crowns like gold, and their faces were as the faces of men. And they had hair as the hair of women, and their teeth were as the teeth of lions. And they had breastplates, as it were breastplates of iron; and the sound of their wings was as the sound of chariots of many horses running to battle. And they had tails like unto scorpions, and there were stings in their tails: and their power was to hurt men five months. And they had a king over them, which is the angel of the bottomless pit, whose name in the Hebrew tongue is Abaddon, but in the Greek tongue hath his name Apollyon.*

The foregoing description defies imagination. What we do know is that these cannot be interpreted as instruments of modern warfare as some have tried to do. These creatures come up out of the Abyss and their King is one called Abaddon or Apollyon, both names signifying "The Destroyer." They are names ascribed to Satan (the Adversary), and it is doubtless he who rules over them.

This text is perhaps best explained by several others. In 2 Peter we are told that; *God spared not the angels that sinned, but cast them down to hell, and delivered them into chains of darkness, to be reserved unto judgment;* (2 Peter 2:4). If, as we have suggested, these are indeed demon forces which are allowed to ascend from the pit, this passage would explain how they initially arrived there and became the prisoners of the abyss for so many millenniums.

Jude tells us of the same group of angels; *And the angels which kept not their first estate, but left their own habitation, he hath reserved in everlasting chains under darkness unto the judgment of the great day.* (Jude 1:6)

When Lucifer rebelled, he drew after him about a third of the innumerable angelic host who rebelled with him. Some of those rebelled still further when; *the sons of God saw the daughters of men that they were fair; and they took them wives of all which they chose. . .There were giants in the earth in those days; and also after that, when the sons of God came in unto the daughters of men, and they bare children to them, the same became mighty men which were of old, men of renown* (Genesis 6:2-4).

The phase "sons of God" is never used in the O.T. to refer to men, but only to the angelic host (Job 1:6; 2:1; 38:7). It is apparent that certain of the fallen angelic hosts actually co-habited with human women. Having polluted the seed of Adam, God cast these fallen angels into the Abyss, and sent a flood to destroy the human race. It is apparently this occasion (the co-habitation with human women) that marks the time when these fallen spirits were thrown into the Abyss which now emerge from there and take the form, not of a man, but of supernatural locusts.

Rev 9:12 *One woe is past; and, behold, there come two woes more hereafter.*

Still the trumpets are not silenced, but sound once more with another loud blast announcing yet another judgment to fall.

Rev 9:13-15 *And the sixth angel sounded, and I heard a voice from the four horns of the golden altar which is before God, Saying to the sixth angel which had the trumpet, Loose the four angels which are bound in the great river Euphrates. And the four angels were loosed, which were prepared for an hour, and a day, and a month, and a year, for to slay the third part of men.*

I spent considerable time reading the old commentators on this passage to see if I could gain any insight on interpretation. What I gleaned was what happens when we attempt to side-step the obvious.

Older commentators seem to shy away from anything which suggests a literal "spirit world" and perhaps that is why they turn to other interpretations. One writer expressed it like this, "We are not to suppose that this is to be taken literally." **(Albert Barnes).**

The problem then is, if we do not take it literally, whose fanciful interpretation are we to believe? As with some of the former events, what is described here is entirely beyond our experience and therefore appears to be incredible. The alternative however, becomes more incredible still, as every man exercises his fertile imagination in an attempt to explain what is herein simply described. So, let us try to follow the text as closely as we can.

The Four Angels

The Trumpet is sounded and a voice comes forth from the horns of the golden altar. The golden altar was the "Altar of Incense" always associated with prayer. From the altar goes forth a command to loose four angels, who are said to be "bound in the river Euphrates." These are loosed and come forth. Once again, we sense that God is in complete control of this event. These angels have been *prepared for an hour, and a day, and a month, and a year.*

How these angels first arrived in this condition we are not told, nor should we conjecture. However, the fact that they were bound would lead us naturally to think that perhaps they were part of that company we saw before, *"And the angels which kept not their first estate, but left their own habitation, he hath reserved in everlasting chains under darkness unto the judgment of the great day"* (Jude 1:6). God may have chosen a variety of locations in which to hold these imprisoned spirits.

The purpose of the angels is stated clearly. It is their task to; *slay the third part of men.* Even with the vast loss of life that would have already occurred during this dark period, this would amount to over a billion individuals. No wonder our Lord said, *And, except those days should be shortened, there should no flesh be saved:* (Matthew 24:22).

And that brings us to the instruments of this devastation, 200,000,000, very mysterious horsemen.

Rev 9:16 *And the number of the army of the horsemen were two hundred thousand thousand: and I heard the number of them.*

Whether or not there is any significance to it, the number was the exact number of militia which the Chinese government announced some years ago that they had at their call.

Rev 9:17-19 *And thus I saw the horses in the vision, and them that sat on them, having breastplates of fire, and of jacinth, and brimstone: and the heads of the horses were as the heads of lions; and out of their mouths issued fire and smoke and brimstone. By these three was the third part of men killed, by the fire, and by the smoke, and by the brimstone, which issued out of their mouths. For their power is in their mouth, and in their tails: for their tails were like unto serpents, and had heads, and with them they do hurt.*

Again, we come to something which John saw that is beyond our comprehension.

Dr. Morris believes that it is a description of an army of demons. Dr. Ryrie, says either it is an army of demons or an army of demon possessed men.

The entertainment industry seems obsessed with monster movies, and who can tell if that is not what we see here. Perhaps it might be well to remind ourselves that there are spiritual armies that do the bidding of God. Elisha was once surrounded by such an army.

> *And when the servant of the man of God was risen early, and gone forth, behold, an host compassed the city both with horses and chariots. And his servant said unto him, Alas, my master! how shall we do? And he answered, Fear not: for they that be with us are more than they that be with them. And Elisha prayed, and said, LORD, I pray thee, open his eyes, that he may see. And the LORD opened the eyes of the young man; and he saw: and, behold, the mountain was full of horses and chariots of fire round about Elisha* (2 Kings 6:15-17).

It would not be much of a leap then to envision an army of demons under the command of their master, Satan. However, while the four angels are certainly literal, John's description of the horsemen is punctuated with words like "as the heads of lions," or "like unto serpents."

These descriptive words are used in other places in Scripture where we know that they are referring to men – men of fierce countenance indeed, but men nevertheless.

> *And of the Gadites there separated themselves unto David into the hold to the wilderness men of might, and men of war fit for the battle, that could handle shield and buckler, <u>whose faces were like the faces of lions</u>, and were as swift as the roes upon the mountains;* (1 Chronicles 12:8).

Benaiah the son of Jehoiada, the son of a valiant man of Kabzeel, who had done many acts; he slew <u>two lion-like men of Moab</u>: also he went down and slew a lion in a pit in a snowy day (1 Chronicles 11:22).

These passages help us understand that what John is describing may be an army of men, even an army equipped with fearsome devices like nothing John had ever seen, and so he describes them in the best way he can.

This may be enough to allow us to suppose that John simply described what he saw in the best terminology he had available and that possibly they may be correct who see this description as a demon-inspired-human-army equipped for twenty-first century combat. Whatever it is, it is a most destructive and terrifying force and it destroys one third of those who remain from the former judgments.

Let's just quickly sum up what we know of the death toll to this point. In Chapter six the Red Horse rides forth to take peace from the earth and men "kill one another." When the Pale Horse rides forth power is given him over the forth part of the earth to kill. Further, in the same chapter we have the great global earthquake and we can only imagine the numbers which must have died as a result of that.

Then in chapter eight, the waters are made bitter and we read that, "many men died of the waters because they were made bitter." Finally, we come to this passage in which a third of those who remain from the former judgments are now killed. The numbers are now incomprehensible.

We turn now to those who were not destroyed by this judgment:

Rev 9:20, 21 *And the rest of the men which were not killed by these plagues yet repented not of the works of their hands, that they should not worship devils, and idols of gold, and silver, and brass, and stone, and of wood:*

---

which neither can see, nor hear, nor walk: Neither repented they of their murders, nor of their sorceries, nor of their fornication, nor of their thefts.

Over and over I have tried to remind us that the ultimate goal of these judgments is that men might be led to repentance. It was the same in Egypt where nine of the ten plagues, terrible as they were, stopped short of the clearly declared action of taking the life of all of the firstborn (Exodus 4:22, 23). However, just as with Egypt, men hardened their hearts against God and proudly went on defying Him, and God at last executed His final and most terrible judgment. The judgments of the Tribulation period are similar. While severe, they are meant to bring a rebellious world to repentance.

The passage above makes clear that when one worships an idol, he is actually worshiping the demon behind the idol. In like manner Paul writes;

> *What say I then? that the idol is any thing, or that which is offered in sacrifice to idols is any thing? But I say, that the things which the Gentiles sacrifice, they sacrifice to devils, and not to God: and I would not that ye should have fellowship with devils* (1 Corinthians 10:19, 20).

The text says that that they further did not repent, *of their murders or of their sorceries.* Murder is always rampant where there is no fear of God, and the word "sorceries," is translated from Gr. Φαρμακεία; pharmakeia which literally translates to drugs, or particularly psychedelic drugs which lead to hallucinations, visions, dreams and mind-altering experiences. This has always been a part of witchcraft and black magic, and the greatly increased use of these in our own time, speaks volumes about our nearness to all that is described here.

In the final analysis, men continue to resist and to rebel and ultimately will find their place in hell, where there are no drugs or even water to alleviate their pains.

REVIEW

- What distinguishes the "Star" in 9:1 from those we saw in the previous chapter?

- What key was he given and who gave it to him?

- What came out of the pit?

- What did these do and how long did they do it?

- Who was exempt from their sting?

- What will it mean when men cannot die?

- Who are these demon hordes that emerge from the pit and how did they get there in the first place?

- What do the 4 angels do which are loosed from the river Euphrates?

- Where will the horsemen they muster come from and how many are there?

- What are the ultimate results of this plague?

Chapter 17 An Angel, A Book, And A Task

Revelation 10:1 – 11

Rev 10:1, 2 *And I saw another mighty angel come down from heaven, clothed with a cloud: and a rainbow was upon his head, and his face was as it were the sun, and his feet as pillars of fire: And he had in his hand a little book open: and he set his right foot upon the sea, and his left foot on the earth,*

As we approach this next chapter, there are several things we should note.   First, this is the last time we hear John pronounce the words that seem to divide these visions, *And I saw . . .* until the opening of chapter twelve. Therefore, we must assume that from this point on, chapters ten and eleven are a single unit.

Second, we need to identify the "angel" who appears here from heaven.   This will be important for our interpretation of the "little book" which is held in His hand. We must establish the identity of this person by his description.   Note carefully what is said: *come down from heaven, clothed with a cloud: and a rainbow was upon his head, and his face was as it were the sun, and his feet as pillars of fire.*

A very similar description is found in the book of Daniel 10:5, 6. And we should remember a former description of Christ found in this book, Revelation 1:13-15.

Since it is certain that the vision in chapter one of Revelation refers to Christ, and most commentators agree that the description found in Daniel refers to a vision of Christ come in His glory, it is very likely that the personage we have before us in this passage in none other than the glorified risen Christ.

Another clue is the fact that He is clothed in a cloud, which always speaks of deity. Consider the following verses.

And he made darkness pavilions round about him, dark waters, and thick clouds of the skies (2 Samuel 22:12).

Thick clouds are a covering to him, that he seeth not; and he walketh in the circuit of heaven (Job 22:14).

Clouds and darkness are round about him: righteousness and judgment are the habitation of his throne (Psalm 97:2).

I saw in the night visions, and, behold, one like the Son of man came with the clouds of heaven, and came to the Ancient of days, and they brought him near before him (Daniel 7:13).

And then shall appear the sign of the Son of man in heaven: and then shall all the tribes of the earth mourn, and they shall see the Son of man coming in the clouds of heaven with power and great glory (Matthew 24:30).

Jesus saith unto him, Thou hast said: nevertheless I say unto you, Hereafter shall ye see the Son of man sitting on the right hand of power, and coming in the clouds of heaven (Matthew 26:64).

Then we which are alive and remain shall be caught up together with them in the clouds, to meet the Lord in the air: and so shall we ever be with the Lord (1Thessalonians 4:17).

Behold, he cometh with clouds; and every eye shall see him, and they also which pierced him: and all kindreds of the earth shall wail because of him. Even so, Amen (Revelation 1:7).

Finally, this person has a book in His hand. Now, while some attempt to make this another book, I find no reason to believe that it is anything else but the same book which was taken from the hand of God by the conquering Lamb. He alone was found worthy to take the book, therefore the one with the book in His hand is Christ.

It is this book, which originally was "sealed with seven seals." However, we have seen all of those seals opened. The book was also said to be written, "within, and on the back side." In other words, after the seals are opened the front side of the scroll would be exposed, and once it is read the back of the scroll can now be read as well.

As we have seen, the front side contained many judgments upon a rebellious and unbelieving world. We shall shortly see that the backside contains the same and will complete the judgments of God.

Now look at the stance of this Person: *he set his right foot upon the sea, and his left foot on the earth.* The setting of a foot is a declaration of ownership or authority. When the early explorers came to this continent, they set their feet upon the land and claimed it for the sovereign they represented. (compare: Joshua 1:2 - 4).

The action here described declares absolute ownership and authority over both land and sea. The planet has a new official owner – it is under new management, and it will soon know His complete sovereign rule.

Rev 10:3, 4 *And cried with a loud voice, as when a lion roareth: and when he had cried, seven thunders uttered their voices. And when the seven thunders had uttered their voices, I was about to write: and I heard a voice from heaven saying unto me, Seal up those things which the seven thunders uttered, and write them not.*

We are not permitted to know the exact content, either of the cry of the Lord, or of the words of the seven thunders, but we can guess from the posture that is taken, and from the sound that was issued forth (*as when a lion roareth*), that it was both a declaration and a challenge. A declaration of His authority and rule, and a challenge to any who would oppose Him.

Rev 10:5-7 *And the angel which I saw stand upon the sea and upon the earth lifted up his hand to heaven, And sware by him that liveth for ever and ever, who created heaven, and the things that therein are, and the earth, and the things that therein are, and the sea, and the things which are therein, that there should be time no longer: But in the days of the voice of the seventh angel, when he shall begin to sound, the mystery of God should be finished, as he hath declared to his servants the prophets.*

This Divine Personage now declares an oath, by the authority of the God who created all that is here, that there should be no more delay. The phrase, *there shall be time no longer*, does not convey, as is implied in the KJV translation, that all time ends and eternity begins. That this is not the case is evident, for before that happens the Judgments continue for some time and Christ will reign upon the earth for 1,000 years.

No, the implication is that God's appointed time for delay, in which He grants space to repent is now ended, and nothing will now prevent His final victory over His enemies. And we are told exactly when that will take place; *in the days of the voice of the seventh angel, when he shall begin to sound, the mystery of God should be finished, as he hath declared to his servants the prophets.*

The terms here seem extremely clear as if the Holy Spirit did not want us to mistake what was said. There is going to yet sound a seventh angel (six have already sounded their Trumpet judgments). When he sounds; no, when he begins to sound, the mystery of God will be finished.

We must determine what is meant by "the mystery of God." I would take it, within this context to refer to all of the prophecies made throughout both the Old and New Testament Scriptures of the glorious Kingdom of Christ. These mysteries, are about to become realities.

There is a sense of finality to this. Yet in the very next verse we are warned that there is more to come.

Rev 10:8-10 *And the voice which I heard from heaven spake unto me again, and said, Go and take the little book which is open in the hand of the angel which standeth upon the sea and upon the earth. And I went unto the angel, and said unto him, Give me the little book. And he said unto me, Take it, and eat it up; and it shall make thy belly bitter, but it shall be in thy mouth sweet as honey. And I took the little book out of the angel's hand, and ate it up; and it was in my mouth sweet as honey: and as soon as I had eaten it, my belly was bitter.*

John is now commanded by the voice from heaven to go and take the "little book," which is now an unsealed book and an open book, out of the hand of the "Angel." We are not told exactly why it is here called a "little book," unless perhaps it is that all of the seals have been opened and all of those judgments are already past. Perhaps it is reduced in size because what is yet to come is reduced in content.

John obediently goes to this Angel personage and requests that the book be given to him. The Angel then tells John what he is to do with the now open book.

He is to, *take it and eat it up*. This is not a strange concept in Scripture. Jeremiah says; *Thy words were found, and I did eat them; and thy word was unto me the joy and rejoicing of mine heart: for I am called by thy name, O LORD God of hosts* (Jeremiah 15:16).

The idea is that the person is to fill himself with what God has written, he is to appropriate for himself God's Word before he is ready to speak that word to someone else.

In Ezekiel, we have a parallel passage to this one in Revelation. Here, the prophet Ezekiel is given a scroll, much like the one we saw in Revelation, "written within and without," and filled with the judgments of God.

> *And when I looked, behold, a hand was sent unto me; and, lo, a roll of a book was therein; And he spread it before me; and it was written within and without: and there was written therein lamentations, and mourning, and woe. Moreover, he said unto me, Son of man, eat that thou findest; eat this roll, and go speak unto the house of Israel. So, I opened my mouth, and he caused me to eat that roll. And he said unto me, Son of man, cause thy belly to eat, and fill thy bowels with this roll that I give thee. Then did I eat it; and it was in my mouth as honey for sweetness (Ezekiel 2:9 – 3:3).*

In the same way John takes the book, open in the Angel's hand and eats it. As soon as he does he experiences a sense of "sweetness" in his mouth. The Word itself is always sweet in the mouth of a believer, but when fully digested, understood, and ruminated upon, he is confronted with a message that will bring glory to God, but disaster to an unbelieving world. As soon as it is eaten, there is a bitterness about what is yet to come.

Rev 10:11 *And he said unto me, Thou must prophesy again before many peoples, and nations, and tongues, and kings.*

Having been thus prepared by "eating" the little book, John is now ready for his recommissioning. He is told that he must "prophesy again." The word used is the Gr. Πάλιν; palin, the idea of *oscillatory* repetition); *once more*, or again."

This is significant because, as we shall see, John will be shortly brought to the end of his first series of visions and a whole new vision will come of details not specifically covered before. This must be our understanding if we are to take Revelation 10:7 seriously. I will have more to say about this when we come to the close of chapter 11.

But now the seventh angel has not sounded, and so John continues in chapter eleven completing the vision now at hand.

REVIEW

- Who do we believe the "mighty angel" seen in 10:1, 2 is?

- What was the "little book" he had in his hand?

- What does it mean that "there will be delay no longer?"

- What does the phrase, "The Mystery of God" mean?

- What was the significance of John "eating the little book?"

- How does John's recommissioning help us to understand what will follow in the book of Revelation?

Chapter 18   2 Witnesses & The 7th Trumpet

Revelation 11:1 – 19

Rev 11:1, 2 *And there was given me a reed like unto a rod: and the angel stood, saying, Rise, and measure the temple of God, and the altar, and them that worship therein. But the court which is without the temple leave out, and measure it not; for it is given unto the Gentiles: and the holy city shall they tread under foot forty and two months.*

We need to observe that we have reached another of the parenthesis found in the book of Revelation. Chapter 9 closes with the sounding of the sixth trumpet, we should have expected the sounding of the seventh as chapter 10 opened. However, once again there is an interlude between the sixth and the seventh trumpets, just as there was between the sixth and the seventh seals where all of chapter 7 is taken up in that interlude. Here chapter 10 serves as an interlude.

Now, each of these interludes is like a parenthetical interruption in the on-going drama in which the movement seems to be halted and additional information is given us. That is what we will continue to see in this chapter up until verse 15.

The chapter begins and ends with a Temple. They are not the same Temple; the first is on earth, and the last one is in heaven, but both are significant in interpreting this passage.

Taking the measurement of something, particularly a plot of ground, or a particular area, always implies taking possession of it.

What John is called upon to measure here is quite evidently a portion of a Temple, called, *The Temple of God*, that is in the earthly city of Jerusalem. The existence of a Temple dedicated to the God of the Bible in the city of Jerusalem implies that such a Temple had been built, since no such Temple exists at this present time.

Just when this Temple will be built or exactly how remains a mystery. We know that at the present time, the Dome of the Rock and the Al Asqa Mosque now occupy Israel's ancient Temple Mount. But despite all that the Arabs have done to try to erase all trace of Israel's claim to this place, there is a growing recognition that Israel has historic rights here.

David first purchased the site by a direct command of God (2 Samuel 24:18 – 24; 2 Chronicles 3:1). All of Israel's Temples, from the first, built by Solomon, to the Second Temple of Ezra's time (greatly enlarged by Herod the Great and sometimes referred to as "the Third Temple"), have rested on this location.

When Titus and his Roman legion destroyed the last Temple (Herod's Temple), as predicted by Christ (Matthew 24:1, 2), no further place of worship existed here until Umayyad Caliph Abd al-Malik ibn Marwan ordered the construction of an Islamic shrine, the Dome of the Rock, on the site of the Temple. The shrine has stood on the mount since 691 AD; the al-Aqsa Mosque, from roughly the same period, also stands in the Temple courtyard.

With the return of Israel to the Land and the establishment of a Jewish State in 1948, there has been an increased desire especially among orthodox Jews to rebuild a Jewish Temple on the site of Solomon's first Temple. A "Temple Institute" was founded in Jerusalem in 1989 to begin research on the project.

The Temple Institute has the following statement of purpose: **"The Temple Institute's ultimate goal is to see Israel**

rebuild the Holy Temple on Mount Moriah in Jerusalem, in accord with the Biblical commandments."

In preparation for the day when the Third Temple will become a reality, the Temple Institute has already prepared all of the Temple articles for worship, including the altars with all their tools, the curtains, the clothing for the priests, and even the musical instruments.

Hence, we must expect the building of the Third (or Forth, depending upon how you count Herod's Temple), Temple, and sometimes referred to as the Tribulation Temple, sometime before or during the Tribulation period. Although Herod's Temple took 40 years in the building, this Temple will likely take a very short period of time, because of the extensive preparations already made.

The question is always, "When will this Temple be built?" There are several possible answers to that question. Some believe that it will be a part of the Covenant that the Anti-Christ will make with Israel which will assure their protection and freedom of worship (Daniel 9:27). That would mean that the Temple would be constructed very early in the seven-year period.

Or, it is possible that it will take place, either just before or just after the invasion of Russia and the Islamic nations, which will happen somewhere toward the end of the first half of the 70th Week. If before the invasion, it would be the flashpoint to cause the invasion, if afterward it would be the result of Islam's total defeat as related by Ezekiel 38, 39.

Finally, we should not forget that within the prophecy of the Temple, is also the clear statement that the City (Jerusalem), will be, at one point, *given unto the Gentiles: and the holy city shall they tread under foot forty and two months.*

In any case, a Temple exists in Jerusalem and John is sent to measure, *the temple of God, and the altar, and them that worship therein.*

God lays His claim to this portion of the Tribulation Temple and to those who are worshipping Him. This action lays the groundwork for what is about to take place.

The Persons of two Prophets

Rev 11:3, 4 *And I will give power unto my two witnesses, and they shall prophesy a thousand two hundred and threescore days, clothed in sackcloth. These are the two olive trees, and the two candlesticks standing before the God of the earth.*

Let's begin by affirming that the two individuals in question are, in fact, two persons and not symbols. I remember teaching on this passage in Romania shortly after the Revolution. It was the first time the men assembled there had ever heard an exposition that interpreted Revelation in a literal fashion.

When I suggested that these two were actual persons, one student, who had attended a well-known seminary in Romania, raised his hand to tell me that, "they always told us in Seminary that the two witnesses were the Old and the New Testament." I responded by saying, "OK, let's try that theory out. How do you get the Old Testament and the New Testament clothed in sackcloth, killed and raised again?" Our students agreed the seminary's interpretation was not tenable.

Next, I want to look at how God introduces these two individuals to us. God begins by calling them His witnesses. The actual word in the Gr. Μάρτυς; martus, is the word from which we get our English word martyr. The word seems to have been originally referring to one who bears witness for Christ, but so often did that testimony end in the witness being put to death, that the word came to refer to one who laid down his (or her) life for Christ.

That is indeed the import here, for as we shall see, that is exactly what these two witnesses (martyrs), do.

God next spoke of them as Prophets; *they shall prophesy a thousand two hundred and threescore days*. The word translated "prophesy" is Gr. Προφητεύω; prophēteuō, means both to foretell the future and also to "speak forth" that is, to bear witness of both sin and the imminent judgment of God. Strong's Concordance notes that the word often denotes "inspired preaching." In other words, imparting a direct message from God.

Note, that the period of the testimony is established. It will be 1,260 days, or half of the Tribulation period. Remember that period lasts for seven years and is divided in two equal time periods. These are found, not only here in the book of Revelation, but in the book of Daniel as well. The period is recorded in Daniel 7:25, and 12:7 as "a time, times and half a time." As becomes clear in a study of Daniel, "a time" is the equivalent of one year, "times" is equivalent to two years, and "half a time" in equivalent to six months, or one half year.

Now the time of the testimony of these witnesses is set at 1,260 days. All prophetic years are 360 days in length, divided into twelve months of 30 days each. So, the time indicated here is the same as "a time, times and half a time," and it is also referred to as 42 months in verse five of this same chapter (see Revelation 13:5).

One of our tasks as we look at this passage, will be to determine which of the two time periods is meant – the first half of the Tribulation (as many believe), or the second half.

The next thing we note, in the descriptive introduction of these men, is that they are clothed in sackcloth. Sackcloth always indicated repentance and mourning over something, either over one's own sin, or the sinful condition of a people or nation.

Next, God refers to them as two Olive trees and two Lampstands.

This simile is taken directly from Zechariah chapter four. The background of that passage was the rebuilding of the Temple by the returned remnant. Joshua, the High Priest, and Zerubbabel (acting as governor), were leading the work. There was strong opposition both from surrounding peoples, even threats of military attack (see Nehemiah 4). There was also opposition from within the Jewish community. The task was momentous, like removing a large mountain, but God promised that it would happen by the power supplied by His Spirit. Zechariah's vision is explained as follows:

Then answered I, and said unto him, What are these two olive trees upon the right side of the candlestick and upon the left side thereof? And I answered again, and said unto him, What be these two olive branches which through the two golden pipes empty the golden oil out of themselves? And he answered me and said, Knowest thou not what these be? And I said, No, my lord. Then said he, These are the two anointed ones, that stand by the Lord of the whole earth (Zechariah 4:11-14).

So, God's message through Zechariah was that His power would be supplied to the two servants of God who led the work in his day, and God's message through John is that the same power will be given to these two martyrs (witnesses), who testify for Him in the final days, the key lesson being, *Not by might, nor by power, but by my spirit, saith the LORD of hosts* (Zechariah 4:6).

The final word of description is found in these words, *who stand before the God of the whole earth* (vs.4).

The true prophet of God is always aware that as he delivers God's message, wherever he is, he stands in the very presence of God and his responsibility is to God alone to rightly deliver the word that was imparted to him. As has been said, he is responsible to "an audience of One," for his performance.

When Elijah the Tishbite delivered his fiery ultimatum to King Ahab, it was not the regal trappings of the palace that engaged his attention, nor the power or authority of the king, but rather his clear awareness that he spoke as one standing in the presence of God and as God's messenger: *As the LORD God of Israel liveth, <u>before whom I stand</u>, there shall not be dew nor rain these years, but according to my word* (1 Kings 17:1).

Having this introduction of the two prophetic witnesses, we will examine the power that these two exert. But even as we do we are compelled to ask the question, "Who are these prophets?" "Do we know them?" "Are there distinguishing characteristics in their ministry that we have seen before and which we might associate with people about whom we are already familiar?"

The Power of the Prophets

Rev 11:5, 6 *And if any man will hurt them, fire proceedeth out of their mouth, and devoureth their enemies: and if any man will hurt them, he must in this manner be killed. These have power to shut heaven, that it rain not in the days of their prophecy: and have power over waters to turn them to blood, and to smite the earth with all plagues, as often as they will.*

In identifying these prophets, we begin with their actions. Let's note the following:

- *If any man will hurt them, fire proceedeth out of their mouth, and devoureth their enemies* (vs.5). Every see this before? The entire first chapter of 2 Kings records something very similar.

The background is the aged Elijah. His prophetic word concerning King Ahaziah angered the King and a company of fifty soldiers was sent out to arrest him. Now the contest became a battle between God's authority and that of the King.

Then the king sent unto him a captain of fifty with his fifty. And he went up to him: and, behold, he sat on the top of an hill. And he spake unto him, Thou man of God, the king hath said, Come down. And Elijah answered and said to the captain of fifty, If I be a man of God, then let fire come down from heaven, and consume thee and thy fifty. And there came down fire from heaven, and consumed him and his fifty (2 Kings 1:9,10).

Actually, this is repeated twice and two companies are destroyed, until the third captain implores mercy and Elijah allows himself to be taken. It was this very incident that Jesus' disciples had in mind when, having been refused by the Samaritans, they asked, *Lord, wilt thou that we command fire to come down from heaven, and consume them, even as Elias did?* (Luke 9:54)

So, the first thing we learn about these witnesses is that the power of God is upon them to demonstrate that the message they bring comes from God. Now look at the next thing we read of them.

(They), have power to shut heaven, that it rain not in the days of their prophecy.

Again, we have seen this before. *And Elijah the Tishbite, who was of the inhabitants of Gilead, said unto Ahab, As the LORD God of Israel liveth, before whom I stand, there shall not be dew nor rain these years, but according to my word* (1 Kings 17:1).

Clearly then, at least one of these two witnesses exercises the power that Elijah had during his ministry. Could this person actually be Elijah?

The final words of the Old Testament are these; *Behold, I will send you Elijah the prophet before the coming of the great and dreadful day of the LORD:*

And he shall turn the heart of the fathers to the children, and the heart of the children to their fathers, lest I come and smite the earth with a curse (Malachi 4:5, 6).

The Rabbis of Jesus' time took these words quite literally and taught that before Messiah would come, Elijah (spelled Elias in KJV), would first appear. This is the question that troubled Jesus' disciples.

> *And his disciples asked him, saying, Why then say the scribes that Elias must first come? And Jesus answered and said unto them, <u>Elias truly shall first come, and restore all things</u>. But I say unto you, That Elias is come already, and they knew him not, but have done unto him whatsoever they listed. Likewise shall also the Son of man suffer of them. Then the disciples understood that he spake unto them of John the Baptist* (Matthew 17:10 – 12).

This response of Jesus is natural in light of the words the angel spoke to Zechariah concerning John; *And he shall go before him in the spirit and power of Elias, to turn the hearts of the fathers to the children, and the disobedient to the wisdom of the just; to make ready a people prepared for the Lord* (Luke 1:17).

There are two possible conclusions we may come to from these verses: (1) That Elijah himself must come and therefore one of these two witnesses must be Elijah, or (2) that another, sent in the power and spirit of Elijah may fulfill the prophecy. I am strongly inclined to the first of these conclusions as I will explain as we proceed.

The next defining thing we read about these witnesses is:

- *(They) have power over waters to turn them to blood, and to smite the earth with all plagues, as often as they will.*

It is impossible for a student of Scripture to read this without seeing the power of Moses in this passage. Exodus, chapters seven to thirteen, records the contest with Pharaoh, in which Moses' initiated the plagues, including the turning of water into blood. So, we see a clear parallel between Moses' actions and that of the witnesses.

Another point of interest is that when Christ was transfigured on the Mount, *there appeared unto them Moses and Elias talking with him* (Matthew 17:3). The event is significant because Jesus had preceded it with these words; *Verily I say unto you, There be some standing here, which shall not taste of death, till they see the Son of man coming in his kingdom* (Matthew 16:28).

In other words, the transfiguration event was a preview of the Kingdom. It is clear that Peter understood it in that way for he would later write:

> *For we have not followed cunningly devised fables, when we made known unto you the power and coming of our Lord Jesus Christ, but were eyewitnesses of his majesty. For he received from God the Father honour and glory, when there came such a voice to him from the excellent glory, This is my beloved Son, in whom I am well pleased. And this voice which came from heaven we heard, when we were with him in the holy mount* (2 Peter 1:16 – 18)

Dr. C. I. Scofield points out that the Transfiguration scene actually reflects all of the features that will be present in the coming Kingdom. Scofield writes:

> "The transfiguration scene contains, in miniature, all the elements of the future kingdom in manifestation:
>
> (1) the Lord, not in humiliation, but in glory. (Mat 17:2).

(2) Moses, glorified, representative of the redeemed who have passed through death into the kingdom. (Mat_13:43); (Luk_9:30-31).

(3) Elijah, glorified, representative of the redeemed who have entered the kingdom by translation. (1Co_15:50-53); (1Th_4:14-17).

(4) Peter, James, and John, not glorified, representatives (for the moment) of Israel in the flesh in the future kingdom (Eze_37:21-27).

(5) The multitude at the foot of the mountain (Mat_17:14); representative of the nations who are to be brought into the kingdom after it is established over Israel (Isa_11:10-12)."
(Dr. C. I. Scofield; Scofield Reference Bible, pp. 1022, 1023)

Hence, it would be easy to conclude that the two witnesses are Moses and Elijah.

However, there is another consideration. While we know that Elijah did not die but was translated into heaven, Moses, on the other hand, did die, and some would argue that the dictum; *It is appointed unto men once to die,* precludes Moses from being one of the witnesses, since both of them are killed and that would involve a kind of second death for Moses.

Well, the argument is not without merit, and while we do not know that the statement in Hebrews is the final word, we might consider the question, "is there any other candidate for the second witness?" And, indeed, we find that there is.

Enoch, the seventh from Adam, was also translated and taken to heaven without dying. But is Enoch eligible? Is he really a prophet? We are not left to wonder.

Jude records Enoch's prophetic ministry in these words:

And Enoch also, the seventh from Adam, prophesied of these, saying, Behold, the Lord cometh with ten thousands of his saints, To execute judgment upon all, and to convince all that are ungodly among them of all their ungodly deeds which they have ungodly committed, and of all their hard speeches which ungodly sinners have spoken against him (Jude 1:14, 15).

Thus, we learn that Enoch was also a prophet, and that his prophetic ministry centered upon the subject of the Lord's coming, and particularly upon His coming in judgment. Therefore, it would seem that while we are not given precise information that these two witnesses are Enoch and Elijah, there seems to be strong evidence that would support that.

One final thought, it is always of interest to me what the earliest Church Fathers thought. Their thoughts may be as much in error as ours, but they were closest to the Apostles and therefore to the inspired revelation. I discovered what they believed in a rather strange way.

I was reading John Gill's Commentary on Revelation. Gill is a Baptist writer, and can be trusted in much of his material, but, like so many Post-Reformation writers Gill carries the baggage of spiritualizing prophetic passages. About the witnesses he writes; "By whom are meant, not Enoch and Elias, <u>as some of the ancient fathers thought</u>, who, they supposed, would come before the appearance of Christ, and oppose antichrist, and be slain by him."

While Gill disagrees with the idea, it is of comfort to me to know that those closest to the Apostles had come to the same conclusion that we have; that is, if these witnesses can be identified, the preponderance of evidence suggests they are Enoch and Elijah.

The Persecution of the Prophets

Rev 11:7, 8 *And when they shall have finished their testimony, the beast that ascendeth out of the bottomless pit shall make war against them, and shall overcome them, and kill them. And their dead bodies shall lie in the street of the great city, which spiritually is called Sodom and Egypt, where also our Lord was crucified.*

The opening phrase reminds us at once that God is in complete control however terrible the situation may become. The two witnesses are commissioned to bear testimony for a stated period of time. When that period is over, the opportunity for repentance for their hearers is also over, and God allows the heart response of a wicked world to their message to be made very clear.

According to this passage they are killed by *the beast that ascendeth out of the bottomless pit.* Now, while we will read a great deal about the Beast in later chapters of Revelation, this is the first time he is mentioned in the book and in such a way as to almost assume we are familiar with him. John certainly was. He spoke often of this one in his epistles (1 John 2:18-22; 4:3; 2 John 7).

In the Gospel of John, Jesus predicted him in these words; *I am come in my Father's name, and ye receive me not: if another shall come in his own name, him ye will receive* (John 5:43).

It is worth noting also that the word translated "Beast" in this text is not the same as that translated "Beast" earlier (as in Revelation 4:6, 7; 5:6).

In these incidences, as we saw, the word was Gr. ζῶον, which means a "living creature." Here, the word is Gr. Θηρίον, thērion; a *dangerous animal:* - a wild beast."

We must note the phrase; *that ascendeth out of the bottomless pit.* As we have noted before, the "bottomless pit" is translated from the word abyss, which refers to a portion of hell.

This passage has some similarities with the fifth Trumpet (Chapter 9), which tells of the release of minions of demons on the earth. To "ascend from the bottomless pit," clearly indicates that this one came from a former captivity in hell.

Some have concluded therefore, that what we have here is a resurrection. A wicked man from the past, released to work his evil again. There are some who have even tried to identify him with such historic figures as Nero, Mussolini, or Napoleon. There are a number of reasons why this does not seem feasible, including the fact that Satan does not hold the power to raise the dead.

What we do know is that this person will come to power through the direct aid of Satan himself. Scripture tells us, *the dragon gave him his power, and his seat, and great authority* (13:2). So, is it a human that came up out of the pit, or is the Beast a composite of human/demon? I can't answer the question, but it must be considered.

Perhaps even more important to our understanding is what this one called, "the Beast" does. He makes war against the prophets and prevails. Now note, that up until now, nothing formed against these two prophetic witnesses could avail. They had power over all their enemies. Now, however, the Beast is given power over them and he kills them.

It is important in trying to understand this to determine the timing of both the witness of these prophets and their death to the entire seven years. Did they prophesy during the first three and a half years, or during the second? Most believe that it was during the first period, but the context of this section makes that problematic.

In the first place, the chapter opens with a description of the Tribulation Temple. That means that a Jewish Temple will have been erected on the ancient Temple Mount in Jerusalem.

As suggested before, it is likely that this will occur at around the mid-way point of this seven-year period. If that is the case, and since the Temple is in evidence during the prophetic ministry of these prophets, we must conclude that their ministry began at the middle of the week and will span the final half of the Tribulation.

In addition, we have already seen that in the preceding chapter (10:5-7), the One holding the "little book" takes an oath that delay will be no longer, but that when the seventh trumpet begins to sound, the mystery of God should be finished. That seems to place us toward the end of the Tribulation Week, not the middle.

Furthermore, as soon as the seventh angel sounds, a heavenly choir resounds with the words, *The kingdoms of this world are become the kingdoms of our Lord, and of his Christ; and he shall reign for ever and ever* (vs.15). The statement is in the present tense, that is, it is an accomplished fact. Therefore, I must conclude that the ending of this chapter brings us as far chronologically, as we will be in Chapter nineteen, when Christ is seen riding forth to take the Kingdom.

On the basis of those two passages, it would seem most likely that the two witnesses had their ministry in the last three and a half years of this period. The chapter ends with the declaration of the coming of the Kingdom and all the events that will transpire at that time. It just seems more likely that the testimony of the two witnesses takes place at this time also.

We are not left to guess about the fate of these two special servants of God. We read, *their dead bodies shall lie in the street of the great city, which spiritually is called Sodom and Egypt, where also our Lord was crucified* (vs.9).

The wicked Beast will not allow their bodies to be buried. To allow a dead body to be exposed and remain unburied was (and perhaps still is), the greatest possible indignity that could be shown.

It is evident that their dead bodies, provided for the Beast, the apparent evidence of his superior power over them, and by extension, over their God. The evidence is short lived.

It is important that we note the location of their death. It is in the city of Jerusalem, now occupied by the Beast. Comparing other Scripture, we know that he will occupy Jerusalem in the middle of the seven-year period (Daniel 9:27; Matthew 24:15; 2 Thessalonians 2:3, 4). Now, the spiritual condition of the city in comparable to Sodom and Egypt. It was the city where our LORD Himself was slain and now the site of the death of His servants.

The Profaning of the Prophets

Rev 11:9, 10 *And they of the people and kindreds and tongues and nations shall see their dead bodies three days and an half, and shall not suffer their dead bodies to be put in graves. And they that dwell upon the earth shall rejoice over them, and make merry, and shall send gifts one to another; because these two prophets tormented them that dwelt on the earth.*

Revelation 11:9 used to present something of a conundrum for expositors. How could all the world simultaneously see an event that occurred in one city - Jerusalem? Now we have no question that it will happen, and there are multiple modes of media that would make it possible, and perhaps more than we know now. Whatever the case, God, centuries ago, told John that people all over the world would simultaneously view the dead bodies of the witnesses – and they shall.

The bodies are allowed to lie, thus exposed to what additional abuse we are not told, for three and a half days. After the third day extreme decomposition would begin to set in. Nevertheless, the bodies are not permitted to be buried.

And during this horrible time, the "earth dwellers" demonstrate their extreme hatred for the witnesses, and their hatred for their message and for their God.

They demonstrate in the streets in the greatest Mardi-Gra type celebration ever staged. The time becomes an international holiday for gift-giving, because the message of righteousness which these two preached, tormented the consciences and upset the minds of those who had given themselves over to the Beast and to the godless revelry of the times.

The Prevailing of the Prophets

Rev 11:11, 12 *And after three days and an half the Spirit of life from God entered into them, and they stood upon their feet; and great fear fell upon them which saw them. And they heard a great voice from heaven saying unto them, Come up hither. And they ascended up to heaven in a cloud; and their enemies beheld them.*

But their merriment is abruptly interrupted by the sudden movement of these two defiled and dishonored corpses. Suddenly, they not only moved but stood up, restored, living and glorified, and as a watching world stood by terrified at what they saw, a great voice said to them, (just what He had said to John and to us in chapter four), "Come up hither."

At that moment a cloud of glory (lit. the glory cloud), surrounded them and they are raised into the skies before the amazed eyes of a watching world.

Rev 11:13 *And the same hour was there a great earthquake, and the tenth part of the city fell, and in the earthquake were slain of men seven thousand: and the remnant were affrighted, and gave glory to the God of heaven.*

Just as occurred when Christ died, an earthquake ensues, but while apparently local in scope, it is nonetheless devastating and a tenth of the city is toppled to the ground.

Considering that we are now talking about modern structures that are built to withstand quakes, this damage is phenomenal.

In addition to the structural damage there are 7,000 lives lost due to the quake and it seems men are forced to acknowledge and glorify God. What this means cannot be construed to imply conversion or repentance, but a simple recognition that there is a Living God who has done what they have just witnessed.

Rev 11:14 *The second woe is past; and, behold, the third woe cometh quickly.*

In Chapter eight, verse thirteen we read; *Woe, woe, woe, to the inhabiters of the earth by reason of the voices of the three angels which are yet to sound.* Now two of those "woes" are past. The first woe was the opening of the abyss to allow hordes of locust-like demons to ascend in smoke upon the earth. The second was the march of 200,000,000 horsemen who slay a remaining third of the human race. Both were certainly "woes" to unsaved rebellious humanity – that is, to the "earthdwellers."

Now the third woe comes with the seventh trumpet. But please notice that there is nothing in this or the other trumpets that spelled woe to God's people. When the final trumpet sounds, it is woe and final doom to rebels, but glory and unspeakable joy to the saints.

Rev 11:15 *And the seventh angel sounded; and there were great voices in heaven, saying, The kingdoms of this world are become the kingdoms of our Lord, and of his Christ; and he shall reign for ever and ever.*

The incontrovertible fact, that the seventh trumpet brings us chronologically to the end of the Tribulation and the return of Christ is acknowledged even by those who do not sense the full finality of these words (vs. 15). The following is quoted from the Bible Knowledge Commentary.

> "The fact that this (the full establishment of the Kingdom), will be fulfilled at the Second Coming makes it clear that the period of the seventh trumpet

chronologically reaches to Christ's return." **(BKC)**

You may view the seventh trumpet encompassing all the remainder of the book up to chapter 19, or you could understand this passage as bringing us to the coming of the Kingdom, and the following chapters to be additional information that covers generally the same period we have just covered from chapters 6 – 11.

Remember, in chapter 10, John is given the "little book" to eat. It is sweet in his mouth as he ruminates upon the coming glory of God, but bitter to his belly as he contemplates the awful judgments that will fall and the final destiny of the wicked.

Immediately after eating the book John is told that he must, *prophesy again before many peoples, and nations, and tongues, and kings* (10:11). We have noted that the word, "again" is the Gr. *palin,* the idea of *oscillatory* repetition. In other words, John is going to prophecy again of some of these same things and with much additional information.

Dr. H. I. Ironside, likened it to "turning over the scroll and reading from the backside." I think that helps us picture what is happening beginning in chapter 12.

In chapter 12, we reverse the scroll, we begin to be introduced to the great actors, for good and for evil in the last days which continues through chapter 13.

Then in chapter 14 through 20 we see the Lamb on Mount Zion with the 144,000, and the final reaping of the earth, the final last plagues and the destruction of Babylon.

After that we arrive at the marriage supper of the Lamb and His final decent in victory to set up His Kingdom.

All of that to say that the seeming triumphant victory recorded in these verses, is exactly what it seems to be, the arrival of the King and the Kingdom.

Rev 11:16-18 *And the four and twenty elders, which sat before God on their seats, fell upon their faces, and worshipped God, Saying, We give thee thanks, O Lord God Almighty, which art, and wast, and art to come; because thou hast taken to thee thy great power, and hast reigned. And the nations were angry, and thy wrath is come, and the time of the dead, that they should be judged, and that thou shouldest give reward unto thy servants the prophets, and to the saints, and them that fear thy name, small and great; and shouldest destroy them which destroy the earth.*

Once again, our attention is drawn to the twenty-four elders, seated on their thrones, who fall prostrate before God in absolute worship and praise because that now, at long last His Kingdom has come and His will is going to be done on earth as it is in heaven.

Verse 17 is translated:

- *because you have taken your great power and have begun to rule* in the ASV.
- *have taken up your great power and are ruling your kingdom* (BBE)
- *You used your great power and started ruling* (CEV).

All of which says the obvious, this is present tense, this is not looking forward in anticipation to a Kingdom that will soon come (as some teach), but is rejoicing that the Kingdom has come. Notice the accompanying events:

(1) Thy wrath is come (2)The dead shall rise and are to be judged; *(3)The Servants of the King will be rewarded, small and great* *(4) Those who have destroyed the earth* (by filling it with iniquity) will be destroyed (no unrighteous will be allowed to enter the Kingdom).

Rev 11:19 *And the temple of God was opened in heaven, and there was seen in his temple the ark of his testament: and there were lightnings, and voices, and thunderings, and an earthquake, and great hail.*

This chapter began with the Temple on earth, it now ends with the Temple in heaven. Notice, it is open, and the ark of the covenant is seen within.

On earth, and in the earthy Temple, the Beast has set up his throne in the very Holy of Holies. But in the heavenly Temple, God's presence is seen and there comes an ominous sound of voices, and thunderings, accompanied by earthquakes and hail.

We are about to look at the second side of the scroll and there are some awesome things ahead. The vision is to prepare us and remind us that the One who dwells between the cherubim is in complete control.

REVIEW

- *How many Temples are there in chapter 11 and where are they?*

- *Give a description of the 2 prophets of chapter 11*

- *Who do we believe the two prophets are any why?*

- *Did the two prophesy during the first or second half of the Tribulation?*

- *How were they killed and how did the world react to their death?*

- *What happens when the 7th Trumpet begins to sound?*

Chapter 19 A Woman, A Child & A Dragon

Revelation 12:1 – 17

When we open chapter 12, we have come to a pivotal point in the book of Revelation. In chapter 10 we saw the announcement; *there should be time* (delay), *no longer: But in the days of the voice of the seventh angel, when he shall begin to sound, the mystery of God should be finished, as he hath declared to his servants the prophets* (Revelation 10:6, 7). These words put us on notice that there is great significance to the sounding of the seventh trumpet.

As we closed chapter 11, the seventh trumpet sounds and according to the "great voices in heaven," *The kingdoms of this world are become the kingdoms of our Lord, and of his Christ; and he shall reign for ever and ever.* It should be noted that this proclamation is in the present tense, therefore, at this point of time, this will be an accomplished feat. I find that in expounding this text, I am captive to that proclamation, and therefore believe that it carries us in time to the actual beginning of the Kingdom, which will be repeated again in chapter 19:11 – 20:4.

It is for that reason that we believe that the two witnesses perform their ministry during the last 3 ½ years of the Tribulation. According to this passage, their ministry immediately precedes the seventh Trumpet Judgment. After their testimony is finished and they are dramatically raised from death and carried up to heaven, the seventh trumpet alerts us to the final descent of Christ from heaven and the declaration that the Kingdom has come. Therefore, the ministry of the two prophets must be in the final 3 ½ segment of the Tribulation.

That raises the next question; what is the remainder of the book of Revelation about?

You will remember that when we were first introduced to the scroll, it had seven seals and was written "within and on the backside." The seven seals have been opened, the seven trumpets came out of the seventh seal, and the seventh trumpet brought us to the commencement of the Kingdom. Dr. H. A. Ironside has suggested that beginning with chapter twelve, the scroll in now reversed, and we are allowed to look at what is on the backside. I think we can see the feasibility of that concept as we look at this next section of the book.

In summary, chapters 12 and 13 will introduce us to the great personalities/entities that act in the last days. Chapter 14 is a kaleidoscope covering a span of time and a variety of subjects, such as the 144,000, Babylon, Beast worshippers, Blessed Martyrs and the reaping of the grain and vintage of the earth. Chapters 15 and 16 cover the final pouring forth of the bowls of wrath. Chapter 17 and 18 cover the fall of Babylon, and 19 brings us to the marriage supper of the Lamb and the descent of the King of Kings and Lord of Lords. In other words, chapter 19 brings us once again to the point where; *The kingdoms of this world are become the kingdoms of our Lord, and of his Christ.*

We in the west are accustom to thinking in a linier fashion, that is, we want each event to flow in a strict chronological order from the first to the last. That is not the pattern of the book of Revelation. In these coming chapters, we will again and again see scenes that are taken from the first half of the seven-year Tribulation and then others that jump to the very climax of the period. In fact some take us to the very beginning of time. If we are prepared for that, it will make understanding this section much easier.

With that preview, let's begin by meeting the great entities which will be in operation in the last days.

Rev 12:1 *And there appeared a great wonder in heaven; a woman clothed with the sun, and the moon under her feet, and upon her head a crown of twelve stars:*

The statement begins by alerting us that what we are seeing is symbolic. The word translated "wonder" in the KJV, is the Gr. *Semeion,* which refers to a sign, i.e., something symbolic. So we should not be looking for a specific person in this vision, but a picture, sign or symbol of some other entity.

There are three symbolic women in the book of Revelation. The first is the woman we now see in this vision. The second is the Great Harlot of chapters 17, 18, symbolic of that corrupt religious and economic system that began in Babylon shortly after the flood and remains in various forms to this time, its final form being revealed in the two chapters just mentioned. The final woman is *the Bride, the Lamb's Wife* whose marriage supper takes place in chapter 19. She is the true Church, united to her Lord Jesus Christ in the eternal bonds of matrimony (Ephesians 5:25-33), and having been faithful to Him, is now gathered to Him and glorified with Him forever.

Having then identified two of the three women, and noting the fact that each is symbolic of a much larger entity, it should not be difficult for us to now identify the woman we see here in chapter 12. The vision is symbolic therefore the woman is not a specific person, but a symbol of something else.

It is important that we understand this, since Roman Catholicism insists that the vision is of the Virgin Mary and much of that Church's worship of her is based upon that interpretation. Wherever Mary is seen in Roman Catholic art or image, she is inevitably crowned with twelve stars and radiance emanates from behind her head to represent the sun. This false interpretation has led to idolatry and must be rejected.

The first clue we get to her real identity is her appearance. She is *clothed with the sun, and the moon under her feet, and upon her head a crown of twelve stars.*

That description should remind us of another vision, or dream, from long ago.

> *And he dreamed yet another dream, and told it his brethren, and said, Behold, I have dreamed a dream more; and, behold, the sun and the moon and the eleven stars made obeisance to me. And he told it to his father, and to his brethren: and his father rebuked him, and said unto him, What is this dream that thou hast dreamed? Shall I and thy mother and thy brethren indeed come to bow down ourselves to thee to the earth?* (Genesis 37:9, 10).

Please note that Joseph's father, Jacob, immediately understood the significance of the symbols. The sun represented Jacob, the moon Jacob's wife Rachel, and the eleven stars the eleven other sons of Jacob. In other words, the symbols in the dream represented the family of Jacob, or Israel.

In the present vision, the stars are increased to twelve, thus representing the twelve tribes of Israel, the sun and the moon add to her glorious appearance, but they may well relate to the promise found in Psalm 72:5 where Israel is said to "fear Thee as long as the sun and moon shall endure." Here they are related to Israel's continual perpetuity.

I think the final confirmation of their meaning is found in Jeremiah 31, where God declares His New Covenant with Israel (the guarantee of their eventual national conversion and salvation). After setting forth the unconditional terms of the covenant, God says;

> *Thus saith the LORD, which giveth the sun for a light by day, and the ordinances of the moon and of the stars for a light by night, which divideth the sea when the waves thereof roar; The LORD of hosts is his name: If those ordinances depart from before me, saith the LORD, then the seed of Israel also shall cease from being a nation before me for ever* (Jeremiah 31:35, 36).

The sun and the moon are the guarantee that Israel will not perish as a nation, and John sees the woman (Israel) clothed with them in his vision. Therefore we conclude that the personage of the Woman, can be none other than the nation Israel.

Rev 12:2 *And she being with child cried, travailing in birth, and pained to be delivered.*

The woman is seen as being with child, and travailing in birth. The entire Scripture story, from the call of Abraham in Genesis 12 promises that Abraham's seed will one day produce the long promised Messiah-Savior, and through Abraham, *shall all the families of the earth be blessed.* Thus the promise travels from Abraham, through Isaac, through Israel. The Jewish prophets constantly foretold His birth.

Furthermore, Israel would not be the Christ-bearer without pain. The vision sees her suffering as a nation as she often had done down through the weary years of waiting, and even in the birth of Messiah, Rachel is left "weeping for her children and will not be comforted for they are not" (Matthew 2:18).

The vision now shifts its focus to a second symbolic personage.

Rev 12:3, 4a *And there appeared another wonder in heaven; and behold a great red dragon, having seven heads and ten horns, and seven crowns upon his heads. And his tail drew the third part of the stars of heaven, and did cast them to the earth:*

We are not left to doubt about the identity of this symbol. Verse 9 will identify the dragon as, *the great dragon . . . , that old serpent, called the Devil, and Satan.* Dr. Henry Morris rightly observes that the vision is of "the woman and the Serpent" harking back to that first encounter in the Garden when the war between the woman and the serpent began.

- 227 -

Morris writes, "John must understand . . . the great cosmic drama which has been taking place in heaven and earth since the very foundation of the world." **(The Revelation Record; pp. 217).**

Although the Dragon is introduced to us here, we are not given the interpretation of his seven heads, ten horns or seven crowns until we get to the next chapter. But what is revealed here is that when the Dragon (Satan) rebelled, he drew a third of the angel hosts after him in his rebellion. I have no idea how many angels that is.

Dr. Renald Shower writes, "Daniel saw a *thousand thousands* plus *ten thousand times ten thousand* angels serving God and standing before His throne waiting to receive His commands. Ten thousand times ten thousand equals one hundred million, but there were thousands upon thousands more. These statements by Daniel and John were intended to relate the fact that there are innumerable hosts of angels serving God (Hebrews 12:22)." **(Daniel – WWBI Course; Renald Showers).**

Please note that we are told that when we get to the heavenly Jerusalem, we will be joined by a still "innumerable company of (holy) angels" (Hebrews 12:22), leading us to the conclusion that if the unfallen angels are still so many that they are innumerable, then the number of the third which rebelled and fell, must have been staggering.

It is worth noting how Revelation reveals many things kept secret since the world began. We have other hints of the great cosmic battle of spirit-beings that has been raging through the ages, but Revelation draws back the curtain and allows us to see it in action.

Rev 12:4b And the dragon stood before the woman which was ready to be delivered, for to devour her child as soon as it was born.

The dragon is seen here as the full manifestation of Satan's world power in the final form of the Beast. Though we shall deal with this later, we should note here that the Beast imagery pictures the final world Empire, that of Rome. It was Herod, an agent of that Empire, that Satan used to try to snuff out the life of the Christ-child as He came into the world by killing all the boy babies in Bethlehem. What John's vision gives us, is a look at the evil force that was in motion behind Herod's action.

Rev 12:5 *And she brought forth a man child, who was to rule all nations with a rod of iron: and her child was caught up unto God, and to his throne.*

There can be absolutely no question as to who is meant here. The Psalmist predicted centuries ago:

> *I will declare the decree: the LORD hath said unto me, Thou art my Son; this day have I begotten thee. Ask of me, and I shall give thee the heathen for thine inheritance, and the uttermost parts of the earth for thy possession. Thou shalt break them with a rod of iron; thou shalt dash them in pieces like a potter's vessel* (Psalm 2:7-9).

The "rod of iron" symbolizes the absolute and inflexible power of His ruling judgments and the phrase appears again in three passages here in Revelation (2:27; 12:5; 19:15). In each instance it describes the reign of Jesus Christ.

Now the next significant thing about this verse (vs.5), is that no mention is made of the earthly life of the Son of God, or His redemptive death or resurrection. The reason for this omission seems to be that the passage is focusing on Satan's attempts to destroy Christ and the fact that He is caught up to heaven demonstrates Satan's failure.

Rev 12:6 *And the woman fled into the wilderness, where she hath a place prepared of God, that they should feed her there a thousand two hundred and threescore days.*

There are many reasons why it is evident that this passage refers symbolically to Israel, and not simply to Mary, Jesus' earthly mother, but this verse is certainly conclusive. It is Israel (not Mary), that will "flee into the wilderness," during the Tribulation.

Exactly where she flees to we are not told. Some believe that the reference is to the "wilderness of the nations." In other words Israel will be once more scattered throughout the whole earth.

Others believe that she will be secured in the ancient city of Petra. This view is an inference from the fact that when the Anti-Christ comes into the Land of Israel during the middle of the Tribulation Week, he will not enter Edom or Moab (Daniel 11:41).

The arguments are inconclusive, but the fact that this "place" is "prepared by God" for her protection and provision certainly makes the idea of a Petra refuge appealing. This we do know, Satan, through his agent the Beast, will make every attempt to destroy the nation Israel, but he will be unable to do so.

Rev 12:7-9 *And there was war in heaven: Michael and his angels fought against the dragon; and the dragon fought and his angels, And prevailed not; neither was their place found any more in heaven. And the great dragon was cast out, that old serpent, called the Devil, and Satan, which deceiveth the whole world: he was cast out into the earth, and his angels were cast out with him.*

All the fluffy, billowy ideas of heaven, with people sitting on clouds and playing harps get a reality jolt in this passage. As long as there is evil in the universe, there will be spiritual warfare in the universe and now we learn that it breaks out in heaven as well.

Michael is not only the great Archangel of God, he is specifically the angel that seems to be associated with the defense of the nation Israel. Daniel writes;

And at that time shall Michael stand up, the great prince which standeth for the children of thy people: and there shall be a time of trouble, such as never was since there was a nation even to that same time: and at that time thy people shall be delivered, every one that shall be found written in the book (Daniel 12:1).

Michael will, therefore, take up the defense of the nation Israel during this period.

In the passage before us, Michael is seen engaging the Dragon, Satan, in all-out warfare. Not only does Michael himself fight, but all the angel hosts who are under his command fight as well. And Satan, and all his angels fight as well, but they are no match for their adversary and their entire host is "cast out of heaven."

The passage reminds us once again that though Satan fell so very long ago, he has had access to the courts of God as is clear in the case of Job, (chapter 1, 2), where he viciously accused a righteous man to God. As a result of Michael's victory, Satan's access is hereafter denied and his activity is now confined exclusively to the earth.

Finally, we must not miss what is said of him as he is flung at last out of the court of heaven. He is first called, *that old serpent.* The word used is Gr. *Archaios,* from which we get the English word archaic. He is the "ancient serpent," who appeared in the Garden to our first parents and has continued his war against God ever since.

He is also called *the Devil and Satan.* The word Devil is from the Gr. Diabolis, and means to falsely accuse or slander, while the name Satan basically means adversary. All of that is bad enough, but do not miss the final phrase; *which deceiveth the whole world.*

Satan's program has been one of deception from the very beginning and he has been eminently successful in that his deception has permeated the entire world. When he is cast out of heaven, we may be certain that his destructive program of deceit will not cease, but only increase.

Rev 12:10 *And I heard a loud voice saying in heaven, Now is come salvation, and strength, and the kingdom of our God, and the power of his Christ: for the accuser of our brethren is cast down, which accused them before our God day and night.*

Verse 10 gives us a clear picture of what Satan has been doing in heaven. He has been accusing us before God day and night. Thankfully, for the child of God his accusations cannot stand. As the hymn-writer has well expressed it;

> *I hear the Accuser roar,*
> *Of wrongs that I have done,*
> *I know them all, and thousands more,*
> *Jehovah findeth none.*

> *Though the restless foe accuses,*
> *Sins recounting like a flood,*
> *Every charge our God refuses,*
> *Christ has answered with His blood!*

Rev 12:11 *And they overcame him by the blood of the Lamb, and by the word of their testimony; and they loved not their lives unto the death.*

The victory over Satan for the believer is clearly set forth here, not only for Tribulations saints, but for saints in our day as well. They overcame him by the blood of the Lamb.

> *Giving thanks unto the Father, . . . Who hath delivered us from the power of darkness, and hath translated us into the kingdom of his dear Son: In whom we have redemption through his blood, even the forgiveness of sins* (Colossians 1:12-14).

Secondly, they overcame him by the word of their testimony. Peter tells us to resist Satan, *steadfast in the faith.* There is nothing that defeats Satan more quickly than the truth. His entire program is built on lies, and when we know and confess truth, he cannot withstand it.

Finally, they overcame Satan by loving God more than they loved life. They took their lives into their own hands and boldly proclaimed their loyalty to Christ even when it meant their certain death.

Remember Rachel Scott, one of those killed in the Colorado High School massacre. Eric Harris and Dylan Klebold, asked each student, "Are you a Christian?" If the student replied, "Yes," they were shot. That is the question they asked Rachel Scott. And without a moment's hesitation, she replied that she was. In the eyes of God, Rachel overcame the real enemy, Satan, and was ushered through the doors of heaven a victor.

Rev 12:12 *Therefore rejoice, ye heavens, and ye that dwell in them. Woe to the inhabiters of the earth and of the sea! for the devil is come down unto you, having great wrath, because he knoweth that he hath but a short time.*

What is good news in heaven, is bad news on earth. Little need be said of this verse for the following verses make abundantly clear the result of Satan's final exit from heaven to earth.

Rev 12:13 *And when the dragon saw that he was cast unto the earth, he persecuted the woman which brought forth the man child.*

As we have already seen, there is more about Israel in these later chapters and this is certainly evident here. Satan has tried to destroy the woman that brought forth the Man Child, even before the Man Child could be born. He used Pharaoh to try to destroy her in Egypt by demanding that every male child be thrown into the river.

He used Haman to try to annihilate Israel in the days of good Queen Esther. He used Adolf Hitler and Joseph Stalin to try to destroy them in the twentieth century, and he will use the power of the Beast to try one final time in the Tribulation.

Rev 12:14 *And to the woman were given two wings of a great eagle, that she might fly into the wilderness, into her place, where she is nourished for a time, and times, and half a time, from the face of the serpent.*

The two wings of the great eagle are reminiscent of God's word to Israel in Exodus 19:4, *Ye have seen what I did unto the Egyptians, and how I bare you on eagles' wings, and brought you unto myself.* I suspect it is the same "eagles wings" that are referred to here and that God will again carry them out of danger.

Note, they are carried to a particular "place." This does seem to suggest perhaps they may be correct who believe Israel will flee to the ancient ruins of Petra. Perhaps not, perhaps it is some other "place." But wherever it is, it is a place prepared where the remnant of Israel can be protected and even fed. In a world where satellite cameras see every part of the globe and can track the movements of a single person, how Israel can be kept safe is not told us, we only know that she is. Perhaps we get a hint in the next verse.

Rev 12:15, 16 *And the serpent cast out of his mouth water as a flood after the woman, that he might cause her to be carried away of the flood. And the earth helped the woman, and the earth opened her mouth, and swallowed up the flood which the dragon cast out of his mouth.*

We have tried to stay as true to literal interpretation as possible except where it is clear that a symbol is being used. Here, it is difficult to picture an overwhelming flood of water originating from anyone's mouth, even the wonder-working dragon. Was the flood cast out of his mouth a flood of water?

Was the flood actually an overwhelming army? Isaiah paints that picture in those words in Isaiah 59:19. Jeremiah sees the armies of Egypt coming up as a flood (Jeremiah 46:7-10). Daniel describes the destruction of the sanctuary as a flood (Daniel 9:26). The sanctuary (Temple) was destroyed by the Roman legions under Titus in 70 AD. So it is not unreasonable to understand this passage as telling us that a command went out the mouth of the Dragon and a vast army was sent out to destroy the nation Israel.

Whichever is true, the thing we should not miss is the result: *the earth opened her mouth, and swallowed up the flood.* I really don't have much difficulty visualizing this. That is exactly what God did in the case of the rebellion of Korah, Dathan, and Abiram .

> *And Moses said, Hereby ye shall know that the LORD hath sent me to do all these works; for I have not done them of mine own mind. If these men die the common death of all men, or if they be visited after the visitation of all men; then the LORD hath not sent me. But if the LORD make a new thing, and the earth open her mouth, and swallow them up, with all that appertain unto them, and they go down quick into the pit; then ye shall understand that these men have provoked the LORD. And it came to pass, as he had made an end of speaking all these words, that the ground clave asunder that was under them: And the earth opened her mouth, and swallowed them up, and their houses, and all the men that appertained unto Korah, and all their goods.* (Numbers 16:28 - 32).

Whether a flood of water or armies, the earth swallowed them up just as the sea had swallowed up Pharaoh and the earth swallowed up Korah. The frustration this caused the Dragon can be clearly seen in the next verse.

Rev 12:17 *And the dragon was wroth with the woman, and went to make war with the remnant of her seed, which keep the commandments of God, and have the testimony of Jesus Christ.*

Satan's insane anger against Israel is not assuaged and so he redoubles his efforts to destroy all that are of the Woman. The Serpent continues to strike at the Woman's seed because they keep God's commandments and bear the testimony of Jesus Christ.

We can be assured that just as deranged, and maniacal tyrants in the past have done, the Dragon, unable to get to the person he wants to destroy, turns to destroy multitudes of others in their place. It was a tactic often used by Nazis and Marxists and will be employed with vengeance and great brutality by the Dragon.

We will see him using other tactics against Israel and the followers of the Lamb in the next chapter.

REVIEW

- When do we believe the 2 witnesses had their ministry and why?

- What do we believe happens to the scroll at the opening of chapter 12?

- Who is the woman clothed with the sun and why do you think so?

- Who is the Man-Child?

- Who is the Dragon?

- Who fought with the Dragon?

- Who won the fight?

- What happened after the fight?

- What weapons did the saints use to overcome the Dragon?

- How did the Dragon try to destroy the woman?

- How did God protect her?

- What did the Dragon do next?

Chapter 20 The Anti-Christ & False Prophet

Revelation 13:1 – 18

Chapter 13, as was pointed out previously, is related to the previous chapter in that, taken together, they introduce us to the great actors for both good and evil in the last days. In the former chapter we met the Woman, the Child and the Dragon. In this chapter we meet two additional actors that are very prominent in the last day – the Anti-Christ and the False Prophet.

Rev 13:1 *And I stood upon the sand of the sea, and saw a beast rise up out of the sea, having seven heads and ten horns, and upon his horns ten crowns, and upon his heads the name of blasphemy.*

A number of other translations say, either "he stood on the sand of the sea," or "the Dragon stood on the sand of the sea." Whatever the textual problems may be, I see no reason to depart from the KJV rendering. John was given this vision. In every other place he rehearsed what he himself saw, so I think we can rest in the wisdom of the KJV translators in this case. John found himself standing upon the sand of the sea.

Although it may seem unimportant, I think we need to ask the question, "What sea?" The reason for this is that when the ancients of John's time, and even those who lived centuries before, living in that area, spoke of the sea they invariably were speaking of only one sea - the Mediterranean Sea. Why is that important? It is important because of several things.

First, the four great Empires that comprise prophetic history (and prophecy), all were located around the Mediterranean sea.

The first, the Empire of Babylon, purposely stretched its domain so as to gain access to what was called, "The Great Sea." Each of the succeeding Empires (Medo-Persia, Greece and Rome), also attempted to encompass the Mediterranean, until Rome actually did and called it "our sea."

Secondly, if the Beast that John sees rising from the sea, was simply from just any sea or "the sea of nations," then he might have originated anywhere in the world. But if, as we believe, the sea here referred to is the Mediterranean Sea, then that would particularize his origin to the area of the former Roman Empire. We believe the Scripture teaches that it is from the final form of that Roman empire that the Beast will arise. Therefore, we conclude that the sea referred to here, is the Mediterranean Sea.

This Beast is said to "rise up out of the sea." That is, this creature arises out of the area of the former Roman Empire. That is significant, because the Roman Empire is the final one seen by the prophets, and it is destine to revive in a diverse form, but with its former power in the last days.

That leads me to make a preliminary identification of the Beast. Many have identified him as the Anti-Christ, and indeed, there is good reason for that conclusion. But I want to suggest that this Beast, as it first emerges, must be understood to be something other than just one man. To understand the significance of the term Beast, we need to go back to the visions found in the book of Daniel. Daniel writes:

> In the first year of Belshazzar king of Babylon Daniel had a dream and visions of his head upon his bed: then he wrote the dream, and told the sum of the matters. Daniel spake and said, I saw in my vision by night, and, behold, the four winds of the heaven strove upon the great sea. And four great beasts came up from the sea, diverse one from another (Daniel 7:1-3).

Daniel was a captive of the Babylonian Empire. By the Providence of God, he was brought to great prominence, influencing the affairs of government over the course of both the Babylonian and Persian Empires until the time of Cyrus. It was to Daniel that God chose to reveal the course of human events during what the Lord Jesus called, "the times of the Gentiles." The phrase describes that time when the Gentile nations will have ultimate influence over the land of Israel, and especially Jerusalem. That time began with the conquest of Jerusalem by Nebuchadnezzar in 586 BC, and will end when Messiah Jesus returns to rule and reign from that city.

God revealed to Daniel that four great Empires would arise before Messiah would come and rule over the earth. These are seen in chapter 2 of Daniel in the form of a great image. The body of the image is divided by the metals used in its construction. The head of gold represented the Babylonian Empire and particularly its first king, Nebuchadnezzar. The arms and breast of silver represented the Medo-Persian Empire. The belly and thighs of brass, the Grecian Empire, and the legs and feet of iron, the Roman Empire.

Please note that this vision, of the four empires in the form of an imposing image, was not Daniel's vision, but rather Nebuchadnezzar's. It was fitting that the first Gentile ruler to conquer the Middle-East, would see his own and future empires in all their glory and power. However, that is not how God revealed them to Daniel. Daniel will see them as four beasts.

In his vision, Daniel sees "the four winds" striving over, note, "the Great Sea." Winds are often symbolic of spiritual forces. The word translated wind is the same word translated spirit. I take it the picture is of mighty spiritual forces stirring up the Great Sea, also symbolic of the nations which controlled the sea.

There comes up out of the sea four "beasts." We are to note that each is "diverse" or different from the others.

Further, as we read we recognize that each beast represents a particular empire. For instance, the first is a lion with wings. It is interesting that the national symbol of the Babylonian Empire was the winged lion. You find them represented in great images guarding the Ishtar Gate that entered the city of Babylon.

The second beast is a bear, higher on one side that the other. The Medo-Persian Empire began as a partnership between the Medes and the Persians. When Cyrus came to power, his mother was a Mede and his father a Persian. The Persian side of the Empire took preeminence.

The next beast is a winged leopard with four heads. The imagery is of the Grecian Empire. The leopard is know both for its ferocity and its speed, and then it is given four wings, so that its speed is emphasized again. Alexander the Great was the first King of Macedon (ancient Greece), who conquered the world, from the straits of Gibraltar to the Indian Punjab, in 13 years. He died at the early age of 33 years. Alexander's kingdom was then divided into four kingdoms, symbolized by the four heads of the leopard.

It should be noted, that except for the symbolism of speed (the 4-winged leopard), the symbol represents, not Alexander himself, that is, not a person, but an empire. That becomes even clearer in another vision of Daniel found in Daniel 8:5-8.

And as I was considering, behold, an he goat came from the west on the face of the whole earth, and touched not the ground: and the goat had a notable horn between his eyes. And he came to the ram that had two horns, which I had seen standing before the river, and ran unto him in the fury of his power. And I saw him come close unto the ram, and he was moved with choler against him, and smote the ram, and brake his two horns: and there was no power in the ram to stand before him, but he cast him down to the ground, and stamped upon him: and there was none that could deliver the ram out of his hand.

Therefore the he goat waxed very great: and when he was strong, the great horn was broken; and for it came up four notable ones toward the four winds of heaven (Daniel 8:5-8).

Note that in this vision, which once again reveals the empires which will come after Daniel's time and particularly those which will affect Daniel's people, the Jews, and Israel, Daniel sees Greece as an "he goat." Once again, the speed of conquest is noted, "he touched not the ground," but here the first King, Alexander is seen as "a notable horn between his eyes."

In verse eight, Daniel refers to it again as "the great horn" and tells us that it was "broken," after which four horns came up to take its place. Here the picture is very clear. The "he goat" is the Empire, (i.e., Greece), and the "notable horn" is Alexander.

Now, what have we learned from this? We learn that in prophetic symbolism, a beast stands for a kingdom or empire, not merely a single individual. Therefore, we will interpret John's vision of the Beast out of the sea, as that of an empire rising to power. Later on, when one of the horns of the Beast assumes all the power of the Empire, then that person himself becomes identified as the Beast.

Now we need to try to identify the significance of the heads, the horns and the crowns.

In the previous visions from the book of Daniel, when Daniel saw the Grecian leopard, it had four heads. We know from history that when Alexander died, his kingdom was divided among his four generals. So, the symbolism of "head" in that case represented a ruler.

The word "head" is translated from the Gr. *kephalē* while the word Gr. *Kephalaion* means "the main or principal thing," in other words, as related to an Empire, it would mean the Leader or Authority.

Here in the Revelation vision we have an Empire (the Beast), with 7 heads, therefore, we have 7 authorities or rulers.

The seven heads have ten horns and each horn is wearing a crown (Gr. *diadēma*). We have already seen that the horn is a symbol of power. Apparently these seven heads have ten areas of power over which they reign. It appears therefore, that <u>what we have is the image of a confederation of power making up the final Beast or Empire of the last days</u>.

Finally, it is important that we do not miss the last characteristic of the Beast, *and upon his heads the name of blasphemy.* Although later translations make the word plural (names), the Greek of the Majority Text or Textus Receptus (i.e., the Received Text), limits it to a singular name.

The word 'blasphemies" may mean a number of things. It may mean a vilification of God, or railing against God, or it may mean, as it does in Matthew 12 (where it is applied to the Holy Spirit), attributing the works of God to someone other than God. Thus, any claim which takes God's work and ascribes it to man or to Satan, is blasphemy. Notice that each of the seven heads is said to have this "name" upon it. Whatever that name is, it is an offence to God.

Rev 13:2 *And the beast which I saw was like unto a leopard, and his feet were as the feet of a bear, and his mouth as the mouth of a lion: and the dragon gave him his power, and his seat, and great authority.*

As soon as we read this further description we at once are reminded of Daniel's vision in Daniel chapter 7. The four beasts mentioned were used as symbols of former kingdoms, and so this final kingdom is a composite of all the former ones – four beasts in one.

It is interesting from history how each succeeding empire tended to absorb certain things from the former one. When Alexander conquered Persia he afterward began to dress in Persian attire.

Each of the successive four empires borrows from the former until the final empire is seen as a composite of all the power and evil of the former ones.

We dare not miss the final statement here: *the dragon gave him his power, and his seat, and great authority.* Satan is so much a part of this final Empire, that he actually appears a part of it.

In Chapter twelve where the dragon is seen waiting to destroy the Man-Child, the dragon himself is seen with seven heads and ten horns and ten crowns upon his heads. In other words, Satan and the Beast seem sometimes to be so merged as to be one and the same.

And note that the "power" (Gr. *dunamis*), is given to the Beast directly by Satan. We will see that power in operation a little later against the saints of God. It is also declared that "his seat", or throne along with his "Great Authority (Gr. *Megus exousia*: that is, "complete, absolute to the highest extent," authority), is derived directly from Satan, the Dragon.

Before we go further, it might be well to remember that the fourth and final empire in all of the visions (Daniel 2, 7, Revelation 13) will be the Empire of Rome. In each of the visions, it is diverse from all others.

In Nebuchadnezzar's dream (Daniel 2), it is seen as splitting in two (two legs) and having its final form in ten toes, with feet of iron mixed with clay. All of that suggests that the final form of this beast is a strange admixture of totalitarian strength (iron), mixed with the clay of populous power (i.e., some form of democratic structure).

Dr. Renald Showers offers the following explanation:

> "Daniel interpreted the iron and clay mixture as follows: just as iron is strong, so the final stage of the Roman Empire would be strong militarily.

Just as clay is characterized by brittleness, so the final stage of the Roman Empire would be characterized by division. Different groups of people would combine with one another to form the final stage of the empire, but they would not adhere completely to one another, just as iron and clay do not combine completely with each other." **(The Most High God; Renald Showers, FOI).**

Dr. Showers concludes that, "the final stage of the Roman Empire would consist of a confederation of nations."

It may seem strange for us to talk about the Roman Empire, when traditional wisdom indicates that it ceased to exist. Perhaps we should review.

Actually, after the Empire held on to its existence for 1,500 years, it is generally recognized as having ended in 476 AD, although the eastern division of the Empire, known as the Byzantine Empire lasted until it eventually fell to the Ottoman Turks in 1453.

But many see the Empire as existing even to this day. In 756, territory was transferred to the Papacy, thus giving the Roman Pontiff, temporal authority. Forty-four years later, in the year 800, the Pope crowned Charlemagne, Emperor of the "Holy Roman Empire," after which the ecclesiastical power of the Church and civil power of the Emperor generally shifted back and forth between ecclesiastical and secular power until the Reformation which began in 1517 under Luther.

Still, Europe conceives of itself as a part of that ancient Empire. When Charles De Gaulle was made President of France in 1958, a press article covering the event stated: "there could be little doubt that much on De Gaulle's mind that day was the coronation of Charlemagne on that snowy day in 800 CE, that made him Emperor of the Holy Roman Empire." In other words, Europe cannot forget her history and the Empire and the present efforts at unification carried forward by the European Union (EU), are designed to eventually recover the glory of the ancient Roman Empire.

Rev 13:3 *And I saw one of his heads as it were wounded to death; and his deadly wound was healed: and all the world wondered after the beast.*

Although this is dealt with in a variety of manners by various expositors, we must attempt to accept it in a manner that is consistent with our view of literal interpretation where ever possible.

What we read is that one of the seven heads was wounded "to death." One of the "Heads," the ruling authorities (I hesitate to use the word King), was given a wound that caused his death. Dr. Ryrie points out that the exact same words are used to refer to Christ's death in Chapter 5:6, and since Christ actually died, we must assume here that the same is meant.

Subsequently to his death, he comes back to life. While many have argued against this possibility, since it is assumed that Satan does not have the power of resurrection, there seems little cause to pit human reason against inspired declaration, and hence we simply must accept the fact that this "Head," this person, came back to life after death.

Later, in chapter 17, we are told; *The beast that thou sawest was, and is not; and shall ascend out of the bottomless pit* (Abyss), *and go into perdition: and they that dwell on the earth shall wonder, whose names were not written in the book of life from the foundation of the world, when they behold the beast that was, and is not, and yet is* (Revelation 17:8).

 BKC, comments on this passage: "The Abyss, is the home of Satan (Rev 11:7) and the place from which demons come (Rev 9:11). This indicates that the power behind the ruler is satanic (cf. Rev 13:4) and that Satan and the man he controls are closely identified. Their power is one. . . The supernatural survival and revival of both the world ruler and his empire will impress the world as being supernatural and will lead to worship of the beast and Satan." **(Bible Knowledge Commentary)**

The result of this will produce an immediate reaction of both fear and awe as the world, "wonders after the beast." It is at this point that the reference to the beast seems to change from referring to a confederate empire, to a particular individual.

Rev 13:4 *And they worshipped the dragon which gave power unto the beast: and they worshipped the beast, saying, Who is like unto the beast? who is able to make war with him?*

Although short-lived, Satan has at last succeeded in the goal he set for himself at the time of his rebellion; *For thou hast said in thine heart, I will ascend into heaven, I will exalt my throne above the stars of God: I will sit also upon the mount of the congregation, in the sides of the north: I will ascend above the heights of the clouds; I will be like the most High* (Isaiah 14:13, 14). At last he has world domination and he is worshipped.

In addition, we read that, *they worshipped the beast,* that is, they worshipped the man who has taken full control and who in himself has become, the Beast.

This should not take much imagination to envision. The world has been worshipping the stars of the music and entertainment world, the sports world, and the intellectual world for decades. Now they have a great leader who has come back from the dead. How natural to worship him, and to fear him, and so the question is asked, *Who is like unto the beast? who is able to make war with him?*

It might be well to reflect on the answer to that question. Daniel in his vision of the last Empire gives us the answer:

I beheld till the thrones were cast down, and the Ancient of days did sit, whose garment was white as snow, and the hair of his head like the pure wool:

his throne was like the fiery flame, and his wheels as burning fire. A fiery stream issued and came forth from before him: thousand thousands ministered unto him, and ten thousand times ten thousand stood before him: the judgment was set, and the books were opened (Daniel 7:9, 10).

The One who created all things and sustains all things can certainly "make war with the Beast" and prevail.

Rev 13:5-7 *And there was given unto him a mouth speaking great things and blasphemies; and power was given unto him to continue forty and two months. And he opened his mouth in blasphemy against God, to blaspheme his name, and his tabernacle, and them that dwell in heaven. And it was given unto him to make war with the saints, and to overcome them: and power was given him over all kindreds, and tongues, and nations.*

It is amazing, but if you look closely, you will see that everything this man is and does, has been given him. Even his words are the words of the power that indwells him, and so when he speaks, Satan is speaking, and we should not be surprised that out of his mouth come further insults to God.

And he does not just insult God Himself, but specifically he blasphemes His Name. The Name was so holy to the Jewish believer that he would not write it or pronounce it for fear he might use it in vain, or disparagingly. Now this world leader uses everything at his disposal to degrade and defile that Holy Name.

In addition, he blasphemes His Tabernacle. The reference here is not to the earthly Tabernacle, but to the very dwelling place of God. The dragon has been cast out of heaven and now he pours forth all his bitterness toward God's eternal Throne.

Finally, he blasphemes those who dwell in heaven. Who are these?

These are that multitude of the redeemed whom he accused before God while they were on the earth and whom he slaughtered out of every kindred, tribe, tongue and nation, and who are now before the Lamb rejoicing (Revelation 7:9-14). But the Beast must vilify them to justify his tyranny.

In addition he was given power to make war with the saints and to overcome them. Finally, he was given power over all kindreds and tongues and nations.

Daniel was told; *Thus he said, The fourth beast shall be the fourth kingdom upon earth, which shall be diverse from all kingdoms, and shall devour the whole earth, and shall tread it down, and break it in pieces* (Daniel 7:23).

However, with all his power, God is still entirely in control and has set a limit on his reign of forty-two months, which comprise the final three and one half years of the Tribulation. Then, as Luther once wrote, "One little word shall fell him."

Daniel describes it like this, *I beheld then because of the voice of the great words which the horn (Beast) spake: I beheld even till the beast was slain, and his body destroyed, and given to the burning flame* (Daniel 7:11).

Rev 13:8 *And all that dwell upon the earth shall worship him, whose names are not written in the book of life of the Lamb slain from the foundation of the world.*

The universal dominance of the Beast, empowered and indwelt by the Dragon, appears to be global, but it is also limited. For there will be those who will not accept his mark or worship him. They are those whose names are in the Lamb's book of life. In other words, they are those who have savingly believed and put their faith and confidence in the Lord Jesus Christ.
The final phrase affirms the fact that Christ's death upon the cross that purchased our salvation, was predetermined by God, who knows all things, before the world began. "*Amazing*

love, how can it be, that thou, my God, should die for me?"

Rev 13:9, 10 *If any man have an ear, let him hear. He that leadeth into captivity shall go into captivity: he that killeth with the sword must be killed with the sword. Here is the patience and the faith of the saints.*

This verse seems to be included for the specific purpose of reminding us, that in the midst of all this evil, justice will prevail, and those who perpetuate evil and bloodshed will themselves suffer, just as they have made others suffer.

The phrase, *Here is the patience and the faith of the saints,* simply means that this is the truth that the saints rest upon in their trials. God, the judge of all, will reward every act whether good or evil.

One final reminder is given us by Daniel:

> *And the kingdom and dominion, and the greatness of the kingdom under the whole heaven, shall be given to the people of the saints of the most High, whose kingdom is an everlasting kingdom, and all dominions shall serve and obey him* (Daniel 7:27).

As Paul reminded us, *Know ye not that we shall judge angels?* (1 Corinthians 6:3)

Rev 13:11 *And I beheld another beast coming up out of the earth; and he had two horns like a lamb, and he spake as a dragon.*

There is a wide variety of interpretation when it comes to this second Beast. Some believe that the second Beast should be called the Anti-Christ, because he mimics Christ (i.e., two horns like a Lamb), that is, he has the appearance of a lamb.

However, Scripture itself resolves this in several places.

And I saw three unclean spirits like frogs come out of the mouth of the dragon, and out of the mouth of the beast, and out of the mouth <u>of the false prophet</u> (Revelation 16:13).

And the beast was taken, and with him <u>the false prophet</u> that wrought miracles before him, with which he deceived them that had received the mark of the beast, and them that worshipped his image (Revelation 19:20).

And the devil that deceived them was cast into the lake of fire and brimstone, where the beast and <u>the false prophet</u> are, and shall be tormented day and night for ever and ever (Revelation 20:10).

Please note that in all three of these texts, the second Beast is referred to as the "false prophet." That is, he is the one who promotes the first Beast and teaches the world to worship him. Therefore, we conclude that the first Beast is rightly called the Anti-Christ.

And so, we have a kind of Satanic Trinity: the Dragon, the Beast (also known as the Anti-Christ), and the second Beast or False Prophet, working miracles and teaching the world to worship the first Beast.

Many believe the second Beast will be Jewish. There are several reasons for this. First, while the first Beast emerges from the sea (a symbol of multiple peoples or nations), the second Beast comes up from the Land. That term is particularly used in relation to the Land of Israel.

Some will object to this saying that the word translated "earth" is the Gr. *gē* pronounced "ghey" (from which New Age earth worshipers get the word Gaia, or "mother earth"). This is the usual Greek word for earth.

While that is true, it is also the word translated "land" in Matthew 2:6, 20, 21 (where it specifically refers to the Land of Israel); 9:26; 10:15; John 3:22; Acts 7:3, 4; 10:39 (where again it is specifically referring to Israel), and in many other places. Hence, it is possible, and from other considerations I think likely, that is the way the word should be translated here.

Secondly, he appears as a prophet. While the Gentile world gives little credence to "prophets," the Jews have always recognized prophets as having a special credibility. Israel is still looking for Elijah to return, and this person will seem to fill that expectation, even calling fire down from heaven (vs. 13), as Elijah did.

Scripture is clear that while there will be a large believing remnant out of Israel (in addition to the 144,000), there will also be those unbelieving Jews, described by Daniel as, *the wicked shall do wickedly: and none of the wicked shall understand; but the wise shall understand.* (Daniel 12:10). These will accept the second Beast and follow him. We therefore understand the second Beast to be Jewish.

David Levi writes of him; "*He spake as a dragon.* Although docile in appearance, his speech will be subtle, seductive, and satanic, structured to lead people away from belief in Christ and into the cunning, corrupt worship of the Antichrist. His word will be law, and those who defy it will pay with their lives." **(Revelation; David Levi, FOI).**

Rev 13:12 *And he exerciseth all the power of the first beast before him, and causeth the earth and them which dwell therein to worship the first beast, whose deadly wound was healed.*

Once again, the text makes reference to that "deadly wound that was healed." Whatever this entails, it most certainly seems to be a notable event and one which will cause a gullible world to wonder.

We read of the first Beast that he received his power and throne and authority from the Dragon. Now we read that the second Beast exercises all of the power of the first Beast. It is obvious then, that all the power for this charade comes directly from Satan.

The program and purpose of the second Beast is to bring the world to worship the first Beast, the Anti-Christ. As we proceed, we will see how he accomplishes this and what means he employs.

Rev 13:13, 14 *And he doeth great wonders, so that he maketh fire come down from heaven on the earth in the sight of men, And deceiveth them that dwell on the earth by the means of those miracles which he had power to do in the sight of the beast; saying to them that dwell on the earth, that they should make an image to the beast, which had the wound by a sword, and did live.*

We have already made reference to the apparent miracle of the fire. Elijah had called down fire on at least two occasions. The first was on Mount Carmel in the contest against the prophets of Baal. Baal was the god of fire, but his prophets were unable to produce it when put to the test.

The second time Elijah resorted to fire was when wicked King Ahaziah attempted to arrest him, obviously with the intent of killing him (2 Kings 1). Two companies of fifty men each were consumed by fire.

But the fire in this text is that, which, though seemingly from heaven, is produced by the Dragon through the instrumentality of the false prophet. Can Satan do that? Well, he did it in the days of Job (Job 1:16), and while prevented from doing so at the contest with Baal, it seems that the old arch enemy is indeed able to produce fire.

But the point of all this is that the prophet's intent is to deceive. Jesus predicted this.

For there shall arise false Christs, and false prophets, and shall shew great signs and wonders; insomuch that, if it were possible, they shall deceive the very elect (Matthew 24:24).

Paul, likewise, expounded on this at length.

> *And then shall that Wicked* (One), *be revealed, whom the Lord shall consume with the spirit of his mouth, and shall destroy with the brightness of his coming: Even him, whose coming is after the working of Satan with all power and signs and lying wonders, And with all deceivableness of unrighteousness in them that perish; because they received not the love of the truth, that they might be saved* (2 Thessalonians 2:8-10)

Paul here describes the workings of this unholy trinity as "all power" (Gr. *Dunamis*), "signs" (Gr. *sēmeion*), the same word which is used to describe the signs of the book of Revelation, and "lying wonders" (Gr. *Pseudos teras*), false miracles and omens. The underlying implication is that the entire show is meant to deceive and to bring a gullible world to the worship of the Beast.

In addition to what has been revealed, Paul also gives us an additional insight into the deception of that day.

> *And for this cause God shall send them strong delusion, that they should believe a lie: That they all might be damned who believed not the truth, but had pleasure in unrighteousness* (2 Thessalonians 2:11, 12).

Note that we are given the rational for this mysterious action by God Himself. Basically, it is that the day of Grace, the time when repentance might come has passed. They "believed not the truth" – past tense. The implication is that they heard the truth, had an opportunity to receive and believe the truth, and had rejected the truth. Now, as a judgment from God, their day of opportunity is past and God Himself sends them a spirit of "strong delusion."

I believe we see a measure of this in the world today especially among the western nations. We have had the truth and the gospel has come to us in abundant blessing. But in the last few decades the west has rejected the truth.

They have turned to the lie of materialism, fostered by the myth of evolution, and now they seem to dwell in the fog of fantasy where such deceptions as gender change, and climate change, and the morality of aborting and dismembering our children to market their body parts is accepted and embraced, while any clear statement of empirical truth is shouted down and rejected out of hand. Perhaps we are in the preparation stage of the "strong delusion" of the Tribulation period.

The final outcome of this delusion and deception is the proclamation of the prophet; *saying to them that dwell on the earth, that they should make an image to the beast, which had the wound by a sword, and did live.* This Scripture, when tied into several others, give us a picture of what happens and when that image actually appears.

Daniel is the first to see it and he wrote; *And he shall confirm the covenant with many for one week: and in the midst of the week he shall cause the sacrifice and the oblation to cease, and* for the overspreading of abominations he shall make it desolate (Daniel 9:27).

Daniel reveals that this Beast will make a covenant with Israel for seven years (*one week*). In the very middle of that seven-year period he will break the covenant, cause Jewish temple worship to cease, and defile the sanctuary in such a way as to make it desolate.

Jesus refers to this same event like this; *When ye therefore shall see the abomination of desolation, spoken of by Daniel the prophet, stand in the holy place, (whoso readeth, let him understand:)* (Matthew 24:15).

What this "abomination" is, we are not told but we are told that God will abandon the Temple because of it. In fact, it is this act which according to the next verse (vs.16) will mark the beginning of Great Tribulation such as the world has never before seen.

Finally, Paul gives us additional insight into this heinous act in the passage we have looked at before in this discussion.

> *Let no man deceive you by any means: for that day shall not come, except there come a falling away first, and that man of sin be revealed, the son of perdition; Who opposeth and exalteth himself above all that is called God, or that is worshipped; so that he as God sitteth in the temple of God, shewing himself that he is God. Remember ye not, that, when I was yet with you, I told you these things?* (2 Thessalonians 2:3-5).

Putting all of those statements together, we conclude that the false prophet constructs an actual image of the Beast and sets it in the Holy of Holies in the Temple. The only other act in history that came near to this was when Antiochus Epiphanies sacrificed a sow on the Temple altar and spread its blood in the sanctuary.

It is clear that the unholy trinity will go to the most outlandish lengths possible to defile, disgrace, and insult the holy One of Israel. We need to keep all this in mind when we read the descriptions of the final judgments. Sometimes we have a tendency to forget that actions have consequences.

Rev 13:15 *And he had power to give life unto the image of the beast, that the image of the beast should both speak, and cause that as many as would not worship the image of the beast should be killed.*

It is not difficult to understand why commentators have difficulty with this verse. It is not that it is difficult to understand, it is only that it is hard to believe.

We have already made the commitment to accept what the Spirit says. Therefore, we can do no other than accept it.

The word translated "life" is (Gr. *Pneuma*), which commonly is translated "breath" or "spirit." So, from the wording it would seem that Satan empowers the false prophet to actually create an image that comes to life.

But we should pause before jumping to that conclusion. Remember that we have been told that there will be "strong delusion" so that people will "believe the lie" and that what will be produced will be, false signs (*pseudos teras),* and omens.

This is not the first time that images have been given the appearance of life. During our time in India, there were constant reports about images that drank milk, or performed other remarkable feats. Roman Catholicism has constantly affirmed that various of its images, especially of Mary, weep. The "faithful" (translate gullible), are encouraged to venerate such idols.

Taken all of what we are told together, I think we can conclude that the appearance of life, breath and speech, falls under that category of false signs and strong delusions. In our own day, modern technology can produce laser holograms that appear in every respect to be the actual person, or object, but are totally an illusion. In any case, those who refuse to pay some form of worship (we are not told exactly what) to the image will be put to death.

It is noteworthy that this image is referred to ten times in seven verses of this book (Revelation 13:14, 15; 14:11; 15:2; 16:2; 19:20; 20:4). In the majority of these the reference is to those who refused to worship the beast or his image, regardless of the temporal consequences.

In any case, this helps us understand better the innumerable multitude of martyrs we met in chapter 7, and we might well be reminded that whatever they endured, they had all the riches of heaven as their reward.

Rev 13:16, 17 *And he causeth all, both small and great, rich and poor, free and bond, to receive a mark in their right hand, or in their foreheads: And that no man might buy or sell, save he that had the mark, or the name of the beast, or the number of his name.*

The pronoun suggests that this is still the false prophet or second Beast that is acting here, although surely the entire trinity of the Dragon (Satan), the Antichrist (who is the political Beast), and the False Prophet are complicit. By exercising his great power, the false prophet will consolidate the worldwide religion in the worship of the Beast and his image, as well as the economy, and commerce through the identifying mark which he will demand.

All of this comes at the very middle of the Tribulation Week, upon a world that has already been devastated by both natural and supernatural disasters. Untold millions have already perished. All ecological systems are totally out of balance. Vast amounts of crops have been destroyed. Sea life has been reduced to a fraction of what it had been. There is extreme suffering and privation around the globe.

Now this man, who has seemed to demonstrate that he possesses para-normal powers, offers a method of total governmental control of all remaining resources.

Although a very poor and inadequate comparison, some of us still remember the days of World-War II when there was government control of consumer goods. A family was only allowed a measured amount of meat, flour, sugar, gasoline, coal, and a whole host of other necessities. And if you could not show your rationing card, you could not get anything. It is apparent that a system similar to that, but much more extreme and stringent, will be put in place.

Finally, note that it is the first Beast's name or number or mark that will enable any commercial transaction.

Having blasphemed the Holy Name of the True and Living God, the Beast now proffers his own name to a deceived and deluded world. And that mark, or name or number could only be obtained by worshippers of the Beast. What irony.

May I make an observation here? The God whose name is now blasphemed and despised, is the One who, *maketh His sun to rise on the evil and on the good, and sendeth rain on the just and on the unjust* (Matthew 5:45).

The Beast, whom now they worship and whose name they bear, kills and destroys any who refuse to bow the knee to him. The world has turned away the Lover of its soul to accept the one who hates everyone but himself.

Rev 13:18 *Here is wisdom. Let him that hath understanding count the number of the beast: for it is the number of a man; and his number is Six hundred threescore and six.*

Numerous attempts have been made to decipher the number of the Beast to learn his identification. Although some have claimed they know, there is no evidence that they have arrived at a sound conclusion, and no two schemes have yielded the same results.

BKC writes, "Probably the best interpretation is that the number six is one less than the perfect number seven, and the threefold repetition of the six would indicate that for all their pretentions to deity, Satan and the two beasts were just creatures and not the Creator." **(Bible Knowledge Commentary)**

The fact is that apparently that wisdom must wait until the Beast is manifest and then His people will surely know. While the world will swim in a cloud of strong delusion, those who put their trust in Him will then see things as in the light of a cloudless day.

REVIEW

- Who stood on the sand of the sea?

- What sea is meant and why?

- How do we identify the Beast as he first emerges from the sea?

- What is the final Empire?

- Seven heads on the Beast refer to seven (what)?

- What do the 10 crowns tell us?

- Where does the Beast get his power?

- What happens to one of his heads?

- How long was the Beast allowed to continue?

- Where did the second Beast come from?

- What is the second Beast sometimes called in other passages?

- What did he build, where and for what purpose?

- The Mark of the Beast allowed him to control (what)?

- The Dragon, the Beast and the False Prophet are sometimes referred to as (what)?

Chapter 21 A Kaleidoscope of Events

Revelation 14:1 – 20

This chapter reads like a series of newspaper headlines. Each one of the seven angels makes a crucial announcement, several provide a line or two of additional information, none tell the whole story. Each trumpets a major event or story from the chapters preceding and following. None seem to be in any specific chronological order.

Perhaps the material of chapter 14 is given us at this point to keep the reader from getting too depressed over the tragic events we have just passed through. The rise of the Beast, the death of the two witnesses, the rise of the second Beast, the pseudo-miracles, the dark deception, the slaughter of so many who believe in and love the Lamb. After all of that, it is most refreshing to open chapter 14 and see once again the 144,000 witnesses of the Lamb, standing triumphant in Him, and six other encouraging visions.

Let's give our attention to this opening vision.

Rev 14:1 *And I looked, and, lo, a Lamb stood on the mount Sion, and with him an hundred forty and four thousand, having his Father's name written in their foreheads.*

It is evident that this is the same company of men we saw in chapter 7. There, they received, *the seal of God in their forehead*.

In chapter 7 we where not told the content of that seal – in this passage we are. They have the *Father's name written in their foreheads.* They are identified forever as His own blood bought, purchased possession. They are owned by Him.

There is however, a question raised by this text, and it is one of location. To state the question most simply, "Where is Mount Zion?" Is it a symbolic reference to heaven? In that case, this is a heavenly scene and the 144,000 would be in heaven.

Although there are those who interpret this passage in that way, there are reasons to reject that conclusion. To understand those reasons, we will need to begin with a search of how the name, Mount Sion (or Mount Zion as the Old Testament usually spells it) is used throughout Scripture.

The first reference we find is in Deuteronomy 4, where it is used to describe the territory conquered by Israel east of the Jordan.

> *And they possessed his land, and the land of Og king of Bashan, two kings of the Amorites, which were on this side Jordan toward the sunrising; From Aroer, which is by the bank of the river Arnon, even unto mount Sion, which is Hermon, And all the plain on this side Jordan eastward, even unto the sea of the plain, under the springs of Pisgah* (Deuteronomy 4:47 – 49)

Here the word translated Sion is the word Hebrew śîy'ôn which means the "peak" or uppermost height, in this case of Mt. Hermon. This verse simply helps us to understand the root idea behind the word.

Later, when David established Jerusalem as his capitol, he fortified the area south of the Temple mount and renamed it Zion. The word appears often in the Psalms. It is the Hebrew tsîyôn, which comes from a root meaning "conspicuous."

Eventually the entire city of Jerusalem was sometimes called by that name. The Psalmist Asaph exults in Mount Zion with these words;

Moreover he refused the tabernacle of Joseph, and chose not the tribe of Ephraim: But chose the tribe of Judah, the mount Zion which he loved. And he built his sanctuary like high palaces, like the earth which he hath established for ever (Psalm 78:67-69).

We see this again in Psalm 48. Actually, all of Psalm 48 is dedicated to the praise and beauty of Zion. In this Psalm the city is seen as a symbol both of the beauty and strength of God. It is titled, *A Song and Psalm for the sons of Korah.*

Great is the LORD, and greatly to be praised in the city of our God, in the mountain of his holiness. Beautiful for situation, the joy of the whole earth, is mount Zion, on the sides of the north, the city of the great King. God is known in her palaces for a refuge. . . As we have heard, so have we seen in the city of the LORD of hosts, in the city of our God: God will establish it for ever. Selah.

We have thought of thy loving kindness, O God, in the midst of thy temple. According to thy name, O God, so is thy praise unto the ends of the earth: thy right hand is full of righteousness. Let mount Zion rejoice, let the daughters of Judah be glad, because of thy judgments. Walk about Zion, and go round about her: tell the towers thereof. Mark ye well her bulwarks, consider her palaces; that ye may tell it to the generation following. For this God is our God for ever and ever: he will be our guide even unto death (Psalm 48:1-13).

So we can establish without controversy that Zion (or Sion) refers to the earthly city of Jerusalem. But does it ever refer to heaven? Well, yes, it seems that is does in one single verse.

But ye are come unto mount Sion, and unto the city of the living God, the heavenly Jerusalem, and to an innumerable company of angels (Hebrews 12:22).

It is on the basis of this one verse, and the fact that the medieval church always thought of Zion as a reference to heaven, that this interpretation comes so naturally. After all, we have all sung, *"We're marching upward to Zion, the Beautiful City of God."*

But how shall we interpret the phrase in this verse? We noted that when we saw this company in chapter 7, God sealed them in order to protect them. We compared a similar passage found in Ezekiel 9:6 where God sealed His servants and commanded the destroying angel; *but come not near any man upon whom is the mark.* Thus, the mark was God's seal of protection.

If we understand this to be a scene in heaven, then we can only assume that this company was among those who were martyred during the tribulation, which seems completely inconsistent with the idea of being sealed by God for their protection.

However, if we see this as a scene taking place in the earthly Sion, then it is a preview of that moment when the Lamb will have come to take His rightful throne and the great company of 144,000 Israelites, who bore witness to Him and survived the terrors of the Tribulation will stand triumphantly with him in the city He now claims as His own. It will be the fulfillment of the promise, *yet have I set my King upon my Holy hill of Zion* (Psalm 2:6).

There is one final matter we have to address. It is the phrase found in verse 3, *the hundred and forty and four thousand, which were redeemed from the earth.* It may seem that the use of the phrase, *from the earth,* suggests that this company has been removed from the earth and that therefore the scene is a heavenly one?

Well, we might conclude that, except that the ASV translates that phrase, *the hundred and forty and four thousand, even they that had been purchased out of the earth.* They were redeemed out from among the earth ones, not out of the earth itself.

The Bible Knowledge Commentary appropriately remarks, "Chronologically the vision anticipates the triumph of the 144,000 still intact at the time of Jesus Christ's return from heaven to earth." **(BKC)**

I take it then that the vision is one in which John is permitted to look forward to an earthly scene of joyous triumph in the Holy City of Zion, at the final victory of the Lamb and those who follow Him.

Rev 14:2 *And I heard a voice from heaven, as the voice of many waters, and as the voice of a great thunder: and I heard the voice of harpers harping with their harps:*

What is heavenly about this scene is the sound which comes down from heaven, of a mighty choir. It is described as "the voice of many waters," and "the voice of great thunder" and it is accompanied by "the voice of many harpers harping." Taken together, it seems evident that what John heard was so magnificent, so majestic, so marvelous and so heavenly that he had difficulty finding words to describe it.

We may well be reminded that music is a gift from God, and though man has distorted it (as he has all of God's gifts), heaven will express the full rapture of music the like of which we have yet to hear. How wonderful that we get a taste of it here, after all the dark shadows of the preceding chapters.

Rev 14:3 *And they sung as it were a new song before the throne, and before the four beasts, and the elders: and no man could learn that song but the hundred and forty and four thousand, which were redeemed from the earth.*

The phrase, "a new song" is found six times in the book of Psalms, once in Isaiah and twice here in Revelation.

In Revelation 5:9 it was the new song of the church triumphant as they celebrated the worthiness of the Lamb to take the book and the open the seals thereof. Here, it is the new song of the 144,000.

The song they sing came from heaven, but it becomes the sole property of the 144,000. What that song is, we are not told, but since their redemption is mentioned in connection with it, I would suggest it must be a song of redemption.

But it is more than that, for there were multitudes that will be redeemed, but only this company could sing this particular song. I'm looking forward with anticipation to hearing it, aren't you?

There is one additional reference to a song in this book. In Revelation 15:3, those who had gotten the victory over the Beast sing the song of Moses.

Although Moses actually wrote (or sang) at least two songs (Exodus 15, and Deuteronomy 32), the song in Deuteronomy was a recitation of God's goodness and Israel's failures. The reference in Revelation 15:3, is to the triumphant song of Moses found in Exodus 15, when God had just given them the victory over the armies of Pharaoh as they crossed the Red Sea. So the song of Moses would be a song of victory.

Rev 14:4a *These are they which were not defiled with women; for they are virgins. These are they which follow the Lamb whithersoever he goeth.*

These next verses tell us in some degree from what this company of men had been redeemed. We are told that they were not "defiled with women." The question then arises, how is one "defiled" by a woman.

Any time a man commits a sexual act with a woman outside of marriage, both are defiled. But Scripture clearly teaches that within marriage, sexual intercourse is both proper and blessed by God Himself.

Listen to what God says in Hebrews 13:4; *Marriage is honorable in all, and the bed undefiled: but whoremongers and adulterers God will judge.* So God specifically says that sex between husband and wife does not defile, but is "honorable." So then, what would make it defiling to these men?

We can best understand this apparent contradiction, by noting that there is something called "ceremonial defilement." There is an instance of this found in Exodus at that time of the giving of the Law.

Moses was commanded by God to "sanctify" the people. The idea was that the people were to be specially consecrated and prepared for this holy occasion. Notice the precise instructions: *And Moses went down from the mount unto the people, and sanctified the people; and they washed their clothes. And he said unto the people, Be ready against the third day: come not at your wives* (Exodus 19:15).

Something that was perfectly normal and blessed by God, was forbidden under these special circumstances, as the people are to fully consecrate themselves to God. The circumstances of the 144,000 where certainly special as well, and so that which would have been otherwise approved, would have defiled them. I think this may help our understanding of this passage.

Finally, this company of men did one thing – they followed the Lamb. Where He went they went, what He did they did. That total commitment to which many have aspired, these men obtained.

Rev 14:4b, 5 *These were redeemed from among men, being the firstfruits unto God and to the Lamb. And in their mouth was found no guile: for they are without fault before the throne of God.*

This verse and a half gives us further insight into what the redemption of this company entailed. They were *redeemed from among men,* that is, their redemption separated them from other men in certain specific ways some of which we have already seen.

They are called, *the Firstfruits unto God and to the Lamb.* The idea of Firstfruits implies that there will be many to follow. We caught a glimpse of some of that in chapter 7 with "a multitude that no man could number." The 144,000 were Firstfruits unto the Lamb in that they were the reward of His sufferings and in them He saw the travail of His soul and was satisfied (Isaiah 53:11). Furthermore, their redemption promised the redemption of multitudes who would come as a result of their testimony.

The next thing we learn about this company is their unflinching honesty. They are said to be "without guile." Webster defines guile by using a string of synonyms: "craft; cunning; artifice; duplicity; deceit; etc."

Truth is increasingly hard to come by in our time. Jesus said of Nathanael, *behold an Israelite indeed in whom is no guile* (John 1:47). Now there are 144,000 Israelites who, like Nathanael, speak only the ungarnished truth.

Finally, they are without fault before the throne of God. These men are remarkable by any standard, but they are still men. The only way that anyone can be without fault before the throne of the One who knows every thought, word and action, is to have all fault, all sin, covered by the blood.

This company are redeemed by that blood, and the sacred blood answers every fault they might have.

Since the blood answers to all my guilt, there is no accusation, no charge, nothing that can stand against me (Romans 4:7, 8; 8:1).

Rev 14:6, 7 *And I saw another angel fly in the midst of heaven, having the everlasting gospel to preach unto them that dwell on the earth, and to every nation, and kindred, and tongue, and people, Saying with a loud voice, Fear God, and give glory to him; for the hour of his judgment is come: and worship him that made heaven, and earth, and the sea, and the fountains of waters.*

Verse six begins John's second vision in this series of visions. John sees an angel (the word actually means, "a messenger"), fly in the midst of heaven. While the word "angel" is sometimes applied to human messengers, as it was in Revelation 1:20, and throughout chapters 2, 3; in this passage there can be no doubt that a heavenly messenger is meant.

The messenger is said to carry the "everlasting gospel," which then raises a question. Are we to understand that the gospel, the good news of God's mercy in Christ through His death, burial and resurrection existed forever – or is something else meant here?

While I have dear friends whom I highly respect who adamantly disagree with me on this point, I must take the position that what is called the "everlasting gospel" in this context, is not the same as the gospel we usually think of when the word is used. Let me explain why I say that.

First, the mere fact that the word "gospel" is used does not mean that the message is the same in every case. The word is translated from the Gr. *Euaggelion* which means simply, "good news." The saving gospel of the grace of God is the best news that was ever heralded, but it is not the only good news that God ever announced.

Second, the gospel of Grace, that gospel of salvation, is not everlasting, in the sense that it existed throughout all time. It existed only in anticipation before Christ, came and died and rose again.

What Christ did is the heart of the gospel for this age. It could not have been preached until Christ did it. It may be argued that we have many instances of what has been called the proto-evangel in the Old Testament, but while this is true, the full revelation of the Gospel of redeeming grace awaited its fulfillment in the work of Christ.

Third, the content of what is called here the "everlasting gospel" is not the same as that of the gospel of Grace. Paul defined the gospel of grace like this:

Moreover, brethren, I declare unto you the gospel which I preached unto you, which also ye have received, and wherein ye stand; By which also ye are saved, if ye keep in memory what I preached unto you, unless ye have believed in vain. For I delivered unto you first of all that which I also received, how that Christ died for our sins according to the scriptures; And that he was buried, and that he rose again the third day according to the scriptures (1 Corinthians 15:1-4).

As indicated before, Christ's death for our sins, His burial, and His resurrection is the heart of that gospel. Now read the content of the "everlasting gospel" as recorded for us here in verse 7.

Fear God, and give glory to him; for the hour of his judgment is come: and worship him that made heaven, and earth, and the sea, and the fountains of waters (Revelation 14:7).

Does that message convey the same content as the one in 1 Corinthians 15? Are these two messages the same? If not, then while both are good news, they are not the same good news.

Dr. C. I. Scofield lists three primary messages that are called "gospels" in Scripture.

The first is the "gospel of the kingdom". This was the good news preached by John the Baptist, Christ and His disciples. It was the glad announcement that the King was present, and the Kingdom was about to be set up. It was a message sent exclusively to Israel, so that they might prepare for the Kingdom by repentance, demonstrated by baptism.

The second major gospel message is what we call the gospel of the grace of God. It is the message that men should turn in faith to Christ for salvation. Jesus Christ, having paid sin's debt in full and satisfied the righteous justice of God, provided everything necessary so that salvation is now offered to all men as a free gift. It has been preached beginning with Pentecost and will be preached as long as men need to be saved.

The third major message which is called the "gospel" is the one found here in Revelation 14 and called the "everlasting gospel." It is defined in these words; *Fear God, and give glory to him; for the hour of his judgment is come: and worship him that made heaven, and earth, and the sea, and the fountains of waters.*

First, it is a message that directs men's fear away from the terrors of the Beast and his slaughter and focuses them on God. It is the message that Jesus gave when he said, *fear not them which kill the body, but are not able to kill the soul: but rather fear him which is able to destroy both soul and body in hell* (Matthew 10:28).

Secondly, it calls upon men to "give glory to God." Giving Him glory would necessitate confessing Him before men, at a time when to do so would mean certain death.

The logic of the appeal made is (1) the time of His judgment has come.

In other words, this is a final opportunity and chance to come to God. Because of that (2), we should worship the Creator and not His creation.

It is a message that declares that God is Sovereign Creator and calls on men to worship Him rather than the creature at a time when idolatry will be rampant (Revelation 9:20).

This is specifically the "everlasting gospel, because it was also the first message to man at the dawn of creation and it has continued down through every age. God is the Creator, He alone deserves our worship, our fear and our reverent trust.

So, when the message of submission to the Beast is being heralded through all the world, the counter message is heralded by an angel of God. That is "good news." And that brings us to the third of John's visions.

Rev 14:8 *And there followed another angel, saying, Babylon is fallen, is fallen, that great city, because she made all nations drink of the wine of the wrath of her fornication.*

This announcement is brief and anticipates the detailed account we get of Babylon's demise in chapters 17, 18. Babylon was the ancient capital of the empire founded by the great rebel Nimrod. But it was more than the capital city, it was the polluted fountain of all idolatry and the source of every form of religious error and rebellion against God found upon earth.

The O.T. prophets spoke of Babylon's idolatry as "madness" (Jeremiah 50:38). But Babylon was not alone in her iniquity. She spread her corruption to every nation under the sun. Jeremiah writes, *Babylon hath been a golden cup in the LORD'S hand, that made all the earth drunken: the nations have drunken of her wine; therefore the nations are mad* (Jeremiah 51:7).

Babylon has been a symbol of all that is contrary to God through the ages. When we get over to chapter 17, we will look deeper into this mystery, but for now it is enough to know that her end is certain, and it is near. In fact, it is certain because the angel repeats the formula, "is fallen, is fallen." Just as in those cases where our Lord would say "Verily, verily," or "Truly, truly," it is to establish that this thing is certain, that is, it will surely come to pass (compare Genesis 41:32).

Finally, simply notice that fornication, whether spiritual or literal, brings down the wrath of God, and those who partake of it will drink the bitter dregs thereof.

Rev 14:9-11 *And the third angel followed them, saying with a loud voice, If any man worship the beast and his image, and receive his mark in his forehead, or in his hand, The same shall drink of the wine of the wrath of God, which is poured out without mixture into the cup of his indignation; and he shall be tormented with fire and brimstone in the presence of the holy angels, and in the presence of the Lamb: And the smoke of their torment ascendeth up for ever and ever: and they have no rest day nor night, who worship the beast and his image, and whosoever receiveth the mark of his name.*

John now sees a third angel. Notice, that the first angel was in verse 6, and the second in verse 8. Now, John sees a third angel and there will be four to follow (verses 15, 17 and 18). So, there are a total of seven angels seen in this chapter of seven visions.

The angel John sees has a cryptic message for those who take the easy path during this time of worshipping the Beast and receiving his mark. Remember from the last chapter what was involved. Unless one had the identifying mark of the Beast upon his hand or upon his forehead there could be no commerce conducted. In other words, one could not buy or sell anything, without that mark.

Actually, there seems to be several reasons for people to receive this mark. As noted above, it was impossible to buy or sell anything without it, so there was a strong commercial reason.

But secondly, there seems to be a "wonder factor" to the worship of the Beast and the acceptance of his mark. Scripture tells us that all the world *wondered after the Beast*.

Considering how easily rock stars and athletic personalities draw vast crowds of wondering fans after them, it is not hard to imagine that with the Beast's apparent ability to perform miracles, there is a strong peer pressure that would surround his worship and identifying with him.

Our present generation is enamored with tattooing themselves with pictures of their heroes. Taking the mark of then Beast would fulfill something of the same purpose.

Finally, there is the obvious "fear factor." In addition to the practical reasons of being able to buy and sell, and the "wonder factor" of following a man who possesses powers like no other man, there is the threat of death to any that fail to fall into line.

> *And he had power to give life unto the image of the beast, that the image of the beast should both speak, and cause that as many as would not worship the image of the beast should be killed* (Revelation 13:15).

The result will be an almost universal worship of and identification with the Beast.

> *And all that dwell upon the earth shall worship him, whose names are not written in the book of life of the Lamb slain from the foundation of the world* (Revelation 13:8).

But while the way of least resistance and the way that seems the safest may seem to be to toe the party line and be politically correct, there will be an awful and eternal price to be paid by those who do.

> *The same shall drink of the wine of the wrath of God, which is poured out without mixture into the cup of his indignation; and he shall be tormented with fire and brimstone in the presence of the holy angels, and in the presence of the Lamb* (Revelation 14:10).

Do not pass lightly over the above words. Let each word sink down deeply as you read. The simile of drinking from the cup of wrath is not new to Scripture. Asaph uses it in Psalm 75.

> *For in the hand of the LORD there is a cup, and the wine is red; it is full of mixture; and he poureth out of the same: but the dregs thereof, all the wicked of the earth shall wring them out, and drink them (Psalm 75:8)*

The picturesque cup is filled with the wrath of an offended God against sin. And the "wicked," (literally, the guilty), will be made to drink it.

Remember that old saying, "take your medicine," meaning accept the punishment of your deeds? Here is the Biblical basis for that saying.

We dare not miss however, that the same simile was used by our Lord Himself as He agonized in the Garden of Gethsemane. Matthew gives the most complete record of that agony:

> *And he went a little further, and fell on his face, and prayed, saying, O my Father, if it be possible, let this cup pass from me: nevertheless, not as I will, but as thou wilt. . .* (And again in verse 42), *He went away again the second time, and prayed, saying, O my Father, if this cup may not pass away from me, except I drink it, thy will be done* (Matthew 26:39-42).

- 277 -

The same scene is recorded in Mark14:36, and Luke 22:42. What Jesus drank was the bitter wine of the wrath of God poured out against us because of our sin. He drank it that we might never have to drink it.

But for those who reject Him, that bitter cup is their destiny. And they shall drink it, *without mixture,* that is, it will be as we say, straight up, there will be nothing to mitigate or mollify the horrible bitterness of its contents. It is called, *the cup of his indignation.*

I said as we opened this chapter that its scenes where somewhat brighter than those of the preceding chapter, and up until now they have been. But this scene is dark indeed. However, it should be noted that it is only dark for those who have rejected the salvation which the Lamb offered and preferred to cast their lot with the Beast.

It has never been popular to speak of hell or eternal torment. It is less so today in this Post-Christian culture. But the truth should not be ignored or avoided; *He shall be tormented with fire and brimstone in the presence of the holy angels, and in the presence of the Lamb.*

The word translated "torment" is Gr. Βασανίζω; *basanizō* , the basic meaning of which is to torture. As might be expected, the word is associated with "pain" and "torment," and it is the promised destiny of all who reject His salvation and prefer the wine of deception poured out by the Beast and the Great Harlot. It is all a matter of deciding which cup you are going to drink.

David expressed it in these words, *What shall I render unto the LORD for all his benefits toward me? I will take the cup of salvation, and call upon the name of the LORD* (Psalm 116:12, 13). If you do as David did, and take the free gift of the cup of salvation, you will never have to taste the bitter cup of the wrath of God which Christ emptied for the redeemed at the cross.

Finally, this passage concludes with these terrible words, *And the smoke of their torment ascendeth up for ever and ever: and they have no rest day nor night, who worship the beast and his image, and whosoever receiveth the mark of his name* (Revelation 14:11).

The most terrifying aspect of hell and the eventual Lake of Fire, is that there is no ending.

When Polycarp was about to be martyred, he told his executioner, "The fires that you have set around me have an end, but the fire God has reserved for the wicked, never ends." The thought is almost incomprehensible.

Years ago I read the words of William Elbert Munsey, the great Methodist preacher from Tennessee and I have never been able to get them out of my mind. He often spoke about eternal retribution, and in one message entitled, "Oh, Eternity," he tried to capture the terror of that concept. I have included a few lines from it here.

"Oh, Eternity! All languages beg at they footstool for one word to tell thy name; and all sciences pile their symbols at thy feet, and implore thee for one illustration of thy length. But thy oracles are dumb because of the dullness of the querist – God can only be thy questioner.

And thy vast pendulum beating to the birth and death of worlds, ever vibrating, goes and comes, and goes and comes forever—and all that we can do *is* to *gaze in* silent wonder.

Oh, Eternity! Mother of cycles, and parent of ages, whose incalculable and incomprehensible value no subtraction can diminish, no addition increase — thou only type of deity, and day of His duration—what must be thy significance when joined to the stern penalty upon sin thou becomest to the lost – *Eternal Death.*

Dreadful phrase! It will be written with a fiery pen upon all the walls of Hell, and seared into every arch by the lightning's blaze, and sounded through every dungeon by the thunder's horrid breath. It is the motto upon the seal of God which fastens the doors of woe.

There are no farewells in Heaven. Such a word never rang in chords of breaking anguish from the harps of the redeemed, or shrieked in their harmonious preludes, or 'danced upon their vibrating strings —also, there are no farewells in Hell - Oh, Eternity! Eternity!!

The thought has made me restless at night, "Knowing the terror of the Lord." May it ring through your ears. It always is the first motive to prompt a sinner to repent.
William Elbert Munsey 1833 - 1877

The troubling picture of the eternal torment of the damned, is followed by this word in verse 12.

Rev 14:12 *Here is the patience of the saints: here are they that keep the commandments of God, and the faith of Jesus.*

The obvious intent here is that it is a comfort to the suffering saints to remember that their enemies, who have so sorely tormented them, will themselves also be tormented by God.

The very principle of justice that dwells somewhere in each heart, cries out that wrongs must be righted and scores be settled.

The saints are exhorted to patience in all their suffering with the knowledge that justice will be done. Paul encourages the Thessalonian believers with the same thought.

We ourselves glory in you in the churches of God for your patience and faith in all your persecutions and tribulations that ye endure: Which is a manifest token of the righteous judgment of God, that ye may be counted worthy of the kingdom of God, for which ye also suffer: Seeing it is a righteous thing with God to recompense tribulation to them that trouble you; And to you who are troubled rest with us, when the Lord Jesus shall be revealed from heaven with his mighty angels, In flaming fire taking vengeance on them that know not God, and that obey not the gospel of our Lord Jesus Christ:
Who shall be punished with everlasting destruction from the presence of the Lord, and from the glory of his power; When he shall come to be glorified in his saints, and to be admired in all them that believe (because our testimony among you was believed) in that day (2 Thessalonians 1:4-10).

Here is the patience of the saints.

Rev 14:13 ***And I heard a voice from heaven saying unto me, Write, Blessed are the dead which die in the Lord from henceforth: Yea, saith the Spirit, that they may rest from their labours; and their works do follow them.***

Not only will justice be done to the wicked, but blessed reward is awaiting those who stand true for Jesus. Although this verse is frequently used at funerals, please note the word, "from henceforth." That sets the correct time in which this verse will become particularly applicable.

It actually looks to that time when during the reign of the Beast, conditions on earth for believers will be so terrible, that death will be preferred to life. The verse actually does not pronounce a blessing on those who die, but says, that those who die in the Lord are supremely blest, to which the Spirit himself says, Amen.

There are two reasons for their blessedness. **First,** they rest from their labors. Remember, that during this time their labors will be performed under extreme opposition and persecution even to a continual threat upon their lives. Laboring under such extreme stress calls for rest.

The **second** reason for the joy they experience is the assurance that God has not forgotten anything they have done for Him. Their works follow them to the Judgment seat of Christ where they will receive a full and glorious reward.

There are yet two final visions in this chapter. The reaping of the earth and the reaping of the vineyard.

Rev 14:14 *And I looked, and behold a white cloud, and upon the cloud one sat like unto the Son of man, having on his head a golden crown, and in his hand a sharp sickle.*

While there is some disagreement about the identity of this person, there really should not be. He comes on a cloud (we have already examined that idea as it relates to deity), he is recognizable as a "son of man," that is, he is a member of the human race – not an angel, and he is wearing a golden crown.

The picture is altogether fitting because the One who is the Son of man is the only One who has the right to judge.

He was tempted in all points like as we are, yet without sin. Though He did not sin He knows all the temptations we endure and the power of them. He knows our weakness for He too was a man. Therefore, He can judge in absolute fairness, and we are assured that He will.

For the Father judgeth no man, but hath committed all judgment unto the Son: That all men should honour the Son, even as they honour the Father.

He that honoureth not the Son honoureth not the Father which hath sent him. Verily, verily, I say unto you, He that heareth my word, and believeth on him that sent me, hath everlasting life, and shall not come into condemnation; but is passed from death unto life. Verily, verily, I say unto you, The hour is coming, and now is, when the dead shall hear the voice of the Son of God: and they that hear shall live. For as the Father hath life in himself; so hath he given to the Son to have life in himself; And hath given him authority to execute judgment also, because he is the Son of man (John 5:22-27).

It is impossible to expound this entire passage, but the main focus for our discussion is the phrase, *the Father judgeth no man, but hath committed all judgment unto the Son;* and the summation, *the Father hath given him authority to execute judgment also, because he is the Son of man.* It is because He is the victorious Son of man that He is now the One who alone is worthy to judge.

In the hand of the Son of man is a sharp sickle. The picture is one of reaping the earth. The simile of reaping is used both for the harvest of the righteous (Matthew 24:30, 31; John 4:35, 36), and for the harvest of the wicked (Jeremiah 51:33). Here, it seems clear that the harvest of the wicked is meant.

Rev 14:15, 16 ***And another angel came out of the temple, crying with a loud voice to him that sat on the cloud, Thrust in thy sickle, and reap: for the time is come for thee to reap; for the harvest of the earth is ripe. And he that sat on the cloud thrust in his sickle on the earth; and the earth was reaped.***

One of the objections raised in identifying this Son of man as the Lord Jesus Christ is that an angel seems to give him a command.

While the translation of the KJV does appear to be in the form of a command, Young's literal translation reads, *Send forth thy sickle and reap, because come to thee hath the hour of reaping, because ripe hath been the harvest of the earth* (YLT). Here it is voiced more as a plea, but in any case, there is no reason to question the identity of the reaper. He is the Son of man the Lord Jesus Christ.

The "harvest" in Revelation 14:15 is said to be "ripe"; Gr. ξηραίνω; xērainō; to *desiccate*; by implication to *shrivel*, to *mature:* - be ripe, wither (away), implies that it is "overripe."

It seems unlikely that this picture could be interpreted as a "spiritual harvest." It appears more likely that it represents a picture of judgment. It would seem then that the harvest of the grain of the earth is related to the following description by Matthew.

> *The field is the world; the good seed are the children of the kingdom; but the tares are the children of the wicked one; The enemy that sowed them is the devil; the harvest is the end of the world; and the reapers are the angels. As therefore the tares are gathered and burned in the fire; so shall it be in the end of this world.*
>
> *The Son of man shall send forth his angels, and they shall gather out of his kingdom all things that offend, and them which do iniquity; And shall cast them into a furnace of fire: there shall be wailing and gnashing of teeth. Then shall the righteous shine forth as the sun in the kingdom of their Father. Who hath ears to hear, let him hear* (Matthew 13:38-43).

The harvest here seems to depict the gathering of all opposition out of the nations before the Kingdom is finally set up. Remember, only saved individuals living at the end of the Tribulation will enter the Kingdom. These will enter in natural, earthly bodies and procreate during the 1000-year reign of Christ.

Once again it needs to be stressed that these visions in chapter 14 are like random announcements of things that are going to happen. They do not happen within the framework of the chapter, but are announced and briefly described.

This harvest and the one about to be described both occur in conjunction with our Lord's victorious return, and chronologically, that will not occur until the closing verses of chapter 19.

Rev 14:17, 18 *And another angel came out of the temple which is in heaven, he also having a sharp sickle. And another angel came out from the altar, which had power over fire; and cried with a loud cry to him that had the sharp sickle, saying, Thrust in thy sharp sickle, and gather the clusters of the vine of the earth; for her grapes are fully ripe.*

Our attention is drawn to another angel (the sixth in this one chapter), that emerges from the heavenly temple. He is also equipped with a sharp sickle and is prepared to reap. He is joined by a second angel (number seven), that is associated with the brazen altar. This is the altar of sacrifice, it is the altar upon which the fires are to be continually burning.

The angel from the altar urges the first angel to, *Thrust in thy sharp sickle, and gather the clusters of the vine of the earth; for her grapes are fully ripe.* The idea behind this harvest is expressed a number of places in Scripture with a particularly vivid picture painted for us by the prophet Joel.

> *Let the heathen be wakened, and come up to the valley of Jehoshaphat: for there will I sit to judge all the heathen round about. Put ye in the sickle, for the harvest is ripe: come, get you down; for the press is full, the fats overflow; for their wickedness is great.*

Multitudes, multitudes in the valley of decision: for the day of the LORD is near in the valley of decision. The sun and the moon shall be darkened, and the stars shall withdraw their shining. The LORD also shall roar out of Zion, and utter his voice from Jerusalem; and the heavens and the earth shall shake: but the LORD will be the hope of his people, and the strength of the children of Israel (Joel 3:12 – 16).

In the second chapter of Joel we have a vision of the great northern invasion which took place earlier in this period. In chapter three of Joel, beginning in verse nine down to verse seventeen, the chapter is devoted to what we know from the book of Revelation as the battle of Armageddon.

It is pictured both in Joel and Revelation as a grape harvest. The clusters are gathered together (the armies of the nations will converge), and the harvester cuts them down.

The scene then shifts from the grapevines to the winepress where the grapes are crushed and the juice extracted. In the same way the slaughter of all these gathered armies together will be so great that is will be like a winepress overflowing with blood. Read the description John gives us.

Rev 14:19, 20 *And the angel thrust in his sickle into the earth, and gathered the vine of the earth, and cast it into the great winepress of the wrath of God. And the winepress was trodden without the city, and blood came out of the winepress, even unto the horse bridles, by the space of a thousand and six hundred furlongs.*

The picture here is almost inconceivable. The city referred to is obviously Jerusalem, the blood is seen to flow 1,600 stadia (about 180 miles), flowing in places to the depth of horse's bridles. It is too awesome to contemplate.

Isaiah sees a similar vision in chapter 63 of his prophecy. Here the focus is upon the One who actually treads the winepress, and we see that it is the Lord Himself.

In the past he tread that winepress and His own blood was spilt. Now He treads the winepress in judgment upon His enemies. Note the future tense of this declaration; *I will tread them in mine anger, and trample them in my fury; and their blood shall be sprinkled upon my garments, and I will stain all my raiment. For the day of vengeance is in mine heart, and the year of my redeemed is come.* Here is the complete passage.

> *Who is this that cometh from Edom, with dyed garments from Bozrah? this that is glorious in his apparel, travelling in the greatness of his strength? I that speak in righteousness, mighty to save. Wherefore art thou red in thine apparel, and thy garments like him that treadeth in the winefat?*
> *I have trodden the winepress alone; and of the people there was none with me: for I will tread them in mine anger, and trample them in my fury; and their blood shall be sprinkled upon my garments, and I will stain all my raiment. For the day of vengeance is in mine heart, and the year of my redeemed is come. And I looked, and there was none to help; and I wondered that there was none to uphold: therefore mine own arm brought salvation unto me; and my fury, it upheld me. And I will tread down the people in mine anger, and make them drunk in my fury, and I will bring down their strength to the earth.* (Isaiah 63:1-6).

So we come to the end of the seven visions of chapter 14 which form a great kaleidoscopic overview of events, meant to inform, encourage and equip the saints. As we so often say, we have the advantage, because God has allowed us to read the final chapter and we know how it ends. He wins! And we win with Him. (1 Thessalonians 5:1 – 9)

REVIEW

- How many visions are there in Chapter 14?
- How many angels are there in this chapter?
- Where do we see the 144,000 standing?
- Name at least four things we learn about this group.
- What is the message of the "Everlasting Gospel?"
- To whom was it preached?
- Who Preached it?
- What city is said to be "fallen" in this chapter?
- Does her fall actually happen in this chapter?
- What doom is pronounced upon the worshipers of the Beast?
- Why was the death of saints pronounced a blessing at this point?
- What two harvests do we see at the close of this chapter?
- Describe each of them.

Chapter 22   A Victory Song Before the Battle

Revelation 15:1 – 8

Rev 15:1 *And I saw another sign in heaven, great and marvelous, seven angels having the seven last plagues; for in them is filled up the wrath of God.*

This chapter begins with another Gr. σημεῖον; sēmeion, or "sign".   We may recall that the book of Revelation was introduced as a book of signs and symbols.

> *The Revelation of Jesus Christ, which God gave unto him, to shew unto his servants things which must shortly come to pass; and he sent and signified (sēmeion) it by his angel unto his servant John* (Revelation 1:1).

Then there are a series of things specifically called signs beginning in Chapter 12.   The Woman clothed with the sun was called a sign, and the Great Red Dragon was also called a sign.   Now John sees yet another sign which he describes as "great and marvelous."

The "sign" is that of seven angels each having a "vial" (or bowl), filled with a plague which, when all seven are poured out, will complete God's judgments upon the earth.

Rev 15:2 *And I saw as it were a sea of glass mingled with fire: and them that had gotten the victory over the beast, and over his image, and over his mark, and over the number of his name, stand on the sea of glass, having the harps of God.*

John's attention is now drawn to that multitude that he sees standing upon a sea of glass before the throne of God. You may recall we first saw this sea in chapter four. There we noted that it corresponds to the laver in the Old Testament Tabernacle and Temple.

The Laver was meant for cleansing, but here, there is no need for further cleansing, for the saints are washed in the blood of the Lamb, and so the sea is made of glass. Made of reflecting glass, it would reflect the glory of the One seated upon the Throne.

It is a strange and mysterious sea, for it is mingled with fire. Fire is always a picture or type of God's judgment upon sin. Hence, as His glory is reflected, so is His disposition toward human sin and iniquity and we anticipate that what we are about to see is an outpouring of God's righteous judgment. Indeed, that is the theme of this chapter.

Upon the sea of glass is a great multitude that *had gotten the victory over the beast, and over his image, and over his mark, and over the number of his name.* It is evident that this is the same *great multitude, which no man could number, of all nations, and kindreds, and people, and tongues,* that we first saw in chapter seven.

There they were identified as, *they which came out of great tribulation, and have washed their robes, and made them white in the blood of the Lamb.* Here we see them again and are told that *had gotten the victory.* What victory?

They had been martyred for their faith and their steadfast refusal to deny Christ and worship the Beast. They had won the victory over the deception of the dragon, and over the spirit of fear, and cowardness of the flesh, and had remained faithful to the end. That is the victory they won and though they laid down their earthly lives, they had won crowns of glory that could never fade away and the harps in their hands suggest they are singing the praises of the Lamb.

Verses 3 and 4 let us in on the anthem this choir is singing.

Rev 15:3, 4 *And they sing the song of Moses the servant of God, and the song of the Lamb, saying, Great and marvelous are thy works, Lord God Almighty; just and true are thy ways, thou King of saints. Who shall not fear thee, O Lord, and glorify thy name? for thou only art holy: for all nations shall come and worship before thee; for thy judgments are made manifest.*

We have made reference to this before. Moses has two songs attributed to him. The first is the great song of deliverance which he sang when Israel was delivered from the armies of Pharaoh at the Red Sea. That song is recorded in full in Exodus chapter 15. The second song is found in Deuteronomy 32 and records the goodness of God and Israel's many failures. It is most likely the first of these that is referenced here. It would be wise to read it again.

Some of their praise is recorded in these words, *Great and marvelous are thy works, Lord God Almighty; just and true are thy ways, thou King of saints. Who shall not fear thee, O Lord, and glorify thy name? for thou only art holy: for all nations shall come and worship before thee; for thy judgments are made manifest.*

Only the Authorized Version (KJV), translated the phrase, *King of saints,* and it is the only place where the concept is found in Scripture. Other translations say *King of nations.* Given the context this may be the preferred translation.

Jesus Christ is indeed, *Lord God Almighty,* and He is absolute truth. He deserves both our worship and our fear, and in the end, *every knee shall bow and every tongue confess that Jesus Christ is Lord to the glory of God the Father* (Philippians 2:10, 11). Indeed, *all nations shall come and worship* before Him.

Already, with the opening of the Seals, and the Trumpet Judgments, His just and righteous judgments have been made manifest, and now, with this final series of judgments, He will complete that manifestation.

Rev 15:5 *And after that I looked, and, behold, the temple of the tabernacle of the testimony in heaven was opened:*

Once again, our attention is directed to the Temple in heaven. But not just the Temple but the repository of the testimony (i.e., the Law). Either *the tabernacle of the testimony* means that the Holy of Holies was opened to reveal the Ark of the Covenant, or that the Ark itself was opened to reveal the naked Law.

Remember that the Law was called by Paul, *the ministration of death, written and engraven in stones* and *a ministration of condemnation* (2 Corinthians 3:7, 9). <u>Whenever God opens the book of the Law, judgment is about to fall.</u>

Rev 15:6 *And the seven angels came out of the temple, having the seven plagues, clothed in pure and white linen, and having their breasts girded with golden girdles.*

Although these are distinctly angels, they are dressed very much like the Jewish Priest. Their purity is noted, and the golden girdle suggests that they are "Deputies of Deity." They proceed from the location of the book of the Law and come out of the Temple to execute the justice which the Law demands.

Rev 15:7 *And one of the four beasts gave unto the seven angels seven golden vials full of the wrath of God, who liveth for ever and ever.*

We have seen the four living creatures now in chapters 4, 5, 6, 7, 14, and again here. They will appear one final time in chapter 19. In all, they are referred to 11 times in the book of Revelation.

Remember that the word translated "beasts" and referring to these four is completely different from that used for the wicked Beast, the Anti-Christ. The word is from the root Gr. Ζωή; zōē, meaning "life." Hence, as we have said, these are four "living creatures" apparently the same as the Cherubim seen by Ezekiel (Ezekiel 10).

These creatures act in response to God and seem to almost be manifestations of His character. If so, then the one referred to here, acts as a manifestation of the righteous indignation and wrath of God against sinful and rebellious man. He distributes seven vials (or bowls), *full of the wrath of God, who liveth for ever and ever.* Hence, he has delivered to these dispensers of wrath the contents that comprise the fullness of God's wrath against the earth dwellers.

Rev 15:8 *And the temple was filled with smoke from the glory of God, and from his power; and no man was able to enter into the temple, till the seven plagues of the seven angels were fulfilled.*

The ninth chapter of Numbers describes how God inhabited a cloud and led Israel through the wilderness. There are a number of occasions in Scripture where the Temple, or the Tabernacle, were filled with what was described as a "cloud." The phenomena occurred at the dedication of both.

> *Then a cloud covered the tent of the congregation, and the glory of the LORD filled the tabernacle. And Moses was not able to enter into the tent of the congregation, because the cloud abode thereon, and the glory of the LORD filled the tabernacle (Exodus 40:34, 35).*

> *And it came to pass, when the priests were come out of the holy place, that the cloud filled the house of the LORD, So that the priests could not stand to minister because of the cloud: for the glory of the LORD had filled the house of the LORD (1 Kings 8:10, 11).*

Some have made a distinction between the "cloud" and the "smoke" apparent in this passage, and indeed the words are different. But a reading of all these instances makes the distinction less certain. Nevertheless, there are two related passages where the word smoke seems to attend the presence of God.

> And mount Sinai was altogether on a smoke, because the LORD descended upon it in fire: and the smoke thereof ascended as the smoke of a furnace, and the whole mount quaked greatly (Exodus 19:18).

> And the posts of the door moved at the voice of him that cried, and the house was filled with smoke (Isaiah 6:4).

Both of the above passages have in common the thought of the holiness of God and the smoke seems to appear almost as a warning. In the first, the Law was being delivered and God would impress those who received it of its absolute character (see Hebrews 12:18 – 21).

In the second, Isaiah has just experienced the death of King Uzziah, whom God smote with leprosy because he had attempted to offer incense as a priest. Again, the awesome judgments of Jehovah were in view. Certainly, the smoke reminds us of that. The Temple is off-limits until the seven plagues of the seven angels were fulfilled.

As we view this short chapter, we see a fearful picture of impending divine judgment upon a wicked world. As we move on through chapter 16, it becomes obvious that this ominous expectation is fully justified.

Why the Plagues

Before we look at the plagues, let's answer the question; Why does God send these plagues and the other judgments upon the earth?

A good place to start to answer that question might be with what God tells us about the plagues in Egypt.

In Exodus 9:29, we have the answer. God told Pharaoh, *that thou mayest know, that the earth is the Lord's.* So, we find that the first purpose of the plagues is to establish God's Sovereign right as Creator and Sustainer to have ultimate control over the earth.

That is a lesson the "earth dwellers" need to learn because with all our talk about man-made climate change, we have greatly weakened the perceived connection between God and the phenomena of nature. The fact that in the later plagues, men curse God, suggests that at least He has made His point, i.e., they see the connection.

Many of the plagues of Egypt are miniature parallels to the plagues of Revelation. They are recorded in Exodus 7 – 11 and they are clearly direct judgments

- Against the human adversary — Pharaoh

- Against all the gods of Egypt (Exodus 12:12)

In the plagues of Revelation once again there will be a human adversary; the Beast and the False Prophet, and the judgments are also upon *"those that dwell upon the earth."*

In addition, God will also be exposing the wicked spiritual powers that have energized these men, as He shows their utter helplessness to prevent His judgments from coming (Isaiah 24:21).

Finally, I am going to suggest that there are at least 5 significant reasons for these judgments. We have mentioned these before, but I want to expand what was said.

1. There is a dispensational significance. Each Dispensation has ended in man's failure and God's subsequent Judgment. The plagues of the Tribulation

period are the Judgment which follows the Dispensation of Grace on an unbelieving world that has rejected God's gracious gift of salvation through His Son.

2. <u>There is a consequential significance</u> (Revelation 16:4 - 7). Some of the plagues are designed as a direct consequence of the evil actions of those upon whom they are poured. Here they are given blood to drink as a consequence of having shed the blood of God's saints.

3. <u>There is a controversial significance</u> (Jeremiah 25:31). God has a controversy with the nations who have consistently flaunted their power and claimed their own right to rule independent of God. The final and most flagrant violator is the Beast, and when God enters into a controversy, He always wins the battle.

4. <u>There is a purifying significance</u> (Zechariah 13:8, 9). The Tribulation period is particularly a time of trial for Israel in which He will purge out those who are not faithful. The remaining remnant will be purified and ready to rule and reign with Him in the Kingdom.

5. <u>There is a merciful significance</u> (2 Peter 3:9, 10). As terrible as the judgments of the plagues are, they are temporary and brief in the light of eternal torment, and they are designed to bring a rebellious world to repentance. That did not happen in the days of Pharaoh and is seems that it will not occur in any broad sense during this time either. Nevertheless, the plagues are not only judgments in their own right, but warnings of eternal doom to come if there is not repentance.

There is always strong and significant reasons for all that God does and there will be strong and significant reasons for each of these plagues.

REVIEW

- What sign did John see as this chapter opens?
- Where is the sea of glass which John saw?
- What does the sea being mingled with fire indicate?
- Who does John see standing on the sea of glass?
- Have we seen this company before - if so, where?
- What did John see open in heaven?
- Why is that significant?
- Who came out of the Temple?
- What "filled the Temple?"
- What does the smoke suggest?
- How many reasons can you give for sending the plagues?

Chapter 23 The Final Vials of Wrath

Revelation Chapter 16:1 – 21

Rev 16:1 *And I heard a great voice out of the temple saying to the seven angels, Go your ways, and pour out the vials of the wrath of God upon the earth.*

As the last chapter closed we saw the seven angels of judgment emerge from the Temple of the Tabernacle of the Testimony. In other words, they came from the Holy of Holies, the repository of the Law, that *ministration of death written and engraven on stone.* As soon as they emerged the entire Temple was filled with smoke so that no one could enter.

Then, out of that smoke-filled Temple came a thunderous (Gr. mega-phone') voice commanding the angels to do their work and "pour out" the vials of God's wrath. The words imply a sudden and complete action. Each successive bowl is dutifully emptied in full upon a rebellious and sinful world.

Rev 16:2 *And the first went, and poured out his vial upon the earth; and there fell a noisome and grievous sore upon the men which had the mark of the beast, and upon them which worshipped his image.*

The earth and the earth-dwellers are the target of these plagues. The first plague produces a sore perhaps similar to a boil. It is described as noisome and grievous.

The word "noisome" is Gr. *Κακός*; Kakos, that which is "*injurious:* - bad, evil, harmful, wicked." "Grievous" is translated from Gr. Πονηρός; ponēros, a word particularly related to evil in a moral sense.

It is the word from which we get our word, pornography. While it seems strange to attach a moral connection to a physical sore, the words do suggest that such a connection may exist. One cannot help but wonder therefore, if these painful and grievous sores are somehow related to sexually transmitted diseases rampant because of a society out of control.

This judgment falls upon all who had taken the mark of the beast and worshipped his image. We therefore recognize this as a restrictive judgment. That is, it falls only upon these specific individuals (though they are apparently the vast majority at that time), and not upon those who had refused or escaped the mark of the Beast.

This is consistent with the judgment pattern of God during the plagues in Egypt.

> *And Moses stretched forth his rod toward heaven: and the LORD sent thunder and hail, and the fire ran along upon the ground; and the LORD rained hail upon the land of Egypt. So there was hail, and fire mingled with the hail, very grievous, such as there was none like it in all the land of Egypt since it became a nation. And the hail smote throughout all the land of Egypt all that was in the field, both man and beast; and the hail smote every herb of the field, and brake every tree of the field. Only in the land of Goshen, where the children of Israel were, was there no hail* (Exodus 9:23-26).

Just as the people of God escaped the plagues of Egypt, so will the faithful escape the plagues God sends during the Tribulation judgments.

Rev 16:3 *And the second angel poured out his vial upon the sea; and it became as the blood of a dead man: and every living soul died in the sea.*

We may remember that the second Trumpet judgment (Revelation 8:8, 9), also was visited upon the sea.

At that time, a third of the sea was affected and was "turned to blood." Now, with the final judgments, the entire sea is stricken and becomes, not only blood, but, as the congealed blood of a dead man. The result is that everything in the sea dies. Are we to take this literally?

When Moses raised his rod over the mighty Nile, God turned it to blood. We are given to understand that the river actually turned to blood. While human blood has many chemical components, we are simply told both in Exodus and here, that it was turned to blood. The Lord, who could change water into wine (John 2), can certainly change it into blood as well.

The composition of the human body is made up of 50% to 74% water. Blood partakes of that same characteristic. So the transformation of water to a form of blood should be quite conceivable.

In chapter 8 a third of the sea creatures die. Here in chapter 16, all that live in the sea die. This is nothing short of an ecological disaster! Imagine, if you can, the stench alone, much less the loss of the oceans as food resources. That is the result of this plague.

To place these plagues in the time framework of the Tribulation Week, it is evident that we are meant to understand that they occur in the latter most part of that period. So many disasters have already taken place and now these final plagues "fill up the wrath of God."

Certainly life could not exist for long under these conditions, and they are meant to send the clear message that God is in control and is about to fully judge the earth and its inhabitants.

It may be observed that the order and object of the judgments in chapters 8 and 9 is, in almost each case, the same as the order we find here in chapter 16 (vis. the sea, then the rivers, then the sun, then the Euphrates, etc.).

As a result some believe that the plagues of chapter 16 are really just a reiteration and expansion of those formerly described. While the similarities are real, so are the differences and, I believe, we must view these as the culminating acts of judgment leading to the great battle which will soon decide the fate of planet earth.

Rev 16:4 - 7 *And the third angel poured out his vial upon the rivers and fountains of waters; and they became blood. And I heard the angel of the waters say, Thou art righteous, O Lord, which art, and wast, and shalt be, because thou hast judged thus. For they have shed the blood of saints and prophets, and thou hast given them blood to drink; for they are worthy. And I heard another out of the altar say, Even so, Lord God Almighty, true and righteous are thy judgments.*

Now, not only the seas, but even the land waters clear back to the fountainheads were plagued by this judgment. The *angel of the waters*, apparently refers to the angel that delivered this plague. He declares God's righteousness in dealing thus with men. They shed the blood of God's dear saints and prophets, and now their blood thirsty violence is visited upon their own heads as they have nothing but blood to drink.

The angel proclaims them worthy of the consequences of their own deeds. So the angel declares God's actions righteous and done in truth. What you will not see in these judgments is God's attribute of mercy. The time for mercy has passed. There was a time when God acted in restraint toward sinful man (Jonah 4:11), but no more. The very justice men once accused God of not exercising, is now administered to them in full, and afterward will follow the eternal judgment of hell.

No wonder we are warned again and again to come to Christ and find His mercy and His grace while the time is right – for there is a future deadline to grace.

Today if ye will hear his voice, harden not your hearts, as in the provocation (Hebrews 3:15).

For he saith, I have heard thee in a time accepted, and in the day of salvation have I succoured thee: behold, now is the accepted time; behold, now is the day of salvation (2 Corinthians 6:2).

Rev 16:8, 9 *And the fourth angel poured out his vial upon the sun; and power was given unto him to scorch men with fire. And men were scorched with great heat, and blasphemed the name of God, which hath power over these plagues: and they repented not to give him glory.*

The balance between the sun's activity and the effects on the earth is crucial. Our sun is a raging inferno of cosmic heat comprised of fiery gases ranging millions of degrees in temperature. It emits a constant stream of particles called the "solar wind" that bathes all of the planets in radiation. This wind is the invisible connection between the sun and the earth, which drives our seasonal changes. This solar wind also affects currents in the ocean, our day to day weather, and our long-term climate variations.

The energy that affects the temperature and climate on earth originates almost exclusively from the sun. The sun's energy passes through space until it reaches earth where presently about 40% gets through to the earth's surface.

The explosive heat of a solar flare and great bursts of electromagnetic energy and particles can sometimes temporarily alter the upper atmosphere. At present the earth's magnetic field has been able to alleviate much of the potential damage from such events, but the future ability of the magnetic field to continue to protect us is uncertain.

The forth angel's bowl is emptied upon the sun. No description is given of the changes this action made, but considering the fragile balance which exists now between the earth and its nearest star, any change would most certainly lead to unprecedented disaster.

The sun is said to *scorch men with fire.* With the slightest attenuation of either the earth's magnetic shield, or the sun's radiant output, the ultraviolet rays would bombard the skin and create unimaginable pain and harm.

Remember that time you went to the beach and forgot your sunscreen? Remember the pain of anything touching your body and the feeling of the heat that radiated from your flesh. Then multiply that by any factor you wish and you can begin to imagine the suffering caused by this fourth plague.

But it is not as much the plague as the reaction of the earth dwellers to the plague that shocks us most. We are told that they, *blasphemed the name of God, which hath power over these plagues: and they repented not to give him glory.*

We are about to see in this last sequence of judgments, the predictable response of a godless, rebellious world to any judgment of God. It is this response that demonstrates beyond anything else, the wisdom and justice of God and the necessity of that isolation ward of the universe we call hell.

John Bunyan, in his book *The Holy War*, tells of a time when hearts are so hard that, "Grace cannot win them and judgment cannot frighten them." When that happens, repentance is impossible and damnation waits impatiently at the door.

Rev 16:10, 11 *And the fifth angel poured out his vial upon the seat of the beast; and his kingdom was full of darkness; and they gnawed their tongues for pain, And blasphemed the God of heaven because of their pains and their sores, and repented not of their deeds.*

As we have noted before, these judgments are selective. God's servants are not "appointed unto wrath" (1 Thessalonians 5:9), and though they may experience the worse that man's diabolical cruelty can devise, they will never taste of the wrath of God here or hereafter. The fifth angel's target is the seat or throne of the Beast.

Gross darkness was the condition of the universe at creation. God, who Himself is Light, spoke light into existence and called it good. Nowhere in Scripture is darkness ever called "good." Darkness is used as a picture of evil throughout God's Word. Weber and Rice might revel in "the magic of the night," in *Phantom of the Opera*, but God takes no pleasure in darkness.

The Apostle wrote, *ye were sometimes darkness, but now are ye light in the Lord: walk as children of light:* (Ephesians 5:8).

The curse of darkness was visited on Pharaoh during the contest in Egypt:

> *And Moses stretched forth his hand toward heaven; and there was a thick darkness in all the land of Egypt three days: They saw not one another, neither rose any from his place for three days: but all the children of Israel had light in their dwellings* (Exodus 10:22, 23).

Now it is visited upon the very seat (throne) of the Beast. And we need to recognize that this was a special kind of darkness which ordinary light sources could not penetrate. There was no light anywhere. Nothing they could do could reverse that. It was darkness that could be felt, and since these plagues come in very rapid succession, the darkness further complicated the pain of the sores they were already suffering. Once again, the response was that of rebellious rage.

Rev 16:12 *And the sixth angel poured out his vial upon the great river Euphrates; and the water thereof was dried up, that the way of the kings of the east might be prepared.*

The river Euphrates has always been considered a dividing line between the west and the orient. Historically, it was at times a formidable obstacle to armies, and military strategy sought to avoid it. Although today it is more of a symbolic obstacle, it proved to be a challenge even as late as the Gulf war.

The text seems clear enough that the river will be literally dried up. As such, it not only removes any actual hindrance, but acts as a symbolic omen to tell the kings of the orient that the time has come for them to engage the west. It must seem almost an invitation to move their vast armies to battle.

Rev 16:13, 14 *And I saw three unclean spirits like frogs come out of the mouth of the dragon, and out of the mouth of the beast, and out of the mouth of the false prophet. For they are the spirits of devils, working miracles, which go forth unto the kings of the earth and of the whole world, to gather them to the battle of that great day of God Almighty.*

In addition to the physical drying of the Euphrates, demonic spirits are at work through the trinity of evil to entice the entire world to battle. John sees these demon spirits in the form of frogs, coming out of the mouth of the Beast and the False Prophet, and the Dragon with deceptive and seducing words to accomplish their purpose.

It is instructive to look back at another instance in which we are permitted to draw back the curtain and get a glimpse of something very similar happening in the realm of the spirit world.

Ahab, the king of Israel, had decided to recover his territory east of the Jordan from Syria. He determined to go to war at Ramoth-Gilead and he invited Jehoshaphat, the godly king of Judah to go with him. But Jehoshaphat wanted a word from the Lord to assure him of the success of this venture.

The four hundred prophets of the apostate religion of Israel, all telling Ahab what he wanted to hear, were of little comfort to the godly Jehoshaphat. "Is there not a prophet of the Lord?" Jehoshaphat asked.

At this Ahab ordered Micaiah, a faithful prophet of Jehovah, to be brought out of prison (that should have been enough to caution Jehoshaphat). Charged by the king of Israel to tell the truth, Micaiah reveals the movement of spiritual forces behind the scenes.

> *And he said, Hear thou therefore the word of the LORD: I saw the LORD sitting on his throne, and all the host of heaven standing by him on his right hand and on his left. And the LORD said, Who shall persuade Ahab, that he may go up and fall at Ramoth-Gilead? And one said on this manner, and another said on that manner. And there came forth a spirit, and stood before the LORD, and said, I will persuade him. And the LORD said unto him, Wherewith? And he said, I will go forth, and I will be a lying spirit in the mouth of all his prophets. And he said, Thou shalt persuade him, and prevail also: go forth, and do so. Now therefore, behold, the LORD hath put a lying spirit in the mouth of all these thy prophets, and the LORD hath spoken evil concerning thee* (1 Kings 22:19-23).

It is a similar situation we have here but on a profoundly larger scale. These spirits will draw all the world to the battle *of that great day of God Almighty.*

Rev 16:15 *Behold, I come as a thief. Blessed is he that watcheth, and keepeth his garments, lest he walk naked, and they see his shame.*

Verse 15 is actually an interruption in the ongoing description of the sixth bowl judgment. The Lord Himself interrupts to encourage, strengthen and assure His people. To do so, He announces His coming. Remember, that this will be His Gr. ἀποκάλυψις; apokalupsis, or His full manifestation; His coming in glory (2 Thessalonians 1:7, 8).

He will *come as a thief* that is, suddenly and unexpectedly. Paul wrote of the same to the believers in Thessalonica.

For yourselves know perfectly that the day of the Lord so cometh as a thief in the night. For when they shall say, Peace and safety; then sudden destruction cometh upon them, as travail upon a woman with child; and they shall not escape. But ye, brethren, are not in darkness, that that day should overtake you as a thief. Ye are all the children of light, and the children of the day: we are not of the night, nor of darkness. Therefore let us not sleep, as do others; but let us watch and be sober (1 Thessalonians 5:2-6).

We are not in darkness about the Lord's coming and He does not want these Tribulation believers to be either. It may be dark, as dark as the world has ever been, but do not lose hope – His promise is still *I am coming!*

They are exhorted to watch for these events, so that they understand the times. They are further to keep their garments. In the literal sense it would refer to the custom of taking off ones garments for sleep. Given the nearness of His coming, they must not be found sleeping, or unprepared.

As we read these warning to those who will live through the Tribulation, it might be well to ask ourselves, if Christ were to come this very moment, how prepared are we for His coming?

The garment in scripture is also a picture of ones spiritual condition. Defiled garments speak of sin, white garments symbolize righteousness. But what of nakedness? Is it possible to be deceived into thinking that I am dressed in His righteousness and yet be found naked?

So with the encouragement, comes also this warning. Better to make your calling and election sure.

Rev 16:16 *And he gathered them together into a place called in the Hebrew tongue Armageddon.*

The word Armageddon has become so familiar around the world that we frequently find it in conversation or in print. If one political party plans to take the nation in a certain direction, it is not unusual to hear the opposition cry, "Armageddon!" Used in that way, the word has come to have the meaning of a disaster. Such is Satan's way of demeaning the full significance of that word and the terror it aught to bring to the heart of any who know what it signifies.

The word is found only here and nowhere else in scripture or in secular writing. It appears to be a conjunction of two words, Hebrew: *Har-Megiddon*; *Har*; meaning; "mountain" and *Megiddon*; meaning; "of Megiddo"). Hence the word would literally mean, the mountain (or mountains) of Megiddo.

Anyone who studies closely a map of Israel cannot help but notice the large valley that stretches from the Mediterranean Sea and runs eastward just north of Mt. Carmel onto the broad plane of Esdraelon. Through that valley runs the Kishon river, called by Deborah and Barak, "that ancient river" (Judges 5:21). It was on that great plain, surrounded by the Mountains of Megiddo, that Sisera met defeat at the hands of a woman. It was near here that Saul fell upon the mountains of Gilboa.

Many centuries later Napoleon would stand looking out over that plain and call it the greatest battlefield in the world. It is in this valley that General William B. Allenby, executed his brilliant defeat of the Ottoman forces in September 1918, thus freeing the holy Land from Turkish rule. And it is here that the final battle for the dominion of the earth will be fought.

It is evident that these "kings" (forces) are drawn into the mid-east by direct demonic design. The question might be, why would Satan do that? We know that his plan is to kill, to steal, and to destroy. But is there something more specific about this? What is behind this move?

Kings always seek their own advantage and glory. What bate Satan used to get the nations to make this move we do not know.

But whatever their motivation was, it appears that Satan deliberately musters them to the mid-east, for a battle he knows all too well is coming.

While Satan denigrates and dismisses the Scripture to those he wishes to destroy, he knows right well what is written therein. He knows that when all these things come to pass the coming of the Lord Jesus with His saints is near. And when that heavenly army arrives, Satan wants to have every advantage he can to meet it. Maybe that is his motivation behind this move of gathering the armies of the earth to one place.

Rev 16:17 *And the seventh angel poured out his vial into the air; and there came a great voice out of the temple of heaven, from the throne, saying, It is done.*

That same voice once shouted, "It is finished," across the Judean hillside from a bloody cross. Back then it was the triumphal announcement that the sin debt was settled, and redemption was accomplished. It was the cry that announced the victory of the Lamb on our behalf that obtained our salvation.

This time, the same voice will trumpet the victory cry "It is done!" It is the cry of the Lion of Judah over the earth. It is the roar of a lion over the prey. It is the victory shout of the conquering King of Kings and Lord of Lords. It signifies that what He has undertaken, He has accomplished!

Rev 16:18-21 *And there were voices, and thunders, and lightnings; and there was a great earthquake, such as was not since men were upon the earth, so mighty an earthquake, and so great. And the great city was divided into three parts, and the cities of the nations fell: and great Babylon came in remembrance before God, to give unto her the cup of the wine of the fierceness of his wrath. And every island fled away, and the mountains were not found.*

And there fell upon men a great hail out of heaven, every stone about the weight of a talent: and men blasphemed God because of the plague of the hail; for the plague thereof was exceeding great.

What is described in these four verses is so dramatic and so interrelated that I have chosen to look at them together as a unit. In them, there are at least seven things we should give attention to: (1) voices of victory, (2) vast earthquakes, (3) vanishing islands and mountains, (4) vanquished capitals, (5) vaunted Babylon judged, (6) violent hail, and (7) a vulgar response.

Voices of Victory:
The final judgment upon the earth brings a chorus of "voices" from heaven along with thunders and lightnings. Those in heaven rejoice and the lightening/thunder display will trump any fireworks celebration ever put on by earthlings and all such celebrations together. Heaven knows how to celebrate the victories of God.

Vast Earthquakes:
The earth itself will shudder and shake from pole to pole. Nothing like it will ever have occurred before and nothing like it after. Isaiah prophesied of it when he wrote; *The earth shall reel to and fro like a drunkard* (Isaiah 24:20).

Vanishing Islands & Mountains:
According to verse 20 whole islands will disappear and mountains will crumble to become mere heaps of rubble. Imagine if you can the topographical destruction and confusion.

The fact is that when King Jesus returns to take control of planet earth, He will receive a world destroyed by its own violence and by the judgments of God. There will be plenty to do to restore it to the pristine condition that will eventually exist during the Millennium. Perhaps that is why Isaiah wrote;

Behold, the Lord GOD will come with strong hand, and his arm shall rule for him: behold, his reward is with him, and his work before him (Isaiah 40:10).

Vanquished Capitals:
The phrase, the cities of the nations, implies capital cities, the control center of each of the nations, and these are destroyed. It must be obvious by now that there is about to be a sea-change in the way earth operates.

Among these is one referred to as "the great city" which we learn will be divided in three parts. Although a number of commentators believe this refers to Babylon (which is specifically mentioned later), I believe it clearly refers to Jerusalem.

Jerusalem is described in chapter 11 as, *the great city* (Revelation 11:8). In that context it is further identified as the place where our Lord was crucified. That could be nowhere else but Jerusalem. This is very likely the same earthquake described in Chapter 11, that followed the resurrection and ascension of the two witnesses.

Remember Jerusalem is not yet "the holy city." It is described as, *spiritually called Sodom and Egypt* (Revelation 11:8). The city has been the location of the worship of the Beast and his image during the final 3½ years of the Tribulation. It is certain that, "the great city" will be ripe for judgment.

Vaunted Babylon Judged:
Since its founding Babylon has been a rival system at war with God. We will get a thorough look at her in the next chapter. Here we learn simply that God does not forget. All the wickedness of the ages has had its fountainhead in Babylon and now she will be given the bitter cup of God's vengeance.

Violent Hail:
From the seventh bowl, comes now a violent hailstorm. Hail has long been a choice weapon in the arsenal of God when the wicked go to war with Him.

Job observed:

> *Hast thou entered into the treasures of the snow? or hast thou seen the treasures of the hail, Which I have reserved against the time of trouble, against the day of battle and war?* (Job 38:22, 23).

In Egypt and later in Canaan, God battled against His enemies with hail.

> *So there was hail, and fire mingled with the hail, very grievous, such as there was none like it in all the land of Egypt since it became a nation* (Exodus 9:24)..

> *And it came to pass, as they fled from before Israel, and were in the going down to Bethhoron, that the LORD cast down great stones from heaven upon them unto Azekah, and they died: they were more which died with hailstones than they whom the children of Israel slew with the sword* (Joshua 10:11).

Having observed this however, this was not like any other hailstorm that had ever occurred. These hailstones are said to be about a talent in weight. A talent represented a weight of about one hundred pounds.

Try to imagine if you can hail stones of that magnitude falling at speed force of up to 300 miles per hour. That is the speed a human body falls in a form of sky diving called "speed diving" to achieve maximum speed. Then imagine the impact.

Several years ago, I was in Legazpi City in the Philippines. I traveled out to the sight of its active volcano and looked at the evidence from former eruptions. There were boulders the size of refrigerators scattered across the ground. Anything within their path was totally destroyed. How devastating this hailstorm must be.

A Vulgar Response:

And men blasphemed God because of the plague of the hail; for the plague thereof was exceeding great. Once again, we have to confess the absolute hardness of our hearts, which apart from divine grace would respond just as these do.

The book of Revelation should settle forever the question of eternal torment. We are eternal beings. We will exist somewhere for all eternity. Hard and unrepentant hearts would turn heaven into hell. Men have the freedom to choose what they will do with Jesus, but they have no freedom to change the consequences of their choice.

As the old poem pleads, *While, it is called today repent, and harden not your heart.*

REVIEW:

- The sequence of these plagues is similar in many ways to that of the Trumpet judgments. Are they the same?

- What city is called, "that great city" in this chapter? How can we be sure?

- Why would the angel say that turning all the waters into blood was a "righteous" act?

- What was the response of men after each of these terrible plagues?

- How does this chapter help us understand the necessity for hell?

- Who will draw the kings of the earth to the middle-east?

- Where will the final battle be fought?

- What is the meaning of the word, Armageddon?

Chapter 24 The Harlot, The Beast & 10 Kings

Revelation 17:1 – 18

The next two chapters (17, 18), develop the theme of the development, the character and the destruction of Babylon. As such, the time period covered in these chapters stretches from the period just after the Noahic deluge and the founding of Babylon, across the centuries as the Babylonian system developed and spread, to its final defeat and the triumphal return of Christ.

The chapters focus primarily on the Tribulation week from the beginning, with the supreme exaltation of the great whore (symbol of the Babylonian religious system), to her destruction and total demise in the middle of the week, and then the final destruction at the end of the 7-years of the commercial, political and social system that is Babylon.

Babylon is mentioned six times in the book of Revelation. She is first mentioned in chapter 14 where her ultimate doom is announced:

> *And there followed another angel, saying, Babylon is fallen, is fallen, that great city, because she made all nations drink of the wine of the wrath of her fornication* (Revelation 14:8).

She next appears in Revelation chapter 16 where her judgment is announced again along with a city referred to as *the great city*, which we saw was a reference to Jerusalem (see also Revelation 11:8), and *the cities of the nations*, which apparently indicates what we would call capital cities.

All of the other references to Babylon are found in these two chapters before us. But Babylon is a major theme in Scripture and in fact appears 296 times, beginning as far back as Genesis chapter 10.

While we cannot fully explore this theme, we need to recognize that Babylon is more than the name of a city. It is the name of a system that began in the city Babylon and spread throughout the entire earth. It is the fullest expression of the system designed and ruled over by Satan, a system that the New Testament often refers to as "the world" (Gr. Cosmos), both the religious and the materialistic parts of that.

> *But if our gospel be hid, it is hid to them that are lost: In whom the god of this world* (system) *hath blinded the minds of them which believe not, lest the light of the glorious gospel of Christ, who is the image of God, should shine unto them* (2 Corinthians 4:3, 4).

> *And you hath he quickened, who were dead in trespasses and sins; Wherein in time past ye walked according to the course of this world* (system)*, according to the prince of the power of the air, the spirit that now worketh in the children of disobedience* (Ephesians 2:1, 2).

> *Love not the world, neither the things that are in the world. If any man love the world, the love of the Father is not in him. For all that is in the world* (system)*, the lust of the flesh, and the lust of the eyes, and the pride of life, is not of the Father, but is of the world* (system)*. And the world* (system) *passeth away, and the lust thereof: but he that doeth the will of God abideth for ever* (1 John 2:15-17).

C. I. Scofield summarizes the world system (cosmos) like this;

> The present world-system, the ethically bad sense of the word, refers to the "order," "arrangement," under which Satan has organized the world of unbelieving

mankind upon his cosmic principle of force, greed, selfishness, ambition, and pleasure.

This world-system is imposing and powerful with armies and fleets; is often outwardly religious, scientific, cultured, and elegant; but, seething with national and commercial rivalries and ambitions, is upheld in any real crisis only by armed force, and is dominated by Satanic principles. **(Scofield Reference Bible pp. 1342)**

The Babylon exposed in these two chapters looks at both the religious aspect of the world system and at its commercial character. If we are to understand the significance of Babylon, a brief history lesson is necessary.

Babylon was man's great attempt to make a name for himself, and to direct his destiny apart from the God of creation and revelation.

Babylon was also the fountainhead of idolatry historically speaking. It birthed the early false religion of Nimrod and his wife Semiramis that formed the basis for every false system of religion since that time. Idolatry is basically a rival system of religion that directs the devotion and worship of its followers, away from God and toward itself.

The Tower of Babel (Genesis 11) seems to have been both a religious and a political venture. During Nimrod's time the signs of the Zodiac were mapped out. God tells us in His Word that the lights in the heavens were for signs (Genesis 1:14), and the great commentator, Joseph A. Siess, has developed this theme in his work, *"The Gospel in the Stars."*

Siess demonstrated that the complete plan of salvation was presented in the great constellations. But Nimrod and his priests perverted the star signs to teach their apostasy and error.
When Nimrod was killed, instead of his religion dying with him, a twist of events made it certain that it would establish itself forever.

Through the truths handed down by oral tradition through Noah's line, the people of Nimrod's empire had learned to expect a great Deliverer to be born miraculously of a woman. When Semiramis gave birth to a child more than a year after Nimrod's death, she explained her condition by claiming that the child was conceived through a mysterious union with the spirit of her departed husband. Thus, the child was believed to be a reincarnation of the departed leader and therefore a "god."

Images of the mother and the child were struck and worshiped throughout the empire. From Babylon the cult spread with its mysteries, its priesthood, its temple virgins, its rites of purgation, and of course its family of gods . . . the great father god who was to be feared and the virgin mother and child god who received love and worship.

This religion was one of mystery, magic, symbolism, and ceremonies of great pomp. Dr. John Walvoord writes, "The chief priests of the Babylonian cult wore crowns in the shape of the head of a fish, in recognition of Dagon, the fish god, with the title, 'Keeper of the Bridge,' that is, the bridge between man and god (Satan – the god worshipped in the mysteries), imprinted on the crowns. The Latin equivalent of the title was Pontifex Maximus, used by the Caesars and later by the Roman Emperors, and was adopted as the title for the Bishop of Rome." **(The Revelation of Jesus Christ; Moody Press 1966; page 248).**

Dr. Walvoord goes on to describe how the early Roman Church tried to adapt customs and superstitions from the Babylonian tradition and reinterpret it into the "Christian" faith. Babylon also had its cleansing rituals, celebrations of special days dedicated to one of its gods, prayers for the dead, and even rosary beads.

This whole system of error was gradually immersed into the Church and forms the framework of the Roman Catholic system.

There can be no serious doubt that Rome today is heir to the faith of Babylon.Everything that is said of this harlot can be said of Romanism today and the parallels are too obvious to be accidental.

Rome is the wealthiest of all international corporations. She has committed fornication with the kings of the earth by her innumerable "concordats," by which she obtains special privilege in turn for her support. She signed a concordat with Napoleon (1801), Mussolini (1929), and Hitler (1933). She cares not with whom she lies, so long as she receives her stipend. (Her concordat with Mussolini earned her the property of Vatican City, plus an outright payment of about $90,000,000). It was the weight of the Papacy that put Franco in power in Spain and that once controlled most of the nations south of the United States border.

The Roman system is famous for its delicacies of gold, fine lace, incense, candles, and every other item mentioned in chapter eighteen. It has for long centuries dealt in the bodies and souls of men and turned the pages of history red with the blood of the true saints of God.

While the subject is far too inexhaustible to be able to deal with it here, we suggest further reading (see "Trail of Blood," J. M. Carroll; "The Two Babylons," Rev. Alexander Hislop; and "The Woman Rides The Beast," David Hunt).

Rev 17:1, 2 *And there came one of the seven angels which had the seven vials, and talked with me, saying unto me, Come hither; I will shew unto thee the judgment of the great whore that sitteth upon many waters: With whom the kings of the earth have committed fornication, and the inhabitants of the earth have been made drunk with the wine of her fornication.*

We need to answer the question why this symbolic woman is called a harlot. Spiritual adultery is often referred to in the Old Testament. It is based on the relationship which Israel had with Jehovah.

She was called the "wife of Jehovah." She had entered into a covenant relationship with God at Mount Sinai. The relationship is comparable to marriage and the partners are expected to be faithful. But while God was faithful, Israel was not and so God charged her with spiritual adultery.

The LORD said also unto me in the days of Josiah the king, Hast thou seen that which backsliding Israel hath done? She is gone up upon every high mountain and under every green tree, and there hath played the harlot. And I said after she had done all these things, Turn thou unto me. But she returned not. And her treacherous sister Judah saw it. And I saw, when for all the causes whereby backsliding Israel committed adultery I had put her away, and given her a bill of divorce; yet her treacherous sister Judah feared not, but went and played the harlot also (Jeremiah 3:6-8).

Jeremiah spent the remainder of chapter 3 describing the betrayal of both the northern and southern kingdoms of their covenant relationship with Jehovah. Ezekiel expounds the same theme in chapter 16 of his prophecy, and the entire book of Hosea deals with the spiritual adultery of Jehovah's wife, Israel.

In similar fashion Christ has a relationship with His Church that is described as Bride and Bridegroom. Ephesians develops this in these words,

So ought men to love their wives as their own bodies. He that loveth his wife loveth himself. For no man ever yet hated his own flesh; but nourisheth and cherisheth it, even as the Lord the church: For we are members of his body, of his flesh, and of his bones. For this cause shall a man leave his father and mother, and shall be joined unto his wife, and they two shall be one flesh. This is a great mystery: but I speak concerning Christ and the church (Ephesians 5:28-32).

It is because of this relationship that Paul writes in 2 Corinthians 11:2;

For I am jealous over you with godly jealousy: for I have espoused you to one husband, that I may present you as a chaste virgin to Christ (2 Corinthians 11:2).

And James accuses the believer of adultery with these words;

Ye adulterers and adulteresses, know ye not that the friendship of the world is enmity with God? whosoever therefore will be a friend of the world is the enemy of God (James 4:3).

This woman, however, is called "the great whore," not the great adulterous. Adultery assumes a relationship to a husband. Whoredom may be committed by one who has no relationship to a husband at all. This woman is the antithesis of the Wife of Jehovah (Israel), or the Bride of Christ (the Church). She is a whore because she has no real relationship to God but has used her religious prestige to purchase earthly and political power to herself. She has given her favors to anyone who would enhance her power or her wealth. This has been her way since her birth.

Nimrod's religion spread across the world to every nation, and while the names of certain deities changed from nation to nation, their essential character and identity remained the same (Jeremiah 7:18; 44:19; Ezekiel 8:14). Dr. H. A. Ironside writes:

"The image of the queen of heaven (Jeremiah chapters 7, 44), with the babe in her arms was seen everywhere, though the names might differ as languages differed.

It became the mystery-religion of Phoenicia, and by the Phoenicians was carried to the ends of the earth. Ashtoreth (Samiramus) and Tammuz, the mother and child became Isis and Horus in Egypt, Aphrodite and Eros in Greece, Venus and Cupid in Italy, and bore many other names in more distant places. Within 1,000

years, Babylonianism had become the religion of the world, which had rejected the Divine revelation."
(Ironside; Lectures on Revelation)

Note that the text says that the great whore *sitteth upon many waters.* We are then told that the many waters are peoples and nations and tongues. Indeed, the religious mysteries of the Babylonian cult have spread to every nation around the world and as the text says again, *the inhabitants of the earth have been made drunk with the wine of her fornication.*

The elixir of Babylonianism (hence of Roman Catholicism), have numbed the consciences of those who drink of her teachings to the need for a genuine work of salvation in their lives. They are assured that the practice of their "religion" will save them in the end, only to be tragically deceived.

Thus, the Babylonian Mysteries spread and in every place her priests courted the favor of the rich and the powerful, the Pharaohs and the Caesars, and the power of the state to sustain her and pay her stipend. In this way she was actually committing adultery with all the world powers and was steeped in the pagan superstition that began in Babylon in Nimrod's day.

These superstitions were so ingrained that rather than exposing them and opposing them, the Church, united under Constantine (313 AD), began to absorb them into itself by renaming them and giving them a "Christian" connotation.

Hence the mother/child cult of paganism, became the Mary and Jesus mother/child, and symbols, festivals and rites of paganism where simply adapted into the Roman Catholic system. The modern heir to the Babylonian mysteries is therefore the Roman Catholic system.

The Babylonian mysteries are foundational to all pagan systems and therefore can be traced in every false religion today.

In the end of the age, it is likely that many of the world's religions will try to unite, and they will no doubt do so under Rome's umbrella. This final form of the apostasy will most likely be the form which John sees riding upon the Beast.

Rev 17:3 *So he carried me away in the spirit into the wilderness: and I saw a woman sit upon a scarlet colored beast, full of names of blasphemy, having seven heads and ten horns.*

There can be no doubt that this is the same Beast that John mentions first in chapter 11, then actually sees and describes in chapter 13, and now sees once again in this chapter. Again, note that the beast is said to be *full of names of blasphemy.* In other words, this Beast has ascribed to himself, the names and attributes that belong only to God.

The horror is that the woman, who in this age pretends to be Christ's own Church, is riding this Beast, whose origin we have learned is satanic. The figure suggests that the Beast is in some sense supporting and carrying the woman, and that the woman is apparently directing and to some extent controlling the Beast.

Rev 17:4, 5 *And the woman was arrayed in purple and scarlet color, and decked with gold and precious stones and pearls, having a golden cup in her hand full of abominations and filthiness of her fornication: And upon her forehead was a name written, MYSTERY, BABYLON THE GREAT, THE MOTHER OF HARLOTS AND ABOMINATIONS OF THE EARTH.*

Gold, scarlet, precious stones and pearls – could anything more closely describe the appearance of the ancient priesthood of the mysteries, or papal Rome, when in full regalia?

The scarlet cassocks of the cardinals, the gold papal crown, the extravagant lace and pearls abounding in ostentatious luxury in contrast to the simple lives and dress of the early Apostles.

It was with the ascendancy of Constantine, that he urged the leaders of the church to begin to adapt the dress of the priests with which the people were familiar. The entire idea of clerical clothing comes, not from Scripture, but from the pagan world.

As Pope Leo is said to have commented to one of his prelates, "We can certainly no longer say with Peter, 'silver and gold have I none.'" To which the prelate is said to have replied, "No my Lord, and neither can we say, 'rise up and walk.'"

The woman is said to have *a golden cup in her hand full of abominations and filthiness of her fornication.* This cup is filled with the practices and teachings of pagan Babylon. The blasphemous assumption of infallibility, the worship of the mother child (even though changing their identity), the establishing of a priestly order (God called it "Nicolaitanism"), the use of candles, bells, beads, orders of virgins, all of it coming directly from pagan Babylon.

Finally, we read, *upon her forehead was a name written, MYSTERY, BABYLON THE GREAT, THE MOTHER OF HARLOTS AND ABOMINATIONS OF THE EARTH.* The defining word, "Mystery," tells us that we are dealing with things which have been disguised and hidden, but which are now being exposed.

Some have asked, "How could Rome be called the Mother of these things when the present form of the Roman Church did not exist until fifth century after Christ?" The answer is, she is the present manifestation of all that Babylon represented, and she has perpetuated Babylon's errors to all her offspring. As we learned before, she has caused all the world to drink of the cup of her fornication.

Rev 17:6 *And I saw the woman drunken with the blood of the saints, and with the blood of the martyrs of Jesus: and when I saw her, I wondered with great admiration.*

Baptist writers from John Foxe* and on have generally held that the Roman Catholic Church martyred some fifty million Baptists beginning in the earliest days of the papists and including the Counter-Reformation period.   * **Foxe's Book of Martyrs**

One Catholic source estimates, "between fifty and sixty-eight million people (not necessarily all Protestants) were killed by the "inquisition" from 1518 and later.* This apparently refers to the Roman Inquisition, the Spanish and perhaps the Portuguese Inquisitions as well. There are even much higher estimates."   *(**This is the time of the Counter-Reformation [my footnote]**).

So even Catholic writers admit a terrible holocaust took place. I wonder what the true number of martyrs is? For remember, as late as the middle of the last century, Rome was persecuting evangelicals in all the countries where she held sway.

We need to look at the phrase, *when I saw her, I wondered with great admiration.* It is not surprising that this translation should confuse those who read it. We can be sure that John did not "admire her" in the usual sense of that word.

Both the word translated "wondered" Gr. θαῦμα; thauma, and the word translated "admiration" Gr. θαυμάζω; thaumazō, are from the same root and while they can imply admiration, it appears from the text that it is more the expression of a desire to know and understand what he has seen. It has been translated, *I wondered with a great wonderment.* I think that becomes clear in the next verse.

Rev 17:7 *And the angel said unto me, Wherefore didst thou marvel?*

I will tell thee the mystery of the woman, and of the beast that carrieth her, which hath the seven heads and ten horns.

The angel asks John, not why he admired the woman, but why he marveled at her (the words *wonder, admiration*, and *marvel* are from the same root). Marvel is defined as that which arrests the attention and causes a person to stand or gaze, or to pause. The thought is that of an inquiry, that is, a desire to know or to understand. I believe that is the way we must interpret this.

Hence, the angel says that he will reveal to John that which he sought, that is, the mystery of the woman and the beast.

Rev 17:8 *The beast that thou sawest was, and is not; and shall ascend out of the bottomless pit, and go into perdition: and they that dwell on the earth shall wonder, whose names were not written in the book of life from the foundation of the world, when they behold the beast that was, and is not, and yet is.*

These verses become particularly perplexing to those who understand the term Beast to always refer to a particular person or individual. Remember, we learned in chapter 13 that the term referred in the first instance to a Kingdom or Empire. We examined Daniel's revelation and found that the word Beast is always used for a Kingdom or and Empire, and not for an individual. Although the term will later apply to one individual, the image of a dragon with seven heads and ten horns is not the Anti-Christ himself, but the Empire from which he emerges.

Therefore, what ascended out of the abyss was not a resurrected person (either Judas, or Nero, or Hitler – as some have conjectured), but a satanically controlled Kingdom (Rome), that disappeared centuries ago (*was not*) but now has reappeared for a time (*now is*).

Rev 17:9 *And here is the mind which hath wisdom. The seven heads are seven mountains, on which the woman sitteth.*

Someone has well observed that no one in John's day would have mistaken this for anything but a reference to Rome, the famous city on seven hills. We have determined above that the woman is representative of Romanism in its final stage and therefore her location is defined so that we cannot mistake her identification.

Rev 17:10, 11 *And there are seven kings: five are fallen, and one is, and the other is not yet come; and when he cometh, he must continue a short space. And the beast that was, and is not, even he is the eighth, and is of the seven, and goeth into perdition.*

We already noted that the seven heads are also seven mountains, and these mountains are also kings (or Kingdoms). We read that five have already come and gone. In John's day the sixth was in power. After that, there seems to be a pause; *the other is not yet come.* This indicates that its coming would be future to John's time of writing, and indeed there is no evidence that it has come yet, so its coming is still future even to us.

As we noted in our study of chapter 13, both Seiss and Walvoord conclude that the Heads, which are kings (which are also mountains), must be interpreted as Kingdoms. A mountain is always a symbol of a kingdom in prophetic symmetry.

> *LORD, by thy favour thou hast made my mountain* (Kingdom) *to stand strong: thou didst hide thy face, and I was troubled* (Psalm 30:7).

> *They shall not hurt nor destroy in all my holy mountain* (Kingdom): *for the earth shall be full of the knowledge of the LORD, as the waters cover the sea* (Isaiah 11:9).

And it shall come to pass in the last days, that the mountain of the LORD'S house shall be established in the top of the mountains (Kingdoms) *and shall be exalted above the hills; and all nations shall flow unto it. And many people shall go and say, Come ye, and let us go up to the mountain of the LORD, to the house of the God of Jacob; and he will teach us of his ways, and we will walk in his paths: for out of Zion shall go forth the law, and the word of the LORD from Jerusalem* (Isaiah 2:2, 3).

Thou sawest till that a stone was cut out without hands, which smote the image upon his feet that were of iron and clay, and brake them to pieces. Then was the iron, the clay, the brass, the silver, and the gold, broken to pieces together, and became like the chaff of the summer threshingfloors; and the wind carried them away, that no place was found for them: and the stone that smote the image became a great mountain (Kingdom), *and filled the whole earth* (Daniel 2:34, 35)

I saw in the night visions, and, behold, one like the Son of man came with the clouds of heaven, and came to the Ancient of days, and they brought him near before him. And there was given him dominion, and glory, and a kingdom, that all people, nations, and languages, should serve him: his dominion is an everlasting dominion, which shall not pass away, and his kingdom that which shall not be destroyed (Daniel 7:13, 14).

The final two passages above are of the same event, the taking of the Kingdom by the Lord Jesus Christ. Note the use of the symbol of a mountain to represent a kingdom in these passages.

I must conclude therefore that these heads, which are mountains which are kings refer to kingdoms, some of which are in the past and some yet future. Let's try to identify them.

When the Bible deals with any subject prophetically, it is always as it relates to Israel. That is, one does not find the kingdoms of the far-east or the west mentioned in prophecy. In Scripture are found only those kingdoms which have affected the nation Israel.

So what kingdoms have affected Israel from the time of her beginning. Well, the first would be the kingdom of Egypt where she spent 400 years and first became a nation. The next would be the kingdom of Assyria which came and carried ten of the tribes captive in 721 BC. Next would be the Babylonian Empire under Nebuchadnezzar that conquered Judah in 586 BC, then the Medo-Persian Empire, then the Greek empire, and finally the Roman Empire.

The text says, "five of these have fallen." In the list above, in John's day, Egypt, Assyria, Babylon, Medo-Persia and Greece (five), had come and gone. They had all indeed fallen.

The text says that, *one is,* in other words the existing empire at the time of John writing, which was Rome [number 6], *and the other is not yet come* [number 7]. It is obvious that Rome was still an empire even long after John's day. Hence Rome would answer to the one that *is.*

Next there is to be *the other* (that) *is not yet come* [number 7]. Since the fall of Rome, no single empire has risen that would answer to this. However, from other prophecies, we can deduce that it will be a composite power made up of parts of the former Roman Empire.

In all probability, the present European Union comes very close to fulfilling this or at least being a precursor to it. This is said to "continue a short space." In other words, this will be only a transitional step toward the final kingdom.

And the beast that was, and is not, even he is the eighth, and is of the seven, and goeth into perdition.

When the final kingdom comes to power [number 8], it will be in the form of an individual leader.

He will come out of the same Empire as the former kings, but he is particularly said to go into perdition. In other words, this one is the one Paul calls, *The man of sin*, and *the son of perdition* and *that Wicked One* (2 Thessalonians 2), and will be ultimately destroyed (Gr. ἀπώλεια; apōleia; implying utter destruction – basically eternal damnation).

Now that we have established the Kingdoms that are seen here, it is important that we realize that the Great Whore, the false religious system of Nimrod, rode upon each and all of them. Joseph A. Seiss makes this abundantly clear in the following passage.

> "On these seven great mountains the woman rides. It is not on one alone . . . but upon the whole seven headed beast that she sits.
>
> These seven powers, each and all, supported the woman as their joy and pride, and she accepted and used them . . . as surely as Rome in John's day, and Greece, Persia, Babylon, Assyria, and Egypt before Rome existed and bore sway on earth as regal mountains, so surely and conspicuously were they each and all ridden by this great harlot. <u>They were each and all the lovers supporters, and defenders of organized falsehood in religion, the patrons of idolatry, the foster friends of all manner of spiritual harlotry</u>."
> **Joseph A. Seiss; The Apocalypse pp. 394**

Rev 17:12 *And the ten horns which thou sawest are ten kings, which have received no kingdom as yet; but receive power as kings one hour with the beast.*

As we have noted before, this final phase of the empire comes into being as a confederation. There are ten kings or rulers in the beginning. Daniel gives us more information about this.

After this I saw in the night visions, and behold a fourth beast (Empire), *dreadful and terrible, and strong exceedingly; and it had great iron teeth: it devoured and brake in pieces, and stamped the residue with the feet of it: and it was diverse from all the beasts that were before it; and it had ten horns. I considered the horns, and, behold, there came up among them another little horn, before whom there were three of the first horns plucked up by the roots: and, behold, in this horn were eyes like the eyes of man, and a mouth speaking great things* (Daniel 7:7,8).

Now we must remember that Daniel's prophecies begin with the Babylonian Empire (the Egyptian and Assyrian Empires were already history when Daniel wrote).

So, when Daniel numbers the empires, he begins with Babylon and the "fourth" refers to Rome. What Daniel sees is in the final stages of that empire.

Daniel sees the ascendancy of the "little horn" which becomes the sole ruler and is identified as the one we call the Anti-Christ. It is at this point that the designation Beast, is no longer applied to the Empire itself, but to the one whom the Empire has brought forth, the "Little Horn" or Anti-Christ.

Rev 17:13, 14 *These have one mind, and shall give their power and strength unto the beast. These shall make war with the Lamb, and the Lamb shall overcome them: for he is Lord of lords, and King of kings: and they that are with him are called, and chosen, and faithful.*

Verse 13 indicates that while the Beast may have come to power as one of the horns (Daniel 7), the other horns give their power over to him completely and he will then reign supreme.

Verse 14 looks ahead to the end and sees the Beast and all of those who follow him making war with the Lamb.

This is a reference to Armageddon and to the outcome of that event which will mean the total victory of Christ and His saints.

However, on a timeline, there are a number of things that will happen before that occurs. As we look at the next verses we get a better understanding of the timing.

Rev 17:15 *And he saith unto me, The waters which thou sawest, where the whore sitteth, are peoples, and multitudes, and nations, and tongues.*

Once again the angel refers to the universal reach of the one he calls *The Whore*. She sits on many waters. The waters are interpreted as representative of peoples, and multitudes, and nations, and tongues.

In other words, just as we learned in regard to the cup of her abominations, she has made all nations drunk with the wine of her fornication, so, we see here her control over the nations. We will try to interpret that clearly as we sum up this section.

Rev 17:16, 17 *And the ten horns which thou sawest upon the beast, these shall hate the whore, and shall make her desolate and naked, and shall eat her flesh, and burn her with fire. For God hath put in their hearts to fulfil his will, and to agree, and give their kingdom unto the beast, until the words of God shall be fulfilled.*

What we have been seeing up until now has been the Woman, riding, and therefore directing in some fashion the Beast. This will be the condition during the first half of the Tribulation period. At the middle of the "Tribulation Week" that all changes.

When the Anti-Christ is proclaimed the world Deliverer and Messiah, and when his image is set up in the Holy of Holies in Jerusalem, the apostate Babylonian Whore will suddenly become a rival system and a political liability rather than an asset.

The true attitude of the kings of the earth toward her is revealed in Revelation 17:16. It is the attitude which men have toward any prostitute, that of patronizing disgust.

Now that the desires of these kings have been satisfied with her, they *"hate the whore, and shall make her desolate and naked, and shall eat her flesh and burn her with fire."* In short, they will totally destroy the One World Apostate Religion and wipe her and her priests and ministers and hierarchy from the earth.

Verse 17 tells us that these wicked kings are actually used by God as His instrument against that which has deceived the world for so long. Wreaking God's vengeance upon her, they destroy her forever. She is no longer needed and so men, who have long seen and known her hypocrisy and sham, turn all of the inbred disgust for her into action and destroy her utterly.

This action thus makes room for the last unified false religion; *they give their kingdom unto the Beast.* Revelation 13:8 tells us that <u>the whole unregenerate world will then be united in the degrading debauchery of worshiping the Beast, and making him their god</u>.

Rev 17:18 *And the woman which thou sawest is that great city, which reigneth over the kings of the earth.*

Certainly, in John's day this verse could have no other meaning than the city of Rome, which indeed reigned over the kings of the earth. But remember, we are dealing with mysteries.

REVIEW ?

- Why is the false religious system called Mystery Babylon?

- Who were Nimrod, Semiramus, Tammuz?

- Who is the heir apparent of all this false religious system in our time?

- What will happen to the Harlot in the middle of the Tribulation Week?

- What worship will then replace the Babylonian cult?

CHAPTER 25   Babylon Destroyed

Revelation 18:1 – 24

A careful comparison of the destruction of Babylon, described in Revelation 17, 18, reveals that these appear to be two different events. The *Great Whore* in Revelation 17, symbolizing the false religious system that Babylon had birthed, was associated with political power but was not the political power itself. Her destruction by the ten kings (17:16), apparently brought no mourning from anyone. By contrast the destruction of Babylon in chapter 18, brings loud lamentation from the earth's political and economic powers.

In chapter 17 that "religious" phase of the Babylonian system was destroyed and consumed by the 10 kings about the middle of the Tribulation. Here, in chapter 18, the destruction of Commercial Babylon comes directly from God, and it is probable that this is an enlarged explanation of what was described in Revelation 16:17 – 19 and is caught up in the destruction that is brought by the final vial or bowl of the wrath of God.

Finally, the destruction of the Whore (Religious Babylon), takes place in the middle of the Tribulation Week. The destruction of the political/economic/commercial Babylon takes place at the very end of that period and immediately before Christ's Second Advent.

However, both phases are identified as *Babylon* since it was the fountainhead of all false religion and satanically framed social, commercial and political systems.

Rev 18:1 *And after these things I saw another angel come down from heaven, having great power; and the earth was lightened with his glory.*

The angel is said to have great power. Peter reminds us that angels are, *greater in power and might* (2 Peter 2:11) than we are. There are ascending ranks of angels and so the greater in order the greater in power. This angel is obviously of a high order in the angelic host and the earth itself was lightened by his presence.

Rev 18:2, 3 *And he cried mightily with a strong voice, saying, Babylon the great is fallen, is fallen, and is become the habitation of devils, and the hold of every foul spirit, and a cage of every unclean and hateful bird. For all nations have drunk of the wine of the wrath of her fornication, and the kings of the earth have committed fornication with her, and the merchants of the earth are waxed rich through the abundance of her delicacies.*

Once again, the announcement of Babylon's fall is given and with it, a description of what followed. Babylon became the habitation of demons, and foul spirits. Where the Spirit of the Lord has departed, wicked spirits always fill the void. Hence, we are given to understand that the entire religious structure, of which the great whore is a symbol, is led and controlled and directed by the forces of Satan himself.

Because of her wealth and power and influence, the rulers have desired her favors and the merchants have profited by her dealings. The phrase, the abundance of her delicacies, is explained in verses 11 – 19 where her delicacies are enumerated and described.

This verse also reminds us that all the world drank at the cup of her false and devilish doctrine for which, both she and they will be judged. In other words, not only the source of the corruption is judged, but those who became partakers of it will be judged as well. And that brings us to the next verse.

Rev 18:4, 5 *And I heard another voice from heaven, saying, Come out of her, my people, that ye be not partakers of her sins, and that ye receive not of her plagues. For her sins have reached unto heaven, and God hath remembered her iniquities.*

Note that the command and invitation comes from heaven, and it is an invitation to those who actually belong to God. Which raises the question, it is possible for true people of faith, born-again believers to be caught up in such a cesspool of iniquity as that represented by the Great Whore? And the answer seems clearly to be, yes. God's people do get involved at times in systems of error, but the call is clearly to come out of them and identify themselves with the One who is the Truth.

Of course, to separate from this world renown but apostate system in the environment that will exist during that time, will carry with it a heavy price. If the Whore is known of old as one *drunken with the blood of the saints and the martyrs of Jesus,* it is unlikely that now, at the very zenith of her power, she would permit any to escape without putting them to death. Nevertheless, the eternal benefit of being received with honor into God's presence will more than compensate for the temporary pain which the Whore can inflict.

Rev 18:6 - 8 *Reward her even as she rewarded you, and double unto her double according to her works: in the cup which she hath filled fill to her double. How much she hath glorified herself, and lived deliciously, so much torment and sorrow give her: for she saith in her heart, I sit a queen, and am no widow, and shall see no sorrow. Therefore shall her plagues come in one day, death, and mourning, and famine; and she shall be utterly burned with fire: for strong is the Lord God who judgeth her.*

Payday someday! How quickly we forget that, *God shall bring every work into judgment, with every secret thing, whether it be good, or whether it be evil (Ecclesiastes 12:14),* and that *every idle word that men shall speak, they shall give account thereof in the day of judgment* (Matthew 12:36).

The Great Whore has disgraced His honor, perverted His Word, glorified herself rather than God, and tormented and killed His saints, and now it is payback time.

The woman represents an earthly system – that is to say, she is not eternal as a person is, therefore she must receive her judgment in time, not in eternity, and that time has now come. The Divine Judge sentences her to reap what she has sown, but we must always remember that the reaping is always greater than the sowing. She must now receive double for all she has done.

As we have already seen, while the ten kings destroyed religious Babylon in the middle of the week, now God himself pours His final vial of wrath upon her to totally destroy her so that we read, *Therefore shall her plagues come in one day, death, and mourning, and famine; and she shall be utterly burned with fire: for strong is the Lord God who judgeth her.*

Rev 18:9, 10 *And the kings of the earth, who have committed fornication and lived deliciously with her, shall bewail her, and lament for her, when they shall see the smoke of her burning, Standing afar off for the fear of her torment, saying, Alas, alas, that great city Babylon, that mighty city! for in one hour is thy judgment come.*

This verse uses the word "city" twice. So, we must ask, are we dealing with the literal destruction of a city in this passage? It is this assumption that has led some in our time to insist that the literal historic city of Babylon must be rebuilt and become the world financial center for this prophecy to be fulfilled. Much of the speculation has centered around the reconstruction effort begun by Saddam Hussein during his late reign. In fact, I don't remember ever reading a writer that believed Babylon would be rebuilt until the Gulf War put the spotlight on this area.

That brings to mind a principle we must not ignore. We must always be careful to interpret world events in the light of prophecy, but we must never interpret prophecy in the light of world events. I fear that is what has happened here.

In my study of this passage I carefully considered those claims. I researched the present state of the city of Babylon and the likelihood that she would become once again the financial, commercial and cultural center of the world. I must confess I found no evidence of that, and a lot of evidence that such is entirely unlikely.

But if we are dealing with a city that embodies the Babylonian system of godless commercialism and corrupt culture, perhaps we might look at what modern city could most closely reflect that. I looked for the top commercial centers of the world and discovered that New York and London top the list, with both cities miles ahead of their nearest rivals.

New York City tops every other city on both versions of the Global City Economic Power Index. New York's metro economy is much larger than London's, with total economic output of $1.4 trillion compared to $836 billion for London.

New York City tops even national economies. The city is comparable to the fourth top national economy on earth. It is larger than Germany and a trillion dollars larger than the economy of the entire United Kingdom. New York City is the top economic, commercial, and cultural center of the world.

The text tells us that the destruction of this city was so traumatic that the commercial world was left weeping. I can't imagine the financial barons of the world getting very upset over a possible destruction of the historic city of Babylon, but I can fully imagine their consternation if New York were to be destroyed.

Now, I am not suggesting that this prophecy is about the destruction of New York City.

It is about the destruction of the Babylonian system of finance, commerce and culture. But if I have to point my finger at an actual city that fully embodies that system, facts would force me to point to New York, at least at the time of writing.

Which raises the question, is it really a city that is destroyed or a system? When the ten kings destroyed the false religious system that is unquestionably centered in Rome, the system was destroyed, but there seems to be no indication that the city of Rome was necessarily destroyed with it. It may be that the same holds for the final destruction of the commercial center as well. Could it be that the entire structure of the world's economy and culture comes tumbling down in a single hour, not as a single city but as a total system?

One of the best researched and clearest reasoned presentations I have read on the end-time Babylon was written by Baptist pastor Rev. Dan Hayden shortly after the Gulf War. Comparing all the Scripture he concluded that the historic city of Babylon is not what is in view in the book of Revelation, but rather the spirit of a system that throughout Scripture is symbolized by the word Babylon. He writes, "The spirit of the Babylonian Empire continues to live in the godless systems of our world as Satan seeks to gain ascendancy over the kingdoms of men. Like Babylon, the world (system) will pass away (1 John 2:17) and will become merely the world that was."

Wall Street hates anything that disrupts the smooth flow of commerce. The utter trauma of the loss of this entire financial/commercial structure will bring a degree of trauma unknown until then. If men jumped to their deaths when the stock market crashed leading to the great depression, how much more will they despair when the entire Babylonian system is destroyed?

Rev 18:11 - 14 *And the merchants of the earth shall weep and mourn over her; for no man buyeth their merchandise any more: The merchandise of gold, and silver, and precious stones, and of pearls, and fine linen, and purple, and silk, and scarlet, and all thyine wood, and all manner vessels of ivory, and all manner vessels of most precious wood, and of brass, and iron, and marble, And cinnamon, and odours, and ointments, and frankincense, and wine, and oil, and fine flour, and wheat, and beasts, and sheep, and horses, and chariots, and slaves, and souls of men. And the fruits that thy soul lusted after are departed from thee, and all things which were dainty and goodly are departed from thee, and thou shalt find them no more at all.*

There is something here that seems reminiscent of Paul's experience in Ephesus.

> *And the same time there arose no small stir about that way. For a certain man named Demetrius, a silversmith, which made silver shrines for Diana, brought no small gain unto the craftsmen; Whom he called together with the workmen of like occupation, and said, Sirs, ye know that by this craft we have our wealth. Moreover ye see and hear, that not alone at Ephesus, but almost throughout all Asia, this Paul hath persuaded and turned away much people, saying that they be no gods, which are made with hands: So that not only this our craft is in danger to be set at nought; but also that the temple of the great goddess Diana should be despised, and her magnificence should be destroyed, whom all Asia and the world worshippeth. And when they heard these sayings, they were full of wrath, and cried out, saying, Great is Diana of the Ephesians* (Acts 19:23-28)

The uproar at Ephesus was not over religion, but over the profit that religion had brought. Just so, the tears of the merchants were not for the loss of the Whore (Babylon), but for the loss of the profit they made from her.

Many follow and seem to be zealous for religion when it is popular and profit can be made by doing so, but quickly forsake it when it is persecuted.

The author John Bunyan said it well, "Those who take up religion to gain the world, will lay it down again for the same." The world is the goal, religion only the means to obtaining it. When it no longer can deliver, it is quickly rejected.

Rev 18:15 – 17a *The merchants of these things, which were made rich by her, shall stand afar off for the fear of her torment, weeping and wailing, And saying, Alas, alas, that great city, that was clothed in fine linen, and purple, and scarlet, and decked with gold, and precious stones, and pearls! For in one hour so great riches is come to nought.*

All gone – all empty. Listen as John reminds us, *And the world passeth away, and the lust thereof: but he that doeth the will of God abideth for ever* (1 John 2:17).

This is exactly why Paul writes, *If ye then be risen with Christ, seek those things which are above, where Christ sitteth on the right hand of God. Set your affection on things above, not on things on the earth. For ye are dead, and your life is hid with Christ in God. When Christ, who is our life, shall appear, then shall ye also appear with him in glory* (Colossians 3:1-4).

Some years ago while I was reading a news magazine I stumbled across an article on insurance. In the article was the picture of a palatial home completely engulfed in flames. In the foreground of the picture a woman had just collapsed into the arms of two firemen, and under the picture were these words, "All we ever gave our lives for is gone." I will never forget that picture, and I cried out to God to keep me from ever giving my life for what fire (or anything else) could destroy in a moment. The world of finance and culture was fully invested in Babylon, and in one hour, it was all gone.

Rev 18:17b - 19 *And every shipmaster, and all the company in ships, and sailors, and as many as trade by sea, stood afar off, And cried when they saw the smoke of her burning, saying, What city is like unto this great city! And they cast dust on their heads, and cried, weeping and wailing, saying, Alas, alas, that great city, wherein were made rich all that had ships in the sea by reason of her costliness! for in one hour is she made desolate.*

Although we cannot be dogmatic, it appears that with the demise of the system of Babylonian religion and economy, the entire commercial market that rested upon her collapsed with it. This initial collapse took place with the destruction of the Whore by the ten kings. It would appear that when that happened the Beast intervened to set up His own system of commerce, a system set up by the Beast and the False Prophet which we know comes at the middle of the week.

> *And he causeth all, both small and great, rich and poor, free and bond, to receive a mark in their right hand, or in their foreheads: And that no man might buy or sell, save he that had the mark, or the name of the beast, or the number of his name* (Revelation 13:16, 17).

Now, as we approach the coming of Christ to set up His Kingdom and the end of the great charade, all that is of the kingdom of darkness is swept away.

Rev 18:20 Rejoice over her, thou heaven, and ye holy apostles and prophets; for God hath avenged you on her.

In this last section we have heard the moans and the wailing of the earth-dwellers over the destruction of Babylon. Now we hear a quite different sound.

The atmosphere is sheer joy in heaven. Up until now, heaven has heard the groans and the prayers of those who were martyred as they cried out for vindication. No more!

Now, and from here on, the music of heaven is an anthem of pure rejoicing. God has won the victory over the great Whore, who for so long a time had blasphemed His name and persecuted His saints. Now this godless system is forever destroyed, and the saints are rejoicing!

Rev 18:21 *And a mighty angel took up a stone like a great millstone, and cast it into the sea, saying, Thus with violence shall that great city Babylon be thrown down, and shall be found no more at all.*

The scene is reminiscent of a passage toward the end of Jeremiah's prophecy. Seraiah, one of the captives of Babylon had been sent from Babylon to Israel and was returning to Babylon. Jeremiah wrote in a book a detailed prophecy of the future of Babylon and gave it to him to take back and read to the captives. Then he instructed him what to do with the book.

> *And Jeremiah said to Seraiah, When thou comest to Babylon, and shalt see, and shalt read all these words; Then shalt thou say, O LORD, thou hast spoken against this place, to cut it off, that none shall remain in it, neither man nor beast, but that it shall be desolate for ever. And it shall be, when thou hast made an end of reading this book, that thou shalt bind a stone to it, and cast it into the midst of Euphrates: And thou shalt say, Thus shall Babylon sink, and shall not rise from the evil that I will bring upon her: and they shall be weary. Thus far are the words of Jeremiah* (Jeremiah 51:61 – 64).

In similar fashion the mighty angel casts a millstone into the waters of the great sea, and proclaims the violent and sudden end of the Babylonian false system.

Rev 18:22 - 24 *And the voice of harpers, and musicians, and of pipers, and trumpeters, shall be heard no more at all in thee; and no craftsman, of whatsoever craft he be, shall be found any more in thee; and the sound of a millstone shall be heard no more at all in thee; And the light of a candle shall shine no more at all in thee; and the* *voice of the bridegroom and of the bride shall be heard no more at all in thee: for thy merchants were the great men of the earth; for by thy sorceries were all nations deceived. And in her was found the blood of prophets, and of saints, and of all that were slain upon the earth.*

Not only is the wealth and luxury gone forever from this harlot, but all the singing, the laughter, the happy occasion, the profitable occupation, the demonic incantations that where the fear and wonder of the earth – all is gone. It is all silent now. As Jeremiah once predicted only doleful creatures inhabit her. She is forever ruined. *The laughter of fools is as the crackling of thorns under a pot.* It is empty and hollow and bitter.

A SUMMARY
These chapters (17, 18) have been the most difficult in our study to interpret and understand of all we have studied thus far. The material they present spans time from the beginning of Babel to the second advent of Christ. These two chapters describe the course of the Babylonian Religious and commercial system from its rise to world power to its final destruction. They should be studied carefully.

REVIEW:
The following facts should be noted:

1. The "Great Whore" represents a false religious system (Babylon was the source of all ancient and modern idolatry).

2. This system bears influence over many people ("sitteth upon many waters" 17: 1).

3. The world rulers have given her what she sought in turn for her favors of support and backing ("the kings have committed fornication..." 17: 2).

4. Her influence has had a stupefying effect upon her subjects so that they have become spiritually insensitive ("inhabitants... made drunk" 17: 2).

5. She has arrogated to herself the titles and prerogatives of God ("full of names of blasphemy" 17: 3).

6. She is extremely wealthy and licentious (17: 4).

7. She is a combination of the religious confusion and error of the ages, and is at the same time the "mother" of it all. This implies that in its final form, "Mystery Babylon" will be a world religious system composed of all apostate religious groups (17:5).

8. She is ever and has ever been the arch foe of true believers (17:6).

9. The seat of her power will be at Rome ("seven mountains, on which the woman sitteth" 17:9).

10. She will come to the zenith of her power allied with and carried by the Beast (17:3).

---

11. When the Anti-Christ (called the Beast) achieves total power, the ten kings who rule with him will totally destroy the great whore (17:16, 17).

12. When she is gone, the world will worship the Beast and he will be the sole means of survival (13:12, 17).

13. Just before Christ's victorious advent, the final vial of His wrath will be poured upon Babylon (the commercial system), and the total destruction of all she represents will occur in a single hour (18:10).

14. There will be great despair and mourning by the earth-dwellers, but heaven will rejoice over her destruction. All the singing, all the joy, all the mirth of this world system will be silent forever, while all the choirs of heaven will sing in thunderous tones of rejoicing (18:9-24).

Chapter 26 A Wedding & A Warrior

Revelation 19:1 – 21

Rev 19:1 *And after these things I heard a great voice* (Gr. megas phone') *of much people in heaven, saying, Alleluia; Salvation, and glory, and honor, and power, unto the Lord our God.*

The expression, "Hallelujah" occurs in the New Testament only four times, all of them in Revelation 19. This chapter has been called the "Biblical Hallelujah Chorus."

- The hallelujahs open the chapter and as the chapter closes the Lake of Fire is opened to receive its first victims.

- Two great suppers are recorded: the marriage supper of the Lamb and the feast of the carrion birds after the War of Armageddon.

- Christ is seen as both the Bridegroom with His Bride, and the Warrior King with His army.

- Two armies are seen on the field of battle, the army of the Beast, and the army of the King of Kings.

Finally, we must not miss the words, *after these things* (Gr. *meta tauta*). It signals a new section in this book, just as it did in Chapter 4:1. This will be the final time this expression appears, telling us that with the beginning of Chapter 19 we are entering the final section of the book of Revelation.

Rev 19:2, 3 *For true and righteous are his judgments: for he hath judged the great whore, which did corrupt the earth with her fornication, and hath avenged the blood of his servants at her hand. And again they said, Alleluia. And her smoke rose up for ever and ever.*

As we closed chapter 18, we saw the end of all the world's pleasure and mirth and joy and music. All production, all craft, all commerce is ended. The pale of a deathly silence falls over the earth as the smoke of the destruction of Babylon ascends.

But in heaven it is very different. Voices are shouting the praises of God and rejoicing has begun. God's justice has fallen at last upon the Great Whore that had shed the blood of martyrs and saints down through the ages. It is as if all the perverted and empty joys of earth are now replaced with the holy and heavenly joys of heaven. God's acts of vengeance are seen as just and right and glory and honor is paid to Him.

And this chorus of praise repeats itself again and again as the pent-up emotions of persecuted and martyred saints, rises in a grand crescendo of thanksgiving and joy. This world likes to talk about getting closure – getting justice - here the saints, at last, see justice served. They had been the victims of the Babylonian world system ruled over by the Beast, now they rejoice in the justice of her utter destruction.

Rev 19:4 *And the four and twenty elders and the four beasts fell down and worshipped God that sat on the throne, saying, Amen; Alleluia.*

The initial anthems of praise seem to have come from that great multitude that no man could number of martyrs out of the Tribulation. But now they are joined by the saints of the Church Age and by the Living Creatures. Choir now joins with choir singing the praises of the Lamb and the glories of His victory.

Rev 19:5 *And a voice came out of the throne, saying, Praise our God, all ye his servants, and ye that fear him, both small and great.*

The praises of heaven's multitude are now endorsed, encouraged and goaded forward by a voice from the Throne. There have been many dark scenes in the book of Revelation, but from this point onward there is only jubilant song and blessing upon blessing for the redeemed. There will be one final battle before the Kingdoms of this world become the Kingdoms of our Lord and of His Christ, but heaven is already having a victory celebration.

Rev 19:6 *And I heard as it were the voice of a great multitude, and as the voice of many waters, and as the voice of mighty thunderings, saying, Alleluia: for the Lord God omnipotent reigneth.*

It would appear here that all heaven joins in this anthem of rejoicing. John said he heard it, someday we too will not only hear it but be a part of it. It was *the voice,* (singular), *of a great multitude.* How significant is that? When there is a multitude, there are usually many voices, shouting many different things. But there is a harmony in heaven and every voice blends with ever other voice in the singular praise of our great Savior.

THE MARRIAGE ANNOUNCEMENT

Rev 19:7 *Let us be glad and rejoice, and give honor to him: for the marriage of the Lamb is come, and his wife hath made herself ready.*

To understand this we need to be clear on who is included in the phrase, *His wife.*

To be sure, Israel is referred to in the Old Testament as the "wife of Jehovah." At Sinai, Israel entered into a voluntary covenant with Jehovah that was like the covenant made between a man and a woman.

But like any marriage covenant, the promises of the covenant must be kept. Israel failed terribly, and multiple passages of Scripture characterize her failure as adultery.

The prophet Jeremiah develops this theme beginning in chapter 3. Ezekiel addresses the same in very vivid language in chapters 16. The entire book of Hosea dramatizes Israel's unfaithfulness, God's judgment in putting her away, His continuing love for her, finally providing redemption and promising to reunite her with Himself at last.

But this wedding, concerns a Bride that is a pure virgin, kept for her Bridegroom. It is that simile, Paul uses in the following passages:

> *For I am jealous over you with godly jealousy: for I have espoused you to one husband, that I may present you as a chaste virgin to Christ* (2 Corinthians 11:2).

> *For this cause shall a man leave his father and mother, and shall be joined unto his wife, and they two shall be one flesh. This is a great mystery: but I speak concerning Christ and the church* (Ephesians 5:31, 32).

The one presented to her lover and Savior is the Church victorious, raptured and judged at the Bema Seat of Christ and prepared to reign with Him forever.

Rev 19:8 *And to her was granted that she should be arrayed in fine linen, clean and white: for the fine linen is the righteousness of saints.*

Each of us who are married remember our wedding. Beside the experience of our own salvation, it is usually the biggest event in our lives.

After all the flowers and finery, the music and train of attendants, the organ strikes a very regal tone and the entire audience stands to get its first glimpse of the bride.

Down the long corridor she comes, breathtakingly beautiful, in flowing white satin and lace (traditionally the symbols of her virgin purity), to be presented to her waiting bridegroom.

So, John pictures for us the heavenly Bride, arrayed like her earthly counterpart, in the white gown of purity, justly bestowed upon her. Paul's words again seem apropos; *This is a great mystery: but I speak concerning Christ and the Church.*

The Marriage of the Lamb will be the greatest and most exciting event the Church will ever experience. She who was despised on earth will be forever exalted to the highest place in heaven and reign with her beloved throughout all eternity.

Rev 19:9 *And he saith unto me, Write, Blessed are they which are called unto the marriage supper of the Lamb. And he saith unto me, These are the true sayings of God.*

After the wedding comes the joyous marriage supper of the Lamb. What all is involved we are not specifically told. Some believe the marriage supper takes place in heaven. Others believe that the entire Millennial Kingdom is to be identified with this event. Some of the evidence for this view is found in the frequent use which Jesus often made of the wedding supper analogy in His parables. Remember, Jesus was speaking to a Jewish audience and many of the parables have a direct application to that nation and its position in the future Kingdom.

We have tried to clearly demonstrate that the Bride here is the Raptured, victorious New Testament Church, the Bride of Christ. If that is kept clearly in mind, then many of the parables which Jesus spoke to His Jewish audience begin to take on a much clearer meaning.

Remember, the Church did not begin until Pentecost.

John the Baptist, the forerunner of the Messiah, recognized that although Jesus would be the Bridegroom, he (John), would not be a part of the Bride, but merely a guest, at the wedding. John said, "I am a friend of the Bridegroom."

He that hath the bride is the bridegroom: but the friend of the bridegroom, which standeth and heareth him, rejoiceth greatly because of the bridegroom's voice: this my joy therefore is fulfilled (John 3:29).

Take, for instance the parable found in Matthew 22:1-14. The entire story is about a King who makes a marriage supper for his son. Those who are first invited represent the Jewish nation. They scoffed at and ignored the invitation. Then the King expands the invitation to all who would respond. And even of those, the guests must be attired in the wedding garment furnished by the King. The entire parable warns Israel about loosing their place at the table. And note that in introducing these remarks, Jesus used the formula, *The Kingdom of Heaven is like. . .* It is heaven's Kingdom set up here on earth and celebrated with a wedding feast.

Jesus uses the same formula in His parable of the ten virgins (Matthew 25:1-13). Once again it was a warning to those who would attend the wedding celebration (the Millennial Kingdom wedding feast). But note, they are not the Bride (that position is reserved for the Church), they are the invited guests. Nevertheless, John says they are blessed to be called to the Marriage Supper of the Lamb.

In the case of the Centurion whose servant Jesus healed with only His word of command, Jesus said; *Verily I say unto you, I have not found so great faith, no, not in Israel. And I say unto you, That many shall come from the east and west, and shall sit down with Abraham, and Isaac, and Jacob, in the kingdom of heaven. But the children of the kingdom shall be cast out into outer darkness: there shall be weeping and gnashing of teeth* (Matthew 8:10-12).

Rev 19:10 *And I fell at his feet to worship him. And he said unto me, See thou do it not: I am thy fellowservant, and of thy brethren that have the testimony of Jesus: worship God: for the testimony of Jesus is the spirit of prophecy.*

This statement by the angel is a golden key to interpreting all prophecy and in fact all of the Word of God. The intent of all the Scripture is to testify to the One to whom all honor and all praise belongs. When we study Scripture, and especially prophetic Scripture, we should understand that its purpose is to reveal Jesus Christ – His person, His perfection, His purposes, His promises, His power, His passion, His patience and His purity. *The testimony of Jesus is the spirit of prophecy.*

Rev 19:11-16 *And I saw heaven opened, and behold a white horse; and he that sat upon him was called Faithful and True, and in righteousness he doth judge and make war. His eyes were as a flame of fire, and on his head were many crowns; and he had a name written, that no man knew, but he himself. And he was clothed with a vesture dipped in blood: and his name is called The Word of God. And the armies which were in heaven followed him upon white horses, clothed in fine linen, white and clean. And out of his mouth goeth a sharp sword, that with it he should smite the nations: and he shall rule them with a rod of iron: and he treadeth the winepress of the fierceness and wrath of Almighty God. And he hath on his vesture and on his thigh a name written, KING OF KINGS, AND LORD OF LORDS.*

The phrase "I saw," is found 39 times in the book of Revelation, and always announces a new vision given to John. Beginning with verse eleven the entire picture takes a drastic change. Heaven is open, and the King is coming.

What is presented to us next is so full and so glorious that we must take each part of the vision, one segment at a time, and explore what we can learn as we do.

There are at least twelve separate parts to this vision.

1. A white horse; and he that sat upon him *was* called Faithful and True,
2. In righteousness he doth judge and make war.
3. His eyes *were* as a flame of fire,
4. On his head *were* many crowns;
5. He had a name written, that no man knew, but he himself.
6. He *was* clothed with a vesture dipped in blood:
7. His name is called The Word of God.
8. The armies *which were* in heaven followed him upon white horses, clothed in fine linen, white and clean.
9. Out of his mouth goeth a sharp sword, that with it he should smite the nations:
10. He shall rule them with a rod of iron:
11. He treadeth the winepress of the fierceness and wrath of Almighty God.
12. He hath on *his* vesture and on his thigh a name written, KING OF KINGS, AND LORD OF LORDS.

Let's look at these 12 things one at a time:

1. (A white horse); ***He that sat upon him was called Faithful and True.*** He is Faithful and True because every promise has been kept and every decision and verdict right. The white horse symbolizes both purity and victory. It was always the choice of the conquering warrior as he would lead his triumphant army to victory.

2. ***In righteousness he doth judge and make war.*** Compare the following verses: Isaiah 31:4; 42:13;

59:16-18; Habakkuk 3:11-13; Zechariah 14:3.

3. ***His eyes were as a flame of fire,*** (comp. 1:14); total penetration – He sees and knows all. His gaze in judgment is the consuming fire of the judgment seat. *Every man's work shall be made manifest: for the day shall declare it, because it shall be revealed by fire; and the fire shall try every man's work of what sort it is* (1 Corinthians 3:13).

4. ***On his head were many crowns;*** (Gr. *diadem* a crown or a headband, sometimes adorned with jewels, formerly worn by monarchs in Asia Minor and other parts of the East. Each of the "many crowns," would symbolize a kingdom over which he was ruler.

5. ***He had a name written, that no man knew, but he himself.*** It is not that the name cannot be read – it is rather that no one can enter into its meaning or significance. Christ is the ineffable, indescribable One (Matthew 11:27).

6. ***He was clothed with a vesture dipped in blood***: Isaiah 63:1-4, not His own blood, but the blood of His enemies.

7. ***His name is called The Word of God.*** Jesus Christ is the full expression of God – *he that hath seen me hath seen the Father* (Jn.14:9)

   John 1:1 *In the beginning was the Word, and the Word was with God, and the Word was God.*

   John 1:14 *And the Word was made flesh, and dwelt among us, (and we beheld his glory, the glory as of the only begotten of the Father,) full of grace and truth.*

John 1:18 *No man hath seen God at any time; the only begotten Son, which is in the bosom of the Father, he hath* <u>declared</u> *him.* (Gr. ἐξηγέομαι; exēgeomai; to *consider out* loud, that is, *unfold:* - declare). <u>Christ, by life and testimony spoke God forth</u>.

8. ***And the armies which were in heaven followed him upon white horses, clothed in fine linen, white and clean***. The Bride is not the army. The army is not the Church. The reference is to the "hosts" of angelic beings that He commands. Notice it is plural "armies." This is the meaning of the expression, *the Lord of Hosts* (found over 484 times in the Old Testament).

   Psalm 46:11 *The LORD of hosts is with us; the God of Jacob is our refuge. Selah.* <u>Read this Psalm</u> in connection with this passage in Revelation. Lord of Hosts (Hebrew: tsebâ'âh; <u>a *mass* of persons organized for war</u>).

9. ***And out of his mouth goeth a sharp sword, that with it he should smite the nations***: *But with righteousness shall he judge the poor, and reprove with equity for the meek of the earth: and he shall smite the earth with the rod of his mouth, and with the breath of his lips shall he slay the wicked* (Isaiah 11:4). *The sword of the Spirit, which is the word of God* (Ephesians 6:17).

   It is from this picture that Luther wrote concerning the defeat of Satan, "One little word shall fell him."

10. ***He shall rule them with a rod of iron:*** Psalm 2 is the Psalm of the triumphant Son. The nations rage against Him, but heaven laughs at their folly. God says, *Yet have I set my King upon my holy hill of Zion.*

Nothing will change that and His rule will be with inflexible justice. As iron does not bend, neither will He.

11. **He treadeth the winepress of the fierceness and wrath of Almighty God.** Joel describes Armageddon like this:

> *Proclaim ye this among the Gentiles; Prepare war, wake up the mighty men, let all the men of war draw near; let them come up: Beat your plowshares into swords, and your pruninghooks into spears: let the weak say, I am strong. Assemble yourselves, and come, all ye heathen, and gather yourselves together round about: thither cause thy mighty ones to come down, O LORD. Let the heathen be wakened, and come up to the valley of Jehoshaphat: for there will I sit to judge all the heathen round about. Put ye in the sickle, for the harvest is ripe: come, get you down; for the press is full, the fats overflow; for their wickedness is great. Multitudes, multitudes in the valley of decision: for the day of the LORD is near in the valley of decision. The sun and the moon shall be darkened, and the stars shall withdraw their shining. The LORD also shall roar out of Zion, and utter his voice from Jerusalem;* and the heavens and the earth shall shake: but the LORD *will be* the hope of his people, and the strength of the children of Israel (Joel 3:9-16).

12. **And he hath on his vesture and on his thigh a name written, KING OF KINGS, AND LORD OF LORDS.** Barnes says that in ancient times, kings would have their title inscribed on their clothing (much like the embroidering of a name or title on a garment today). This title is inscribed both on His garment and on His flesh. Pilate once inscribed this title to be

displayed on the cross – *This is Jesus of Nazareth, King of the Jews.* It was a title of scorn. This will be a title of glory. There is none higher than He. He is King over all.

Rev 19:17,18 *And I saw an angel standing in the sun; and he cried with a loud voice, saying to all the fowls that fly in the midst of heaven, Come and gather yourselves together unto the supper of the great God; That ye may eat the flesh of kings, and the flesh of captains, and the flesh of mighty men, and the flesh of horses, and of them that sit on them, and the flesh of all men, both free and bond, both small and great.*

I remember, when I was a boy, my father took me to tour the battlefield at Gettysburg, Pennsylvania. Back then, nearly eighty years had past since the bloodiest battle of the Civil War was fought on those fields with a combined death toll of over 8,000 men.

In spite of the years that had passed, I noticed something I had never seen before anywhere else I had been. Circling overhead were birds of prey. Almost everywhere we went on the battlefield one of two (sometimes more) carrion birds circled overhead.

They are no longer in evidence these days. I've toured the scene many times since then and failed to see anything but an occasional hawk or vulture, but nothing like what I saw as a boy. Apparently, the birds have forgotten, what they still remembered back then.

When a battlefield becomes a great killing ground the carrion birds gather to eat the flesh of the dead. But preceding Armageddon, God actually summons them to prepare for the greatest feast of human flesh the world has ever seen. One of my professors called it, "the clarion call to the carrion birds."

Rev 19:19 *And I saw the beast, and the kings of the earth, and their armies, gathered together to make war against him that sat on the horse, and against his army.*

The campaign of earth's armies into the Middle East was originally intended to destroy Israel, in the last great effort to frustrate her prophetic destiny and thus defeat the purposes of God. But in the midst of their efforts, *then shall appear the sign of the Son of man in heaven: and then shall all the tribes of the earth mourn, and they shall see the Son of man coming in the clouds of heaven with power and great glory* (Matthew 24:30).

When Christ descends upon the fray, the armies will forsake their battle with Israel and turn to fight the One on the white horse. The sequence of the battle is laid out by Zechariah:

> *For I will gather all nations against Jerusalem to battle; and the city shall be taken, and the houses rifled, and the women ravished; and half of the city shall go forth into captivity, and the residue of the people shall not be cut off from the city. Then shall the LORD go forth, and fight against those nations, as when he fought in the day of battle. And his feet shall stand in that day upon the mount of Olives, which is before Jerusalem on the east, and the mount of Olives shall cleave in the midst thereof toward the east and toward the west, and there shall be a very great valley; and half of the mountain shall remove toward the north, and half of it toward the south. And ye shall flee the valley of the mountains; as you fled from before the earthquake in the days of Uzziah king of Judah: and the LORD my God shall come, and all the saints with thee* (Zechariah 14:2-5).

Rev 19:20 *And the beast was taken, and with him the false prophet that wrought miracles before him, with which he deceived them that had received the mark of the beast, and them that worshipped his image. These both were cast alive into a lake of fire burning with brimstone.*

The mystery that surrounds the destiny of these two individuals is as deep as that of their existence in the first place.

It is evident from previous Scripture, that these two are totally controlled and possessed by Satan so that their actions, their words, their apparent miraculous power all flow from the Evil One himself.

Now, they are cast "alive" into the Lake of Fire, where we will find them a thousand years later, still alive and suffering. How that could be possible we are not told, nor do we need to suppose. God is God, and certainly their punishment fits the crime, for they deceived the entire world and caused multitudes of deluded followers to perish, while slaughtering those who were the true servants of God.

These two have, along with their master, had their hour of fame and power upon the stage of time. Now they will disappear forever, except for a brief moment when we are allowed to see them still burning in a lake that never will be quenched and into which all who have rejected grace will eventually be cast. The judgments executed by the King of Kings will be swift and final.

Rev 19:21 *And the remnant were slain with the sword of him that sat upon the horse, which sword proceeded out of his mouth: and all the fowls were filled with their flesh.*

As soon as the Beast and the False Prophet are taken, panic will seize upon all who were following them. Their destruction will be immediate.

Dr. Henry Morris describes it like this; "They will not have long to wait, A mighty cutting wind sweeps across their ranks, up the 180-mile column of massed men and horses, proceeding like a slicing sword, directly from the powerful Word of the majestic Rider . . . Like grapes trampled in a winepress, the blood bursts from their veins and death is instantaneous. Soon the great trough is flowing with blood. . . "

(The Revelation Record; Henry Morris)

Zechariah also describes it in detail:

And this shall be the plague wherewith the LORD will smite all the people that have fought against Jerusalem; Their flesh shall consume away while they

stand upon their feet, and their eyes shall consume away in their holes, and their tongue shall consume away in their mouth (Zechariah 14:12)

Thus the doom of all the enemies of the King is settled in a moment. There is another matter of business to settle, but Satan's fate comes in the next chapter. As this chapter opens we see heaven opened. As it closes, we get a glimpse of eternal hell – the Lake of Fire.

One of the many questions which the book of Revelation answers is the question of justice. Even unsaved individuals have a sense that injustices need to be settled, and wrongs need to be made right. Is right to be "forever on the scaffold and wrong forever on the throne?" The book of Revelation answers with a resounding, "NO!" Judgment will come, righteousness and truth will prevail, there will be payday someday.

Abraham once ask God the question, *"shall not the Judge of all the earth do right?* That question is forever resolved here. Yes, God will come. Yes, He will enter into judgment. Yes, He will punish the wicked and vindicate the righteous. Yes, He will set everything right. The Psalmist David described it in these words;

Say among the heathen that the LORD reigneth: the world also shall be established that it shall not be moved: he shall judge the people righteously. Let the heavens rejoice, and let the earth be glad; let the sea roar, and the fulness thereof.

Let the field be joyful, and all that is therein: then shall all the trees of the wood rejoice before the LORD: for he cometh, for he cometh to judge the earth: he shall judge the world with righteousness, and the people with his truth (Psalm 96:10-13).

REVIEW:

- What is "opened" at the beginning of this chapter?

- What are those in heaven rejoicing about?

- What grand announcement is made?

- Who did we identify as the Bride, the Lamb's wife?

- Where and when do you believe the Marriage Supper of the Lamb will take place?

- How many descriptive phrases are given of the Rider on the White Horse?

- How is justice finally meted out as the chapter closes?

CHAPTER 27   A Millennium in One Chapter

Revelation 20:1 – 15

Chapter 20 picks up where chapter 19 left off. There is more "unfinished business," to care for and God never leaves things uncared for. The chapter begins with the word "And," (Gr. Kai), which is most commonly used to indicate a sequence of things or events. The most natural reading of the text suggests that is precisely what it does here.

Rev 20:1 - 3 *And I saw an angel come down from heaven, having the key of the bottomless pit and a great chain in his hand. And he laid hold on the dragon, that old serpent, which is the Devil, and Satan, and bound him a thousand years, And cast him into the bottomless pit, and shut him up, and set a seal upon him, that he should deceive the nations no more, till the thousand years should be fulfilled: and after that he must be loosed a little season.*

It is amazing to me how people so easily stumble over the simplest difficulty in the interpretation of Scripture. Some have asked, "How could a chain hold Satan who is a spirit?" The answer of course, is, "the same Person who made Satan, made the chain." We are dealing with spiritual things, and wisdom dictates that we allow God to tell us what will happen, and allow Him to determine the way it happens.

But there is a far more urgent question raised by these verses, and one that will determine your entire understanding of prophetic things. That question is this; "Is the thousand years really a thousand years, or is that only symbolic?"

As simple as that question sounds, the answer given will largely determine your view of future things, your understanding of the Church, your view of the nation Israel and the covenant promises, your view of the resurrections, the judgments, in short, just about everything concerning the future.

There are generally three answers, and these frame the three positions that are defined theologically by the words, A-Millennial, Post-Millennial, and Pre-Millennial. Let's briefly define each.

1. **A-Millennial** (usually spelled without the hyphen). This view had no place at all in the early Church. For the first two hundred years of Church History, the basic position of the writing theologians was clearly a belief in a literal, earthly, kingdom that would last a thousand years. But several factors began to change that perspective.

First, was the resistance of the Jewish nation to the gospel. Many reasoned, if the Jewish nation is going to refuse their Messiah, then perhaps their refusal cancels the covenant promises of an earthly kingdom in which they will participate and in fact play the leading role.

This led to reinterpreting the promises of the Old Testament and "spiritualizing" them, that is, teaching that they are fulfilled in the spiritual promises to the Church. In this system, the New Testament Church has become, "spiritual Israel," and there is no future for Israel as a nation.

In addition to the stubborn unbelief of the Jewish nation, certain of those who taught a literal thousand-year kingdom, did so in such materialistic, and political terms that spiritually minded people were repulsed. All of this came together and was defined in Augustine's work, "The City of God."

To the Amillenial, these passages that speak of a thousand years are simply symbolic and Amillennials are not clear about what they may symbolize. Amillennialism became the position of the Roman Catholic Church and after the Reformation, many of the Reformed Churches simply accepted and defend that position.

2. The second position is called **Post-Millennialism**. The word implies that Christ's coming will occur after the thousand years. However, the thousand years itself is not taken literally, but believed to refer to the Church age. In this scheme, the gospel is believed to eventually triumph and much (or most), of the world to be converted. The idea is based largely on a misinterpretation of the parable of the woman and the leaven (Matthew 13:33), where the leaven is interpreted as the "gospel." Since the leaven is said to *leaven the whole lump*, it was taken to mean that all the world would eventually be effected by the gospel and be converted. It is believed that this converted multitude will bring a condition of peace and prosperity on earth (i.e., the conditions of the Kingdom), and when things are right, Christ will return.

Post-Millennialism seems to have been defined and popularized (if not invented), by Daniel Whitby, a 17th century writer. It was popular with many in the Missions movement, believing that their efforts would eventually affect a world-wide turning to Christ. Songs like, "We've A Story to Tell To The Nations" whose chorus says, "And the darkness shall turn to dawning, and the dawning to noon day bright, and Christ's great Kingdom shall come to earth, the Kingdom of love and light," promoted the idea.

Although Post-Millennialism still finds some friends among certain Charismatic groups, the horrors of two world wars and continued global conflict have made it difficult to convince anyone that the world is preparing for Christ's Kingdom. The more recent development of Dominion Theology carries a form of Post-Millennialism, "Kingdom Now" teaching.

In response, if the condition of the earth we are living in now is the Kingdom, the candid observer would conclude that there is not much about the Kingdom to merit our excitement.

3. Finally, there is the **Pre-Millennial** position. Pre-Millennialism was the basic position held by the early church as is clearly demonstrated in their writings.

Papias (A.D. 60–130) the bishop of Hierapolis had heard the Apostle John. Papias "related that they had heard from John how the Lord used to teach about the coming Kingdom. He is recorded as saying: "there will be a millennium after the resurrection from the dead, when the personal reign of Christ will be established on this earth."

Along with his witness could be cited **Polycarp** (A.D. 70–155), bishop of Smyrna and disciple of the Apostle John; **Clement of Rome,** who wrote a letter to an early church around A.D. 95; **Ignatius of Antioch,** a disciple of the Apostles John and Peter and **Theophilus of Antioch** (A.D. 115–181), who wrote one of the first accounts of primitive church history and affirmed their millennial persuasions.

Pre-Millennialism recognizes a distinction between God's program with Israel and that of the Church, believes in a future conversion and future destiny for the nation of Israel, believes that the language of Revelation 20 should be taken literally, and that it clearly teaches a 1000 year Kingdom of Christ on earth before the final judgment. That is the position of this writer.

Now perhaps we need to look again at what the opening verses of this chapter say.

Rev 20:1 - 3 *And I saw an angel come down from heaven, having the key of the bottomless pit and a great chain in his hand. And he laid hold on the dragon, that old serpent, which is the Devil, and Satan, and bound him a thousand years, And cast him into the bottomless pit, and shut him up, and set a seal upon him, that he should deceive the nations no more, till the thousand years should be fulfilled: and after that he must be loosed a little season.*

This is not the first time in this book that the "bottomless pit" has been cited. In chapter nine it was opened to allow a horde of demons to escape that tormented the "earth-dwellers" for five months. In chapters eleven and seventeen, the Beast is said to "ascend out of the bottomless pit (i.e., out of the deepest regions of hell), and now here, Satan is banished and confined to the bottomless pit during the entire one thousand years of Christ's Kingdom reign on earth.

That banishment will result in the removal of the great outside source of temptation – the devil. Enticement to all forms of sin is thus eliminated during this time (comp. James 1:14, 15). And what will that accomplish? It will mean that any sin, any disobedience, any rebellion that occurs cannot be blamed on Satan. Flip Wilson's famous; "The Devil made me do it," quip will no longer work. When sin occurs, it will be seen to clearly originate in the corrupt heart of man himself and not any outside influence.

This is of specific significance in Dispensational teaching. Dispensationalism teaches that each distinct Dispensational period constitutes a test. Man has been tested in a state of innocence, under the guidance of his conscience, under the restraint of human government, under his response to the promise of God, under the Mosaic Law, under the offer of Grace, and now he is tested a final time, during the direct, personal reign of Messiah on earth.

Not only has faith given way to sight, and error and darkness to truth and light, but Satan is bound and all external enticement to sin has been removed.

Yet, at the close of this Golden Age, our text tells us that Satan will be loosed for a little season. That will be all that is necessary for the internalized rebellion against the Righteous King to manifest itself and verses 7-10 tell us man's response and its ultimate outcome.

We will examine these verses in a moment, but perhaps this would be the time to answer a question that is often raised when discussing the 1000-year Millennial Reign of Christ. The question is, "Why is an earthly, millennial reign necessary?" Let me list the reasons:

- The Necessity to Fulfill God's Decree that Man have Dominion over the Earth (Genesis 1:26, 27; Hebrews 2:5-8). Christ, the God-man will reign.

- The Necessity to realize what Peter called, *The Restoration of all things which God hath spoken by the mouth of His holy prophets* (Acts 3:19-21). During this Millennial period all unfulfilled prophecy will be fulfilled.

- The Necessity to Silence the Claim that Man's reason for sinning rests outside himself in the conditions and environment that surround him. Now, without any external enticement to sin, man continues to sin, and in the final moments of the age openly rebels against the goodness and grace of the King.

- The Necessity to fulfill all the unfulfilled promises to National Israel (see the Abrahamic, Palestinic, Davidic, and New Covenants).

- Finally, and simply because God has decreed that there shall be a Millennial Reign of His Son on earth. (I deal with each of these in depth in my book

Dispensationalism in a Post-Modern Age; see pp. 119-122).

For anyone who is willing to take the plain words of Scripture seriously, the earthly, Millennial, reign of Jesus Christ on David's throne, is a certainty.

Rev 20:4 *And I saw thrones, and they sat upon them, and judgment was given unto them: and I saw the souls of them that were beheaded for the witness of Jesus, and for the word of God, and which had not worshipped the beast, neither his image, neither had received his mark upon their foreheads, or in their hands; and they lived and reigned with Christ a thousand years.*

This passage is crucial to our understanding and so we need to approach it carefully and take it one phrase at a time. The first thing John saw was thrones. Thrones are places of authority and power. John next says that he sees; *they who sat on them.* Who are these people who are now seated in places of great authority and power, and to whom the right to make judgment is given?

In order to fully answer that question we must remember that *no prophecy of the Scripture is of private interpretation* (2 Peter 1:20). That means, we must not take a single verse and attempt to interpret it apart from other Scripture on that same subject. So, the question we are attempting to answer is, who are these people who John sees seated on these thrones?

The remainder of the verse tells us who some of them are. They are those who were beheaded because they refused the mark of the Beast. In other words, these are the martyred saints of the Tribulation. But notice they are not alone. After John sees the thrones and certain persons seated on them, that little conjunction "and" appears again; *and I saw the souls of them that were beheaded. . . etc.* In other words, along with those he had already seen seated upon thrones, John also sees these Tribulation Martyrs. They are resurrected and will also reign with Christ during His 1000-year Kingdom.

Now, that should make us ask, who else will be reigning? To answer that question we must first answer the question, who else has experienced resurrection? Well, the apparent order of Scripture is:

1. Christ (who is the "Firstfruits") was resurrected and certain Old Testament saints were resurrected with Him (Matthew 27:52, 53).

2. The Church is resurrected and raptured (1 Thessalonians 4:13-18). According to God's promise, we shall also reign with Him (2 Timothy 2:12; Revelation 5:10). Furthermore, He promised the 12 Apostles a specific jurisdiction, vis., *ye also shall sit upon twelve thrones, judging the twelve tribes of Israel* (Matthew 19:28).

3. Finally, at Christ's Second Advent, Tribulation saints are resurrected, along with the remainder of the Old Testament saints (Daniel 12:2, 3; Revelation 20:4).

What we learn then is that along with the Tribulation martyrs specifically named here, all the saints of all the ages will be resurrected and have assigned jurisdictions over which they are given authority during the Millennial reign of Christ. All of these are included in what John calls, the First Resurrection. It is thus designated because it is "First" in both time and kind. That is, it precedes what John calls the "second Resurrection," and it involves only those who are the redeemed.

We will see that the "second Resurrection" is such because it is "second" (being after the final segment of the First Resurrection), and it involves only the lost of all the ages. Which brings us to our next verse in the text.

Rev 20:5, 6 *But the rest of the dead lived not again until the thousand years were finished. This is the first resurrection. Blessed and holy is he that hath part in the first resurrection: on such the second death hath no*

power, but they shall be priests of God and of Christ, and shall reign with him a thousand years.

If there is any question about either the timing or the participants in the resurrections, this verse makes it abundantly clear. The final phase of the First Resurrection occurs preceding the Kingdom, thus allowing all the redeemed of the ages to participate in and experience that Golden Age for which prophets and sages have looked since the beginning of time, and as such, they are both *blessed and holy.*

There is also an equally clear implication here that those who are part of that second resurrection are neither blessed nor holy and have a most terrible fate awaiting them.

One final glimpse is given of this great Kingdom period. *They shall be priests of God and of Christ, and shall reign with him a thousand years.* What does all of that entail? We are not told. In fact, the entire Millennial Kingdom is passed over in just three verses.

If the Millennium is as important as we Premillennialists say it is, why is there no more description given of it here? I think the answer to that is twofold. First, it is not the purpose of the Holy Spirit here to expound to John all the glories and the wonder of the Kingdom. His purpose seems to be to assure John that all the saints will be there to enjoy it, just as God has promised and as they have believed through the centuries.

Secondly, there is abundant testimony in both the Old Testament Scriptures and the parables of Jesus to the reality and the nature of the Kingdom. The following are meant to be samples and certainly not an inclusive list of such passages.

1. Psalms 2; 22:27-31; 24; 45; 48; 67; 72; 96; 110
2. Isaiah 2:1-5; 9:6, 7; 11:1-9; 12:1-6; and 60 - 66
3. Jeremiah 31:31-40; 32:36-44; 33:1-26
4. Ezekiel 43:1-7
5. Daniel 7:9-14

6. Joel 3:16-21
7. Amos 9:11-15
8. Micah 4:1-8
9. Zephaniah 3:14-20
10. Zechariah 8:1-8; 14:9-21

Likewise, our Lord spoke a great deal about His coming Kingdom. In fact, until Israel had clearly rejected Him, Most of His teaching concerned the Kingdom, with this difference. Since He, the King, was then in the midst of them, He often spoke of the Kingdom as something that was present. Only when His Kingdom offer was clearly rejected and He Himself destined for the cross did He begin to speak of the Kingdom as something future.

In Matthew 5-7 our Lord describes the character of the Kingdom and those that will inhabit it. He spoke of it again in 8:11,12; and in 11:11, 12. In Chapter 16:28 He said that some of them living in that day would actually "see" the Kingdom. After six days He took Peter James and John to a high mountain and was transfigured before them, Moses and Elijah being with them. Peter later understood that event as singular proof of the certainty of the coming Kingdom and of *the Power and coming of our Lord Jesus Christ* (2 Peter 1:16-18).

Finally, in chapters 24 and 25 of Matthew, Jesus predicts in stark detail the events which will finally culminate in the Kingdom, His coming in great glory, and the accounting that will take place of His servants. I believe that Revelation has little to say about the actual details of the Kingdom, because the rest of Scripture has already said so much.

Rev 20:7 - 9 *And when the thousand years are expired, Satan shall be loosed out of his prison, And shall go out to deceive the nations which are in the four quarters of the earth, Gog and Magog, to gather them together to battle: the number of whom is as the sand of the sea.*

And they went up on the breadth of the earth, and compassed the camp of the saints about, and the beloved city: and fire came down from God out of heaven, and devoured them.

If a thousand years with the Lord is as a day (2 Peter 3:8), it seems here to be even shorter as we are transported immediately to the terminal end of the earthly Millennial Kingdom, and to the release of Satan from his prison. What follows demonstrates that he is unchanged after his former defeat and confinement. He goes immediately out to once again deceive the nations. He is still the great liar, deceiver, murderer and thief that Jesus once said that he was (John 8:44).

What should give us pause however, is his unbelievable success in being able to once more convince men that they can successfully rebel against God. What is that phrase, "History teaches us that man learns nothing from history?" And even more, what this teaches us is that man is utterly corrupt and sinful, just as God has said that he is, and that he, like his spiritual father the devil, is a rebel at heart.

Satan once again, and for the final time, is able to muster multitudes who are ready to pit their puny strength against the God who spoke them into being and to whom they owe their very existence. And this is all the more remarkable because of the character of the Kingdom itself.

For one thousand years, justice has at last reigned on this planet. The negative destructive elements of the curse have been nullified. Peace, safety, and plenty, have prevailed over the entire globe. For a thousand years the planet has not known war, or famine, or poverty.

What Jesus did when presenting the Kingdom here on earth He will do again. All who come with sickness, or infirmity of any kind will be healed.

Indeed even the animal kingdom will rest and the lion will lie down with the lamb and a little child shall lead them. What could man possibly want more than what the Kingdom provides?

In spite of it all, man's sinful nature will desire to break the traces of restraint and return to the slime pits of sin. He will resent the righteous commandments of the King and a festering hatred will burn deep within his fallen nature.

When the Deceiver tempts him to rebel and to throw off the yoke of the King, he will respond in such great numbers that the only way the writer can express it is to compare it to the invasion of Gog and Magog – *their number is as the sand of the sea.*

The object of the final and futile crusade is again the Holy City of Jerusalem. As the Psalmist said, *Beautiful for situation, the joy of the whole earth, is mount Zion, on the sides of the north, the city of the great King.* Psalm 48:2).

Yet we read, *They went up on the breadth of the earth, and compassed the camp of the saints about, and the beloved city.* The words suggest a rebellion that encompasses every corner of the earth.

If there was ever any doubt about the depth of human sin and depravity, this final failure should forever put it to rest. Man is incurably evil and apart from a redeeming work of Divine grace he is fit for nothing but the punishment and destruction to which he is destined.

The response of the King is swift and total - *fire came down from God out of heaven, and devoured them.* Perhaps this is what the Holy Spirit had in mind when He inspired the Psalmist to write; *There is a river, the streams whereof shall make glad the city of God, the holy place of the tabernacles of the most High.*

God is in the midst of her; she shall not be moved: God shall help her, and that right early. The heathen raged, the kingdoms were moved: he uttered his voice, the earth melted. The LORD of hosts is with us; the God of Jacob is our refuge (Psalm 46:4-7).

Rev 20:10 *And the devil that deceived them was cast into the lake of fire and brimstone, where the beast and the false prophet are, and shall be tormented day and night for ever and ever.*

At last he meets his final doom - To be stripped of all pretension of glory or power and to be humiliated before the gaze of the entire universe.

> *How art thou fallen from heaven, O Lucifer, son of the morning! how art thou cut down to the ground, which didst weaken the nations! For thou hast said in thine heart, I will ascend into heaven, I will exalt my throne above the stars of God: I will sit also upon the mount of the congregation, in the sides of the north: I will ascend above the heights of the clouds; I will be like the most High. Yet thou shalt be brought down to hell, to the sides of the pit. They that see thee shall narrowly look upon thee, and consider thee, saying, Is this the man that made the earth to tremble, that did shake kingdoms; That made the world as a wilderness, and destroyed the cities thereof; that opened not the house of his prisoners?* (Isaiah 14:12-17).

Satan's final repose is in the Lake of Fire, where the Beast and False Prophet were thrown at the beginning of the thousand-year kingdom. Notice, they are still there, suffering the torments of eternal fire after a thousand years, and will remain there for all eternity.

Satan and his cadre will soon be joined by all the multitudes of individuals who have followed him and been deceived by his wiles.

Demon hosts will join their master in the howling madhouse of the universe, and together they will forever suffer the judgment of a Righteous God.

Rev 20:11 *And I saw a great white throne, and him that sat on it, from whose face the earth and the heaven fled away; and there was found no place for them.*

Again John tells us, *And I saw.* By now we know that the words are meant to alert us that a new vision is before the writer. John tells us that he saw "a Great White Throne," and that he saw the One who occupied that throne.

We need not ask who is upon the throne for Jesus Christ has told us, *For the Father judgeth no man, but hath committed all judgment unto the Son* (John 5:22). He who once stood at the judgment seat of Caiphas and later before Pilate, now ascends the throne of judgment to judge those who once judged Him. Once they pronounced the sentence upon Him. Now He will pronounce an eternal sentence upon them.

There is something about His face (Gr. *Πρόσωπον;* prosōpon *visage; countenance, appearance;* by implication *presence*). From His presence, yes, from His appearance everything is swept away. The rendering is strong; (Gr. *Φεύγω;* pheugō; to *run away* (literally or figuratively); by implication to *vanish.*

Our text seems clear enough, it appears that the present earth and the heavens, that is, the entire created universe will be dissolved. I realize that there are those who have difficulty with this. Some argue that the first Law of Thermodynamics confirms that energy/matter may change form, but the amount of energy/matter remains constant. It is called the "Law of the Conservation of Energy."

But the laws and principles of this present created universe are not applicable to what is to come.

Consider how many times Jesus spoke about the present heaven and earth passing away (cf. Matthew 24:35; Mark 13:31; Luke 16:17; 21:33). If that were not sufficient it seems that Peter certainly leaves no doubt.

> But the day of the Lord will come as a thief in the night; in the which the heavens shall pass away with a great noise, and the elements shall melt with fervent heat, the earth also and the works that are therein shall be burned up.

> Seeing then that all these things shall be dissolved, what manner of persons ought ye to be in all holy conversation and godliness, Looking for and hasting unto the coming of the day of God, wherein the heavens being on fire shall be dissolved, and the elements shall melt with fervent heat? Nevertheless we, according to his promise, look for new heavens and a new earth, wherein dwelleth righteousness (2 Peter 3:10-13).

When we come to the next chapter it opens with these words; *And I saw a new heaven and a new earth: for the first heaven and the first earth were passed away; and there was no more sea* (Revelation 21:1).

The Bible Knowledge Commentary says, "The present universe was created like a gigantic clock which is running down, and if left to itself, would ultimately come to a state of complete inactivity. Inasmuch as God created the universe and set it in motion for the purpose of enacting the drama of sin and redemption, it would seem proper to begin anew with a new heaven and a new earth suitable for His eternal purpose and built on a different principle." **(Bible Knowledge Commentary)**

So we conclude that even matter itself is dissolved and there is nothing of a material universe left. The words, *There was found no place for them,* say to me, they no longer exist.

Which now leads us to conclude that there will be nowhere for the lost to hide. There is nothing but this Great White Throne, upon which sits the Lord Jesus Christ and this scene apparently occurs in some sort of ethereal space.

Rev 20:12 *And I saw the dead, small and great, stand before God; and the books were opened: and another book was opened, which is the book of life: and the dead were judged out of those things which were written in the books, according to their works.*

We are next told who is assembled before that Throne. John says it is, "the dead."

As far as I have been able to discern that description is never used of a believer. Believers are said to "sleep", (that is, their bodies sleep), but they are always consider alive. Jesus, quoting the Old Testament said, *I am the God of Abraham, and the God of Isaac, and the God of Jacob? God is not the God of the dead, but of the living* (Matthew 22:32).

The very way in which this mass of people are described, implies at once their condition. They have never received the gift of eternal life and are therefore dead in trespasses and sin and are soon to suffer a second death as well.

Notice that "small and great" are there. No one escapes this appointment. *It is appointed unto men, once to die, but after this the judgment* (Hebrews 9:27).

Lastly, note that God keeps books. Someone asks, is it really a literal book? The answer is, it doesn't matter. We now keep volumes of information in digital format on very small devices. The point is that the record of every man and woman, boy and girl that ever lived is kept by God and He can retrieve it in an instant.

But along with the "books" is the Book of Life. We will examine that at the end of this section.

Rev 20:13 *And the sea gave up the dead which were in it; and death and hell delivered up the dead which were in them: and they were judged every man according to their works.*

Verse thirteen underscores the truth just stated in the previous verse. Man is made of dust. The book of Revelation brings to a climax much that began in the book of Genesis. God told the sinning and fallen Adam, *In the sweat of thy face shalt thou eat bread, till thou return unto the ground; for out of it wast thou taken: for dust thou art, and unto dust shalt thou return* (Genesis 3:19). Now God tells us that no matter where that dust has fallen, into a grave or into the sea, it will reform and again reconstitute the body of the presently dead.

The phrase, death and hell, signifies the condition of the lost at death. The word death refers to the condition of the body, the reference to hell refers to the abode of the lost soul. Now both are reunited to stand in the judgment.

Men sinned in the body, and they will be judged in the body. The judgment is one of works, that is, what they did while living. The scope of that judgment includes both actions, words and even thoughts. Jesus warned that every idle word would be brought into judgment and that to lust after a woman is to commit adultery in the heart.

Actions, motives and effects will be evaluated, that is, not only the deed itself, but the corresponding results it produced on others. Imagine the result of examining the actions of totalitarian governments whose pogroms have cost untold suffering and loss of life to so many. Imagine the sentence of an entertainer who has influenced thousands of youth to a promiscuous and irreverent lifestyle, not only corrupting them but condemning them to hell as well.

Three of the gospels record the sobering words of Jesus, *It were better for him that a millstone were hanged about his neck, and he cast into the sea, than that he should offend one of these little ones* (Luke 17:2).

In short, nothing will escape His judgment and everything will be given a just and fitting retribution.

The implication of such a judgment is to affix the appropriate punishment to the crime. In other words, this judgment strongly implies degrees of punishment, something Jesus spoke about when he told the parable of the careless servant.

> *And that servant, which knew his lord's will, and prepared not himself, neither did according to his will, shall be beaten with many stripes. But he that knew not, and did commit things worthy of stripes, shall be beaten with few stripes.*
>
> *For unto whomsoever much is given, of him shall be much required: and to whom men have committed much, of him they will ask the more* (Luke 12:47,48).

Rev 20:14, 15 *And death and hell were cast into the lake of fire. This is the second death. And whosoever was not found written in the book of life was cast into the lake of fire.*

The final declaration of this sad section is that everyone who comes to the judgment of the Great White Throne will be cast into the Lake of Fire to receive the eternal torment appropriate to their sins. Body and soul reunited stand trial and body and soul are cast into the Lake of Fire.

We are told here that this constitutes what Scripture calls, the *second death*. What does that mean? Let me answer that by saying what it does not mean. It does not mean annihilation. In other words, nothing said here implies that these who are thrown into the Lake of Fire go out of existence.

The word death always implies a separation. When Adam disobeyed God he "died" spiritually, that it, he was separated from all communion and fellowship with God.

When a body dies there is a separation. The spirit separates from the body, leaving the body in a state of death. When the lost are cast into the Lake of Fire it is eternal separation from God, from good, from all that is pleasant, a separation to a state of pain that constitutes a living death.

That it does not constitute annihilation is clearly shown by the fact that the Beast and the False Prophet (both of them men), are still seen suffering in the Lake of Fire a thousand years after they arrived there. In fact verse 10 says that they will be tormented forever and forever.

The words forever and forever are significant. It is the same identical phrase which is used to describe the duration of the throne of God in Hebrews 1:8; *But unto the Son he saith, Thy throne, O God, is for ever and ever: a sceptre of righteousness is the sceptre of thy kingdom.*

The meaning is "unto the ages of the ages." As both a description of the length of God's reign and the length of the torments of the Lake of Fire, the meaning is clearly, unending and eternal.

Finally, once again reference is made to the Book of Life. Because there seems to always be a troubling question about this book, I want to take this occasion to examine all the pertinent passages on the subject. We can begin with the first mention of the book, in the prayer of Moses.

> *And Moses returned unto the LORD, and said, Oh, this people have sinned a great sin, and have made them gods of gold. Yet now, if thou wilt forgive their sin; and if not, blot me, I pray thee, out of thy book which thou hast written. And the LORD said unto Moses, Whosoever hath sinned against me, him will I blot out of my book* (Exodus 32:31-33).

While some have supposed that this book refers merely to the genealogical records which the Jews were famous for keeping, it must be noted that this is a "*book which thou* (God) *hast written.*" If it is a record of the living, it is one that God is keeping.

Here the sense seems clearly to be that those who are "blotted out" are delivered to physical death. The book seems to be a record of the living. That becomes even clearer when contemplating a verse from Isaiah. *And it shall come to pass, that he that is left in Zion, and he that remaineth in Jerusalem, shall be called holy, even every one that is written among the living in Jerusalem* (Isaiah 4:3).

That being the case the sense seems to be that those who are alive are in the book of the living and those who die are removed.

Daniel, likewise speaks of a book in which certain names are inscribed. It is possible that his meaning is that those who have lived through the tribulation and survived, shall experience deliverance from the sufferings and dangers they experienced.

> *And at that time shall Michael stand up, the great prince which standeth for the children of thy people: and there shall be a time of trouble, such as never was since there was a nation even to that same time: and at that time thy people shall be delivered, every one that shall be found written in the book* (Daniel 12:1).

As far as I can tell, that is the extent of references in the Old Testament to the book of life. But the New Testament refers to it as well. There are just two places where the book of life is mentioned before the book of Revelation, but it is referred to seven times in the final book. We will begin with the references in the Gospel and the Epistle.

> *Notwithstanding in this rejoice not, that the spirits are subject unto you; but rather rejoice, because your names are written in heaven* (Luke 10:20).

Here our Lord was cautioning his disciples who had just returned from a preaching tour and found that, *even the demons are subject to us through thy name* (Luke 10:17), to refocus on the miracle of their own salvation, and not on the power they had against Satan. Their names were written in heaven. Where? Doubtless in that book of life so often referenced before.

In the epistle to the Philippians, Paul pleaded for unity on the grounds that their names were all written in the family album – the book of life.

> *And I intreat thee also, true yokefellow, help those women which laboured with me in the gospel, with Clement also, and with other my fellowlabourers, whose names are in the book of life* (Philippians 4:3).

Which brings us now to the seven references found in the book of Revelation. While some of the references in the Old Testament seem to refer to a record of those who are living (i.e., have physical life), there can be no doubt that the New Testament references clearly refer to something more. It is to those who have spiritual life, in other words, those who are born again and are children of God. So that we can compare the references in Revelation easily, I have listed them below:

> *He that overcometh, the same shall be clothed in white raiment; and I will not blot out his name out of the book of life, but I will confess his name before my Father, and before his angels* (Revelation 3:5).

> *And all that dwell on the earth shall worship him, every one whose name hath not been written from the foundation of the world in the book of life of the Lamb that hath been slain.* (Revelation 13:8 ASV)

The beast that thou sawest was, and is not; and shall ascend out of the bottomless pit, and go into perdition: and they that dwell on the earth shall wonder, whose names were not written in the book of life from the foundation of the world, when they behold the beast that was, and is not, and yet is (Revelation 17:8).

And I saw the dead, small and great, stand before God; and the books were opened: and another book was opened, which is the book of life: and the dead were judged out of those things which were written in the books, according to their works (Revelation 20:12).

And whosoever was not found written in the book of life was cast into the lake of fire (Revelation 20:15).

And there shall in no wise enter into it any thing that defileth, neither whatsoever worketh abomination, or maketh a lie: but they which are written in the Lamb's book of life (Revelation 21:27).

And if any man shall take away from the words of the book of this prophecy, God shall take away his part out of the book of life, and out of the holy city, and from the things which are written in this book (Revelation 22:19).

Conclusion: God appears to have a book which records the names of all those who have eternal life. Because of God's infinite foreknowledge their names were written in the book before the world was even created. The reference to "blotting out" a name, is found only once and there God assures the reader that He will not blot out that name.

There is, however, one verse that seems to suggest that a name, once a part of the book, may be removed. It is, *And if any man shall take away from the words of the book of this prophecy, God shall take away his part out of the book of life.*

Albert Barnes believes the meaning is, "not that his name had been written in that book, but that he would take away the part which he might have had, or which he professed to have in that book." If that interpretation is correct, then it would harmonize with every other passage of Scripture which assures the believer that his salvation is completely secure in Christ.

Whatever is concluded then about the Book of Life, we can be sure that is does not contradict that clear and certain assurance given by our Lord himself:

And I give unto them eternal life; and they shall never perish, neither shall any man pluck them out of my hand. My Father, which gave them me, is greater than all; and no man is able to pluck them out of my Father's hand. I and my Father are one (John 10:28-30).

REVIEW

- What are the three positions theologians have on the Millennium.

- Which of the three does the author hold?

- Name five reasons why the Millennial reign of Christ is a necessity.

- Why does Revelation spend 14 chapters to cover the 7-year Tribulation, and only one chapter to cover the 1,000 year Millennium?

- Where does the Judgment of the Great White Throne take place.

CHAPTER 28 "I Make All Things New"

Revelation Chapter 21:1 – 27

Rev 21:1 *And I saw a new heaven and a new earth: for the first heaven and the first earth were passed away; and there was no more sea.*

"And I saw," is the Holy Spirit's way of notifying us that we are about to see something new. The phrase appears 21 times in the book of Revelation and each time it alerts us to a new vision. Here it is a new vision of something completely new - a new heaven and a new earth.

As I mentioned in our study of Chapter 20, there is considerable debate among expositors as to whether the new Heaven and earth are a renovated or rejuvenated version of the old, or whether the old are actually destroyed and the new created. Frankly, I don't believe it is a matter of great consequence as if some doctrine rested upon it. I tend to favor Dr. John Walvoord's conclusion:

> "The most natural interpretation of the fact that earth and heaven flee away is that the present earth and heaven are destroyed and will be replaced by the new heaven and new earth. This is also confirmed by the additional statement in Revelation 21:1 where John sees a new heaven and a new earth replacing the first heaven and the first earth which have passed away."

I believe the determinative statement is found in chapter 20, verse 11:

> *And I saw a great white throne, and him that sat on it, from whose face the earth and the heaven fled away; and <u>there was found no place for them</u>.*

If *there was found no place for them*, that means they ceased to exist, and that seems clear enough. What we have here in chapter 21 is a newly created heaven and earth in the very strictest sense of that word.

No more sea implies an entirely different hydro-cycle. Although a river is mentioned it cannot run to the sea, rise through evaporation and then fall again as rain. Solomon had observed that cycle long ago when he wrote; *All the rivers run into the sea; yet the sea is not full; unto the place from whence the rivers come, thither they return again* (Ecclesiastes 1:7).

That will no longer be the case and the absence of a sea, which is essential to the present order, underscores again the fact that a new earth is ordered in a new way. One more thing to note is that the present seas have acted as barriers to total contact between people groups. Those barriers will no longer be there.

Rev 21:2 *And I John saw the holy city, new Jerusalem, coming down from God out of heaven, prepared as a bride adorned for her husband.*

We made a point of noting that the Bride of Christ is the Church. But this verse does not say that what John saw was the Bride, only that the city was adorned as a bride. The point, of course, is that just as a bride is decked with all things beautiful, so this city is arrayed with beauty and glory. The wonder, the beauty was so great that John could only describe it as a bride adorned.

I remember when I was quite young (maybe 6 or 7), my Grandmother took me on the train to Louisville, Kentucky, to attend the wedding of a nephew of hers. It was a great formal wedding and I had never seen a bride in full bridal attire before. I remember thinking that she was the most beautiful lady I had ever seen. Brides are meant to have that effect on us, and that is the effect the city had upon John.

Rev 21:3 *And I heard a great voice out of heaven saying, Behold, the tabernacle of God is with men, and he will dwell with them, and they shall be his people, and God himself shall be with them, and be their God.*

I have often pointed out that none of God's purposes will be frustrated by either man's sinfulness or Satan's schemes. God intended to have fellowship with man when he was first created, and He will achieve that condition in the eternal state. But in that day, those with whom He has fellowship will be perfected, and they will love him with all their hearts.

There is a precious intimacy to these words. Words like "dwell with them," "shall be His people," He will be "their God." Those are relational words spoken with great affection.

Rev 21:4 *And God shall wipe away all tears from their eyes; and there shall be no more death, neither sorrow, nor crying, neither shall there be any more pain: for the former things are passed away.*

Some have asked why there are tears in heaven to be wiped away. Some have even tried to tie this verse to the Judgment Seat of Christ and taught that we will be weeping because of our many failures which the Judgment Seat will reveal. It is an interesting sentiment, but it really has no basis in the text.

The point is that tears will be one of the things that will be "no more." One of the most precious phases in the book of Revelation is the simple, "no mores". There are many things in the present order which are painful, and distasteful, and which bring sadness and tears. One of the things this phrase assures us of is that those things are gone forever.

In verse 1 we read there will be "no more sea." Now we read there will be no more death, no more sorrow, no more crying, no more pain.

Actually, the "no mores" begin back in Chapter 3 where we read;

Him that overcometh will I make a pillar in the temple of my God, and he shall go no more out: and I will write upon him the name of my God, and the name of the city of my God, which is new Jerusalem, which cometh down out of heaven from my God: and I will write upon him my new name (Revelation 3:12). In the very promises to the churches God anticipates and announces what we now see in Chapter 21 and will, one day experience.

In chapter 7 we read; *They shall hunger no more, neither thirst any more; neither shall the sun light on them, nor any heat* (Revelation 7:17). No more hunger!

In chapter 20 we learn that there will be no more deceiving devil; he should deceive the nations no more (Revelation 20:3). While this specific verse deals with the condition in the Millennium, it will certainly be true of the eternal state.

Finally, in chapter 22 we read; *And there shall be no more curse: but the throne of God and of the Lamb shall be in it; and his servants shall serve him* (Revelation 22:3). No more curse – all that is past for the former things are passed away. What a provision God has made for us! Eden restored!

Rev 21:5 *And he that sat upon the throne said, Behold, I make all things new. And he said unto me, Write: for these words are true and faithful.*

All things new! I like that. I have had a personal passion all my life to take that which is old and worn and often seemingly beyond repair and bring it back to usefulness again, beautifying it with fresh paint or finish. I've done that to furniture, cars, equipment and even houses. I like to make things new. And apparently God does as well, but I am sure when He makes it new, it will be completely new.

All of this was apparently so wonderful that John hesitated to write it down, and has to be commanded to "write," and assured that all that he has heard is "true and faithful."

We can have absolute confidence in what we read here, for just like Abraham, *we look for a city which hath foundations, whose builder and maker is God* (Hebrews 11:10),

Rev 21:6 ***And he said unto me, It is done. I am Alpha and Omega, the beginning and the end. I will give unto him that is athirst of the fountain of the water of life freely.***

I love to hear God say, *It is done*, don't you? All His works are done in truth and reflect His great goodness, and he never leaves anything undone. Everything which He has determined He will accomplish – praise His name!

Then He proclaims one final time, *I am Alpha and Omega, the beginning and the end.* He brought it all into existence and He is the goal that everything moves toward. It is all about Jesus!

The blessed invitation in this verse is to the reader, that is, to you and me. There will be no thirst in heaven, but praise God for that blessed thirst we experience now which leads us to drink of the water of life. This theme of spiritual thirst and God's provision can be traced throughout Scripture.

In Isaiah we read; *Ho, every one that thirsteth, come ye to the waters, and he that hath no money; come ye, buy, and eat; yea, come, buy wine and milk without money and without price* (Isaiah 55:1).

Jeremiah laments; *For my people have committed two evils; they have forsaken me the fountain of living waters, and hewed them out cisterns, broken cisterns, that can hold no water* (Jeremiah 2:13).

In John chapter 4, Jesus says to a Samaritan woman; *If thou knewest the gift of God, and who it is that saith to thee, Give me to drink; thou wouldest have asked of him, and he would have given thee living water. . . , Every one that drinketh of this water shall thirst again: but whosoever drinketh of the water that I shall give him shall never thirst; but the water that I shall give him shall become in him a well of water springing up unto everlasting life* (John 4:10 – 14).

And at the Feast of Tabernacles, as the priest was pouring out an oblation of water at the altar, Jesus cried; *If any man thirst, let him come unto me, and drink. He that believeth on me, as the scripture hath said, out of his belly shall flow rivers of living water* (John 7:37, 38).

He is, and has always been the only source of true satisfaction. Even as He shows us what will be in eternity for the child of God, He invites those who have not drunk, and yet are experiencing that blessed thirst that leads them to want to drink, to come and drink freely of the water of Life.

Which leads me to this: It is often the sense of emptiness and longing in the human heart that eventually draws someone to Christ. Dr. Donald Grey Barnhouse used to end each benediction with the words, "And for those who have never come to Christ; Lord, give them a spirit of restlessness, until they rest in Thee." Oh, blessed restlessness -- blessed thirst that brings us to the Savior.

Rev 21:7 *He that overcometh shall inherit all things; and I will be his God, and he shall be my son.*

Once again, the Lord address those who are "overcomers." Let us remind ourselves once again who these are.

> *For whatsoever is born of God overcometh the world: and this is the victory that overcometh the world, even our faith. Who is he that overcometh the world, but he that believeth that Jesus is the Son of God* (1 John 5:4,5)?

Please note that the same human author penned the book of 1 John and the book of Revelation.

The word "overcomers" is not found in any other book of the Bible. I think we should let John define who is considered an "overcomer." It is everyone who has placed their faith in Jesus as Son of God and Savior and is born of God. That should end the discussion.

But we must not miss what is in store of these "overcomers." *They shall inherit all things.* That is completely inline with what Paul wrote to the Roman believers; *And if children, then heirs; heirs of God, and joint-heirs with Christ; if so be that we suffer with him, that we may be also glorified together* (Romans 8:17).

Who are heirs? Who will inherit all things? Not some elite corps of super saints, but everyone who is a child of God. It is a birthright, not a reward.

And lest someone trip over the phrase, *if we suffer with Him*, the thought is that if we belong to Him, we will suffer with Him. Paul affirms the idea of our inheritance in two additional passages.

> *And if ye be Christ's, then are ye Abraham's seed, and heirs according to the promise* (Galatians 3:29).

> *That being justified by his grace, we should be made heirs according to the hope of eternal life* (Titus 3:7).

Please note that in both of these passages it is clear that those who inherit everything are those who are His family by faith and are justified by His grace. If we belong to Him, we are joint-heirs with Christ. That is, all that belongs to Him, belongs to us.

Furthermore, God says that not only will we inherit all things, but we will be His sons. The word for "sons" here is a different word than is commonly used. John usually uses the Greek word teknon when speaking of sons (1 John 3:2). Teknon can be translated son, or it may also refer to a child (one who has not reached maturity).

But here he uses the word huios. The word implies "immediate kinship."

Dr. J. Vernon McGee writes of this, "Believers in the church are one of the peoples of God, but they are more. They are the sons of God in a unique and glorious fashion." It is that which God is expressing in this passage.

Rev 21:8 ***But the fearful, and unbelieving, and the abominable, and murderers, and whoremongers, and sorcerers, and idolaters, and all liars, shall have their part in the lake which burneth with fire and brimstone: which is the second death.***

What has been said in the positive, is now reiterated in the negative. Who are they who are not His heirs, who will not enjoy eternal life but rather are destined for eternal death?

Let's list them:

- *The fearful*: Fear is the very opposite of faith. Faith places our trust in Jesus Christ and rests in His grace. Fear produces doubt and distrust and is so serious that it can damn a soul to hell.

- *The unbelieving:* This is a step beyond fear. Fear is defined as timidity, whereas the word **apistos** implies an unwillingness to believe. There are a great host of people in our time who count themselves intellectuals and who refuse in the face of clear and irrefutable facts to believe. They too are doomed.

- *The abominable:* This word is most interesting. At its root it means "to stink." It only appears twice in the New Testament, but it means that which is detestable, to God. There is an awfully lot in our present culture that clearly falls into this category. Those who laugh and scorn all that is good, and embrace that which is evil, are an abomination to God. This is closely akin to the experience of Lot living in Sodom, where we read that God; *delivered just Lot, vexed with the filthy conversation of the wicked: For that righteous man dwelling among them, in seeing and hearing, vexed his righteous soul from day to day with their unlawful deeds* (2 Peter 2:7,8). If Lot's sensitivities were offended by those around him, how much more are the sensitivities of God offended constantly by sinners. These are condemned.

- **Murderers:** The word translated "murderers" is the Gr. Φονεύς; phoneus which always means of *criminal intent* [or at least *intentional*] homicide. It is necessary to clarify this because this is what the sixth commandment forbids. When the more general term "kill" is used, all kinds of misconceptions arise. It is the criminal intentional murder of another individual that is condemned by the law, not defensive or accidental killing.

- **Whoremongers:** Our English word implies the sale of sexual services just as the word "fishmonger" would be one who sells fish. Webster defines it as; "practice of unlawful commerce in sex. It is applied to either sex, and to any kind of illicit commerce." Actually the Greek word Gr. Πόρνος; pornos; is broader. The technical definition is to *sell*; a (male or female) *prostitute,* that is a *debauchee* (*libertine*). We often judge the prostitute, but forget those who feed the market and create the trade and the, often violent persons who employ those who are caught up in it. All of that will be judged and nothing of it will enter heaven.

- **Sorcerers:** Webster defines a sorcerer as one who deals with, "Magic; enchantment; witchcraft; divination; the assistance of evil spirits, or the power of commanding evil spirits." That certainly encompasses the general thought, but the actual Greek word translated Sorcery is (Gr.φαρμακεύς; pharmakeus; a *drug*, that is, spell giving *potion*; a *poisoner*, a *magician*: - sorcerer). Because potions and drugs have been used in witchcraft to conjure evil spirits and to prepare the mind for their control, the word is used to describe both drugs and sorcery.

- **Idolaters:** The sense of the word used here very definitely refers to "image worshipers." So what if the "image" is of the Virgin Mary, or Saint Paul, or even an image of Jesus Christ? Image worship is forbidden in the Word of God. Images are a fantasy of reality, and their worship leads to the worship of devils. Consider this exhortation from Paul:

  > *What say I then? that the idol is any thing, or that which is offered in sacrifice to idols is any thing? But I say, that the things which the Gentiles sacrifice, they sacrifice to devils, and not to God: and I would not that ye should have fellowship with devils* (1 Corinthians 10:19, 20).

- **All liars:** Adam Clark comments "Gr. Καὶ πᾶσι τοῖς ψευδέσι· Every one who speaks contrary to the truth when he knows the truth, and even he who speaks the truth with the intention to deceive; i.e., to persuade a person that a thing is different from what it really is, by telling only a part of the truth, or suppressing some circumstance which would have led the hearer to a different end and to the true conclusion."

The final verdict is that all these shall have their "portion" (Gr. τὸ μέρος; their share, what belongs to them, their right {for those who want to insist on "their rights"}), in the lake which burneth with fire and brimstone. This is the second death, and there is no recovery from that verdict.

So, what the passage declares is that those who are given to these things, or whose lives are characterized by these things, will not have any part in the glorious eternal Kingdom of God.

Please note that this passage means to give assurance to the redeemed that these things will be part of the "no mores" in heaven, that is, they will never enter there.

It is not intended to cause fear or apprehension among those who have ever lived this type of life. Having committed one or more of these sinful acts in the past does not bar you from the Holy City.

Consider this: A similar list is found in Paul's letter to the Corinthian Church where we read; *Know ye not that the unrighteous shall not inherit the kingdom of God? Be not deceived: neither fornicators, nor idolaters, nor adulterers, nor effeminate, nor abusers of themselves with mankind, Nor thieves, nor covetous, nor drunkards, nor revilers, nor extortioners, shall inherit the kingdom of God* (1 Corinthians 6:9,10).

Just like the passage in Revelation, this one declares unambiguously that those who practice these things have no place in God's eternal Kingdom. But there is a note of grace in Paul's message.

He writes, *And such were some of you: but ye are washed, but ye are sanctified, but ye are justified in the name of the Lord Jesus, and by the Spirit of our God* (1 Corinthians 6:11).

Though some of the saints once performed these evil deeds, the blood of Christ has washed, and justified them and made them new creatures in Christ (2 Corinthians 5:17). But we are warned that those who continue in these things will be damned.

Rev 21:9 *And there came unto me one of the seven angels which had the seven vials full of the seven last plagues, and talked with me, saying, Come hither, I will shew thee the bride, the Lamb's wife.*

One of the seven angels who had poured out the final bowls of God wrath had shown John the Great Whore that sat upon the Beast. Now an angel from that same group, perhaps the same one, shows him the glory of the Bride, the Lamb's wife.

Rev 21:10 *And he carried me away in the spirit to a great and high mountain, and shewed me that great city, the holy Jerusalem, descending out of heaven from God,*

Recognizing that we are dealing with things eternal, perhaps we should gather all the information about each part of the city together as best we can and then describe it. I have tried to do that in the following pages by gathering the descriptive verses together that seem to describe one feature of the city. Doing that, we will look at:

1. The Overall Appearance of the City

2. The Dimensions of the City and the Walls

3. The Gates of the City

4. The Foundation & The Walls

One thing we know – it is a city, and it is the city looked for and longed for by the people of God through the ages.

> *By faith Abraham, when he was called to go out into a place which he should after receive for an inheritance, obeyed; and he went out, not knowing whither he went. By faith he sojourned in the land of promise, as in a strange country, dwelling in tabernacles with Isaac and Jacob, the heirs with him of the same promise: For he looked for a city which hath foundations, whose builder and maker is God* (Hebrews 11:8-10).

THE OVERALL APPEARANCE OF THE CITY

Rev 21:11 *Having the glory of God: and her light was like unto a stone most precious, even like a jasper stone, clear as crystal;*

Rev 21:18 *and the city was pure gold, like unto clear glass.*

Rev. 21:21 *and the street of the city was pure gold, as it were transparent glass.*

Rev 21:22 *And I saw no temple therein: for the Lord God Almighty and the Lamb are the temple of it.*

Rev 21:23 *And the city had no need of the sun, neither of the moon, to shine in it: for the glory of God did lighten it, and the Lamb is the light thereof.*

Rev 21:24 *And the nations of them which are saved shall walk in the light of it: and the kings of the earth do bring their glory and honor into it.*

Rev 21:26 *And they shall bring the glory and honor of the nations into it.*

Whatever else John is attempting to convey by his description of this city, it seems clear that it appears almost iridescent. The light shines out from within the city through the transparent walls. Two things are immediately evident. First, the glory and light of the city come from within. Second, there is nothing that is hidden, nor is there anything that needs be hidden - there is full transparency there.

There is no temple in the city: *for the Lord God Almighty and the Lamb are the temple of it.* I'm not sure all that means, but during this age, the body of believers is the "temple of God." He resides in us through the Holy Spirit. He is "in us." Are we to assume that in the eternal city, we are in a very specific sense, "in Him?"

Next, John tells us about the source of the light; *the glory of God did lighten it, and the Lamb is the light thereof* (vs.23).

John tells us, in his epistle that the infinite God *is light and in Him is no darkness at all* (1 John 1:5). He further exhorts us to "walk in that light." Apparently, we are literally going to do just that in the New Jerusalem.

Finally, we read that; *the nations of them which are saved shall walk in the light of it: and the kings of the earth do bring their glory and honor into it* (vs.24). This has given some expositors a problem since they have difficulty conceiving the idea of "nations" in the eternal state. Actually, the word translated "nations" is; (Gr. ἔθνος; ethnos; tribe or race). Apparently, God will preserve our various ethnicities in the eternal state.

It is precisely statements like this that have led some to conclude that chapters 21 and 22, of Revelation, go back and actually reveal conditions during the Millennium rather than the eternal state. They ask, "How can there be 'nations' in the eternal state?" "How can they bring the glory of nations into eternity?"

While these are valid questions and while there is no clear answer to them, there are other things here that indicate clearly that we are dealing with the eternal state and not looking back at the Millennium. For instance, verse 22 clearly teaches that there will be no temple in the New Jerusalem. Yet the entire later part of Ezekiel is dedicated to a detailed description of the Millennial Temple. If there is a Millennial Temple and there is no temple in this city, then we are not looking here at Millennial scenes, but eternal ones. We conclude therefore, that whatever the problems are, what Revelation 21, and 22 does is give us a glimpse into the eternal state, not a back-view of the Millennium.

So there will be the distinctions of ethnicity in eternity. There is a certain glory to all that God has created. I recall a former student of mine at Bharat Bible College in India. He was of African descent, and so had a much darker complexion than the Indian students.

He once said, "A bouquet of the same colored flowers is very beautiful, but one of different colors is more beautiful still. Apparently, God prefers a bouquet of many colors." Perhaps that is the answer to verse 24.

THE DIMENSIONS OF THE CITY AND WALLS

Rev 21:15 *And he that talked with me had a golden reed to measure the city, and the gates thereof, and the wall thereof.*

Rev 21:16 *And the city lieth foursquare, and the length is as large as the breadth: and he measured the city with the reed, twelve thousand furlongs. The length and the breadth and the height of it are equal.*

Rev 21:17 *And he measured the wall thereof, an hundred and forty and four cubits, according to the measure of a man, that is, of the angel.*

As has been often pointed out, you don't measure what you don't own. The act of measuring implies first and foremost that this is purchased territory. The Lamb was worthy to take the title deed to the former earth, He is now worthy to hold all authority over the future earth as well.

Have you ever tried to picture what this verse describes? The city is said to be 12,000 furlongs (or stadia) in length and width, which is approximately 1,500 miles. Those figures present no particular difficulty for us, until we read that the city is also 12,000 furlongs or 1,500 miles high. Now we have a dilemma.

The question would then be, are we looking at a cube, a pyramid or perhaps a sphere containing a city of the dimensions indicated here? Dr. Ironside believed it was in the shape of a pyramid. Others see it as a cube. There were a number of items in the Tabernacle that were "four-square." In each instance the shape suggested the perfection of what the object symbolized.

J. Vernon McGee has an interesting suggestion. He believes it is a cube within a sphere. In his commentary on Revelation he actually has a draft of how he conceives the New Jerusalem might look.

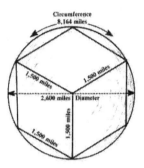

Frankly, I do not think we can come to any conclusion. We are dealing with something that is beyond our present concepts of time and space. All we can do at present is to accept the record God has given us and learn what we can from it.

Finally, we come to the measurement of the walls, that is of the height of the walls.   We are told that they measure 144 cubits in height or about 216 feet. It has been pointed out that the walls of ancient Babylon were 200 feet high. The intention of those was, of course, for protection.

Here, the walls are a bit higher but while they are built of jasper (one of the hardest substances known), they are designed, not for safety, but for beauty.

THE GATES OF THE CITY

Rev 21:12, 13 *and had twelve gates, and at the gates twelve angels, and names written thereon, which are the names of the twelve tribes of the children of Israel: On the east three gates; on the north three gates; on the south three gates; and on the west three gates.*

Rev 21:21 *And the twelve gates were twelve pearls; every several gate was of one pearl:*

Rev 21:25 *And the gates of it shall not be shut at all by day: for there shall be no night there.*

You've never seen gates like these! John sees the gates of the city, which he then tells us, are open continuously. Each gate is a single pearl, and each bears the name of one of the tribes of Israel.

Whatever else this may teach us, it is clear that the distinctions between Israel and the Church carry forward into eternity. The twelve tribes are mentioned by name in the gates of the city, while the twelve Apostles of the Lamb are named in the foundations. The writer to the Hebrews tells us about the heavenly Jerusalem:

> *But ye are come unto mount Sion, and unto the city of the living God, the heavenly Jerusalem, and to an innumerable company of angels, To the general assembly and church of the firstborn, which are written in heaven, and to God the Judge of all, and to the spirits of just men made perfect, And to Jesus the mediator of the new covenant, and to the blood of sprinkling, that speaketh better things than that of Abel (Hebrews 12:22-24).*

Note that in that heavenly Jerusalem are:

1. An innumerable company of holy angels

2. The plenary session of the Church (meaning the entire body)

3. God Himself

4. The spirits of Old Testament saints (apparently this is before the last phase of the First Resurrection).

5. Jesus Christ as mediator of the New Covenant and the blood upon which that covenant rests.

We conclude then, that both Israel and the Church will be present in the New Jerusalem and that each will retain its identity along with the specific identities of the various ethnic groups of redeemed peoples.

THE FOUNDATION AND WALLS OF THE CITY

Rev 21:14 *And the wall of the city had twelve foundations, and in them the names of the twelve apostles of the Lamb.*

Rev 21:18-20 *And the building of the wall of it was of jasper. And the foundations of the wall of the city were garnished with all manner of precious stones. The first foundation was jasper; the second, sapphire; the third, a chalcedony; the fourth, an emerald; The fifth, sardonyx; the sixth, sardius; the seventh, chrysolite; the eighth, beryl; the ninth, a topaz; the tenth, a chrysoprasus; the eleventh, a jacinth; the twelfth, an amethyst.*

The Apostles are always associated with that which is foundational. In Paul's letter to the Ephesian Church he makes this point:

> *Now therefore ye are no more strangers and foreigners, but fellowcitizens with the saints, and of the household of God; And are built upon the foundation of the apostles and prophets, Jesus Christ himself being the chief corner stone; In whom all the building fitly framed together groweth unto an holy temple in the Lord: In whom ye also are builded together for an habitation of God through the Spirit* (Ephesians 2:19 – 22).

Note that the Apostles were foundational for the building of the Church; their names now appear in the foundation of the Holy City.

Therefore, we can be sure that the Church will inhabit this glorious city.

As we come to the listing of the various stones, commentators are in complete disarray as to their appearance. Many have tried to describe each one, but I find no two lists that match. Suffice it to say that the beauty of this city is beyond description and is greater than we can conceive.

In Agra, India, stands the world famous Taj Mahal, one of the seven wonders of the world. Shah Jahan attempted to build an almost heavenly sepulcher when he constructed the Taj Mahal as a final resting place for his favorite wife. He built it of pure white marble and then inserted precious stones into its outer surface to catch the light and refract radiant beams of color.

Sadly, as the ages have passed (the mausoleum was constructed in 1643 AD), thieves have removed many of the lower stones which were then replaced by simply painting the original color of the stone in the place where it had been. In contrast, the stones in the eternal New Jerusalem, will never be stolen and never be marred.

Rev 21:27 *And there shall in no wise enter into it any thing that defileth, neither whatsoever worketh abomination, or maketh a lie: but they which are written in the Lamb's book of life.*

Revelation 21:8, and 21:27 both remind the reader that only redeemed people will inhabit and enjoy what God has provided. In this verse, one more time we are warned that nothing will enter that will ever defile or threaten the perfection of our eternal home. We will see this affirmed again in the next chapter.

That is blessed news. There will never be another rebellion. No angel or man will ever again fall. No one will ever again challenge the absolute sovereignty of God.

Every living thing is now confirmed in righteousness and holiness and all the blessings and the joys of that sin-free condition will exist for all eternity. What a Salvation! What a Savior!

REVIEW:

- Is the New Heaven and the New Earth a completely new creation, or a renovation of the present heaven and earth?

- What is the significance of there being "no more sea?"

- Why does John describe the New Jerusalem as a Bride?

- How many of the "no mores" can you name?

- To whom does the phrase, "him that overcometh," refer?

- Describe as best you can the Holy City, the New Jerusalem.

- What two groups do we know will be in the City and why?

- What does the word "nations" actually mean?

CHAPTER 29 A Final Warning & Invitation

Revelation CHAPTER 22:1 – 21

Rev 22:1, 2 *And he shewed me a pure river of water of life, clear as crystal, proceeding out of the throne of God and of the Lamb. In the midst of the street of it, and on either side of the river, was there the tree of life, which bare twelve manner of fruits, and yielded her fruit every month: and the leaves of the tree were for the healing of the nations.*

The first six verses of this chapter complete the description of the New Jerusalem begun in chapter twenty one. The description begins with a *pure river of water of life, clear as crystal, proceeding out of the throne of God and of the Lamb.* This should not be confused with the river which Ezekiel saw (Ezekiel 47:1-12). In the first place, Ezekiel's vision of the river is Millennial, whereas the vision here concerns the eternal state. There are a number of other differences as well.

Ezekiel's river flowed forth from under the temple and ran eastward. The river increased in depth as it ran, Ezekiel measured it to his ankles, his knees, his loins and finally over his head (*waters to swim in*). There is no indication that the river here in Revelation 22 was such a stream.

There are "many trees" beside Ezekiel's river, here there is only the "tree of Life." Ezekiel's stream runs down into what we know as the Dead Sea and "heals the waters" so that everything lives wherever the river flows. The river here in Revelation flows down the middle of the street of the city. Many other differences could be cited, but these should suffice to demonstrate that we are talking about two entirely different rivers.

Notice that these waters are called, *a pure river of water of life,* and that they flow from *the throne of God and of the Lamb* indicating that God Himself is the source. As John declares in his first epistle, *And this is the record, that God hath given to us eternal life, and this life is in his Son. He that hath the Son hath life; and he that hath not the Son of God hath not life* (1 John 5:11, 12). He is evermore the source of the water of life.

The text tells us that on either side of the river *was the tree of life.* Whether this is to be understood as a single tree which spans the river and under which the river runs, or that "the tree of life" designates the kind of trees which lined the river is uncertain. The picture is not entirely clear, but this we know; the tree that was no longer accessible to Adam and Eve is now the possession of all the redeemed, and all may freely eat of it.

The tree is said to bare twelve *manner* (kind) of fruit. As we have pointed out before, there is much here that is entirely different from anything that we have experienced – and that should help underscore the fact that we are dealing with a heaven and earth that is completely "new" and the laws that govern nature with which we are familiar, are no longer operating.

There is another statement here that should get our attention. This fruit is produced each month and there are twelve months. Apparently we will continue to mark some kind of "time" even in eternity. Perhaps the song writer was completely on the mark when he wrote, *"When we've been there ten thousand years, bright shining as the sun; We've no less days to sing God's praise, than when we'd first begun."*

The leaves of the tree are said to be, *for the healing of the nations.* Once again we are reminded that there will be national or ethnic identity in the eternal city. But the phrase has troubled some. If this is the eternal state, why should anything need "healed?" Perhaps the answer lies in the translation.

The word translated "healing" is Gr. Θεραπεία; therapeia, from which we get our word therapeutic. Greek scholar Wuest suggests that the word is used in the sense of that which maintains health. The thought is not that there is a sickness that must be healed, but rather that there is health that is sustained. Once again these are not verses about the Millennium, regardless of certain nuances we may not fully understand.

Rev 22:3, 4 *And there shall be no more curse: but the throne of God and of the Lamb shall be in it; and his servants shall serve him: And they shall see his face; and his name shall be in their foreheads.*

Revelation constantly takes us back to Genesis and we are made to hear once again those fateful words; *cursed is the ground for thy sake; in sorrow shalt thou eat of it all the days of thy life; Thorns also and thistles shall it bring forth to thee; and thou shalt eat the herb of the field; In the sweat of thy face shalt thou eat bread, till thou return unto the ground; for out of it wast thou taken: for dust thou art, and unto dust shalt thou return* (Genesis 3:17-19).

Now we hear the blessed words, *and there shall be no more curse.* Eden fully restored. Furthermore, the throne of God and of the Lamb are present – they are "in it." No more distance between God and redeemed man. Full and complete fellowship restored – we walk once more with God in the cool of the day. Everything lost in the fall, is completely and abundantly restored. What blessing!

And if that were not enough, we get to see his face. Our faces are made to communicate our feelings more than any other part of the body. If we are sad, our faces show it. If we are happy, we show it in our expression. Love, hate, peace, concern, anger and pleasure are all evident in our faces. What will we see in His face?

Paul anticipates it when he writes; *That in the ages to come he might shew the exceeding riches of his grace in his kindness toward us through Christ Jesus* (Ephesians 2:7).

And then, we are forever identified as His purchased possession. His name is in our forehead.

There are four places in this blessed book where we are told that we shall wear the "seal" that bares His name.

1. *Saying, Hurt not the earth, neither the sea, nor the trees, till we have sealed the servants of our God in their foreheads* (Revelation 7:3). This passage is in relation to the sealing of the 144,000 out of Israel.

2. *And it was commanded them that they should not hurt the grass of the earth, neither any green thing, neither any tree; but only those men which have not the seal of God in their foreheads* (Revelation 9:4). It seems quite evident here that during the Tribulation period, the "seal" of God, which is His mark of ownership, is likely invisible to the eye, but visible to Him and to the angels. Perhaps, that which may not be seen in time, will be evident in eternity.

3. *And I looked, and, lo, a Lamb stood on the mount Zion, and with him an hundred forty and four thousand, having his Father's name written in their foreheads* (Revelation 14:1). Here again the reference is to the 144,000 out of Israel that are His witnesses. As we saw when we studied chapter 14, this scene looks forward to that time when they are gathered, with the Lamb, and stand victoriously in the earthly city of Jerusalem, as they prepare for the full establishment of the Kingdom.

4. Finally, we come to the text before us in which, as has already been noted, it appears that this seal of identification is clearly seen. *And they shall see his face; and his name shall be in their foreheads.*

As believers during this Dispensation, we are sealed by the Holy Spirit, which is God's guarantee that we will be safely delivered to glory. That same guarantee of ownership is given considerable attention in the final testimony of the book of Revelation.

Rev 22:5 *And there shall be no night there; and they need no candle, neither light of the sun; for the Lord God giveth them light: and they shall reign for ever and ever.*

The final description of our eternal condition is found here in verse 5. It is another reminder that darkness is forever past. There will be no night there, neither will we need candle or even the sun, for God Himself, always the source of light and life and blessing, will provide all that we need.

Now, some have pointed out that this verse does not say that there will be no sun, but only that there will be no need of sun. I suspect that if there is no need for it, it will likely not be there.

In any case, we are to understand that God Himself will give all those who are present there light. *This then is the message which we have heard of him, and declare unto you, that God is light, and in him is no darkness at all* (1 John 1:5).

I cannot help but believe that we are not only talking about physical light which can be seen, but that light which enlightens the understanding so that we may know what we could not know at present. After all, this is one of the promises of the Word; *For now we see through a glass, darkly; but then face to face: now I know in part; but then shall I know even as also I am known* (1 Corinthians 13:12).

God has placed within each of us an insatiable desire to know. It is what drives us to search and experiment and study. In eternity we shall share something of the knowledge which belongs to the One who created us in His own image.

And lastly we are told one final time that we will reign with Him. It has always been God's desire to give man authority and dominion. God gave dominion to the First Adam, and he surrendered it to Satan. Now the Last Adam, who has fully recovered it, shares it with those He has redeemed.

All that our reign entails we are not told, but we may be sure that there are glorious things ahead that will excite our imagination, for; *Eye hath not seen, nor ear heard, neither have entered into the heart of man, the things which God hath prepared for them that love him* (1 Corinthians 2:9).

Rev 22:6 *And he said unto me, These sayings are faithful and true: and the Lord God of the holy prophets sent his angel to shew unto his servants the things which must shortly be done.*

Often in this world we are reminded that if something seems "too good to be true," it usually is and we are likely to be disappointed. That will never be the case in eternity. What John has been seeing and hearing has been so far beyond his present experience that he has to be reminded that, *these sayings are faithful and true.*

I am reminded of that passage from the book of Hebrews in that great Hall of Faith, the eleventh chapter. After telling us of many who had forsaken worldly wealth, fame, home and country because they desired an eternal reward, the writer says; *But now they desire a better country, that is, an heavenly: wherefore God is not ashamed to be called their God: for he hath prepared for them a city* (Hebrews 11:16).

Don't miss the thought here. These had all forsaken much in the expectation of something better. Will God disappoint them? Will He have to be ashamed of what they receive? Will they regret the sacrifices made in the world they forsook? Never! God will not be ashamed, He has fully prepared more than they could ever have imagined or expected.

So weary pilgrim, travel on, keep the faith, fight the fight, there is a crown and a throne waiting.

Once again we are reminded that these are God's words. God sent his prophets, not just John, but down through the centuries of time - his prophets, Moses, Job, Isaiah, Ezekiel, and a host of others, so that we His servants should not be in the dark.

Think of how privileged we are. The world agonizes over the future wondering what it holds. We are allowed to see it in advance. *Ye, brethren, are not in darkness, that that day should overtake you as a thief. Ye are all the children of light, and the children of the day: we are not of the night, nor of darkness* (1 Thessalonians 5:4, 5).

Our text tells us that these things will "shortly come to pass." But more than twenty centuries have passed since John wrote these words. Are we to assume they cannot be trusted? No, the word translated "shortly" is (Gr. *En* τάχος; tachos, a *brief* space of time, that is, in *haste:* - quickly, shortly, speedily).

Our problem is that when we read "shortly" we mentally translate "soon." That is not the thought here. The idea is, that when these things happen, they will happen quickly, or speedily. It carries the same sense in the following verse.

Rev 22:7 *Behold, I come quickly: blessed is he that keepeth the sayings of the prophecy of this book.*

This reference to blessing is the sixth beatitude in the book of Revelation, the seventh is in Revelation 22:14. The first blessing, in chapter one verse three, is similar to this one in Revelation 22:7, in that it pronounces blessing on the reader who not only reads, but keeps (obeys) these sayings.

1. Blessed is he that <u>readeth</u>, and they that hear the words of this prophecy, and <u>keep</u> those things which are written therein: for the time is at hand (Revelation1:3).

2. And I heard a voice from heaven saying unto me, Write, Blessed are the dead which die in the Lord from henceforth: Yea, saith the Spirit, that they may rest from their labors; and their works do follow them (Revelation14:13).

3. Behold, I come as a thief. Blessed is he that watcheth, and keepeth his garments, lest he walk naked, and they see his shame (Revelation16:15).

4. And he saith unto me, Write, Blessed are they which are called unto the marriage supper of the Lamb. And he saith unto me, These are the true sayings of God (Revelation19:9).

5. Blessed and holy is he that hath part in the first resurrection: on such the second death hath no power, but they shall be priests of God and of Christ, and shall reign with him a thousand years (Revelation 20:6).

6. Behold, I come quickly: Blessed is he that keepeth the sayings of the prophecy of this book (Revelation 22:7).

7. Blessed are they that do his commandments, that they may have right to the tree of life, and may enter in through the gates into the city (Revelation 22:14).

Rev 22:8, 9 And I John saw these things, and heard them. And when I had heard and seen, I fell down to worship before the feet of the angel which shewed me these things. Then saith he unto me, See thou do it not: for I am thy fellowservant, and of thy brethren the prophets, and of them which keep the sayings of this book: worship God.

This is the second time John has fallen before the angel, overwhelmed by what he has seen and heard. In that state of wonder and amazement, John falls before the angel in an impulse to worship. He was rebuked, but, if we can read these words and they do not move us emotionally as they moved John, perhaps we need to check our spiritual pulse.

As in the former case, the angel restrains John and demands that he – worship God! We may well be thankful that John faulted in these instances in order that we might know how very essential it is that our worship be directed to God alone. If it is unlawful to worship a glorious angel, who is of a higher order than we, dare we direct worship toward earthy and temporal things? These two passages bring us up short to realize the seriousness of faulty worship.

Rev 22:10 *And he saith unto me, Seal not the sayings of the prophecy of this book: for the time is at hand.*

The command to John here is the exact opposite to that given to Daniel. God's command to him was; *But thou, O Daniel, shut up the words, and seal the book, even to the time of the end* (Daniel 12:4).

Now however, in this age, the time is, *at hand*. The prophetic passages of the New Testament declare Christ's coming to be imminent, that is, it can happen at any moment. This entire age therefore is considered *the time of the end*. Not only is the book of Revelation "unsealed," but through the prophecies found in it, a great many of the prophecies of the book of Daniel are made clear. Both prophetic books are open to the spirit-taught earnest believer.

Rev 22:11 *He that is unjust, let him be unjust still: and he which is filthy, let him be filthy still: and he that is righteous, let him be righteous still: and he that is holy, let him be holy still.*

This verse decrees that there is coming a time when there will be no more opportunity for change. It will be too late then to repent – in fact, it will be impossible. God decrees that eternity establish a solid-state condition where nothing changes. There can never be another rebellion or another fall. But neither can their be a transformation of evil to good. The character of every individual will be what it is as he enters the eternal state.

In one sense it takes us back to the first pages of Scripture and to Eden and points out a very important fact. Had God not kept the fallen Adam from the Tree of Life, he would have lived forever, but lived in his sinful state. There could have been no redemption, and no change in the awful, fallen condition of our first father. God in His great grace saved Adam from eternal tragedy by casting him out of the Garden of Eden and hence saving him from partaking of the Tree of Life while still in sin (Genesis 3:22, 23).

Now, as we approach the final words of the Book we see redeemed man invited to partake freely of the Tree of Life. Having been transformed they will live forever in the state of righteousness which God provided in Christ. We read, *Blessed are they that wash their robes, that they may have the right to come to the tree of life, and may enter in by the gates into the city* (Revelation 22:14).

Those who have not been redeemed will now also live forever in the unchanged state; *the fornicators, and the murderers, and the idolaters, and every one that loveth and maketh a lie* (Revelation 22:15).

Not only will they be outside the pale of eternal bliss, but they will be fixed in their character so that nothing will affect change any more. Just as the righteous cannot sin any longer, so the unsaved will be what they are for eternal ages. No wonder someone has referred to hell as, "the madhouse of the universe."

Rev 22:12 *And, behold, I come quickly; and my reward is with me, to give every man according as his work shall be.*

Once again, the word quickly simply means suddenly, but let us not miss the promise; *my reward is with me, to give every man according as his work shall be.*

There will be an accounting and the reward for those who were faithful will be greater than human minds can imagine. Let's remember His promise; *Truly I tell you, whoever gives even a cup of cold water to one of these little ones because he is a disciple will never lose his reward* (Matthew 10:42 ISV).

Rev 22:13 *I am Alpha and Omega, the beginning and the end, the first and the last.*

Five times Christ has declared Himself to be the first and the last. The words Alpha (first letter in the Greek alphabet) and Omega (last letter in the Greek alphabet), carry the poignant message that He is before everything and it is to Him that all history moves and in Him all prophecy is fulfilled.

Rev22:14,15 *Blessed are they that do his commandments, that they may have right to the tree of life, and may enter in through the gates into the city. For without are dogs, and sorcerers, and whoremongers, and murderers, and idolaters, and whosoever loveth and maketh a lie.*

In all translations except the KJV, the verse reads; *How blessed are those who wash their robes so that they may have the right to the tree of life* (ISV).

The Bible Knowledge Commentary comments on this as follows; "In the manuscripts followed by the KJV, the expression "those who wash their robes" is translated "that do His commandments." In this case it seems that "wash their robes" is the preferred reading.

These two verses (vs. 14, 15), set forth a contrast: blessings on those who wash their robes and who do His commandments; yes, the blessing of the tree of life and the eternal city; and curses on those who are excluded. They are again listed here, beginning with the word "dogs."

As used in this context the word never refers to actual animals, but those who stoop lower than animals. Moses makes that abundantly clear in the Law:

There shall be no whore of the daughters of Israel, nor a sodomite of the sons of Israel. Thou shalt not bring the hire of a whore, or the price of a dog, into the house of the LORD thy God for any vow: for even both these are abomination unto the LORD thy God (Deuteronomy 23:17, 18).

Hebrew parallelism makes it quite evident that Moses here refers to a sodomite as a dog. It is in this way that the word is used in several places in Scripture.

Sorcerers are again listed. As usual, the word translated is Gr. *pharmakia* implying that the sorcery is also involved in drugs. Drugs have the power to put one in a transcendental state where the mind can easily be manipulated by demons. It has been a part of witchcraft and occultic practice for centuries.

Rev 22:16 *I Jesus have sent mine angel to testify unto you these things in the churches. I am the root and the offspring of David, and the bright and morning star.*

Verse 16 brings us back to realize that this entire revelation, this book, was given to the churches. It is tragic that the churches make so little use of it. The vision of the future and the hope of eternal blessedness is what strengthens the saints to stand in the hour of trial and temptation. In the days just ahead we will need this assurance more than ever. "The best is yet to come," is not a trivial sentiment, but a glorious fact for the believer.

The declaration, *I am the root and the offspring of David,* is meant to remind us that Christ is "of the seed of David according to the flesh," but is also the One from whom David sprang. He is the root, the Creator, the beginning, the first cause, as well as the first born.

Note, that while the reference to David links Him to Israel, the phrase, *the bright and morning star,* relates Him to the Church. He is that "Star" which arises in the darkest period of the morning as Zechariah tells us in Luke's Gospel; *whereby the dayspring from on high hath visited us, To give light to them that sit in darkness and in the shadow of death, to guide our feet into the way of peace* (Luke 1:78, 79).

Just as He arose once in the dark days of Israel's servitude under Rome, so He will once more arise in the darkest hour the world will ever see.

Rev 22:17 *And the Spirit and the bride say, Come. And let him that heareth say, Come. And let him that is athirst come. And whosoever will, let him take the water of life freely.*

Note, that there is a two-fold source giving this invitation. The Bride, which of course refers to the Church gives it. That is, it is the task of the entire Church on earth to call a lost world to come to Christ.

But the call would be ineffectual if it were not for the Holy Spirit who likewise extends that call to the heart and conscience of everyone who hears it. So the call to salvation comes from the Church (which means it must come from those of whom the Church is composed vis. you and me), and from the Holy Spirit, who convicts and draws the sinner to Christ.

This is the wonderful invitation extended to every generation up to the coming of Christ. Those who recognize their need and realize that Christ is the provider of salvation are exhorted to come while there is yet time before the judgment falls and it is too late.

And anyone who effectually "hears" (i.e., who hears with the heart and responds in faith), may join those others calling "come." And all that sense within themselves that gnawing hunger and burning thirst that the world leaves us with, are invited to come – to come to the only One who can fill the need of an empty heart. And when they come, they will receive the water of life freely.

This ancient truth was heralded by Isaiah centuries ago in the words, *Ho, every one that thirsteth, come ye to the waters, and he that hath no money; come ye, buy, and eat; yea, come, buy wine and milk without money and without price* (Isaiah 55:1). And it is still true today; *the* (free) *gift of God is eternal life through Jesus Christ our Lord* (Roman 6:23).

Rev 22:18 *For I testify unto every man that heareth the words of the prophecy of this book, If any man shall add unto these things, God shall add unto him the plagues that are written in this book:*

What can you add to the Bible? Can you increase its comfort in sickness, sorrow, and death? Can you improve on its sublime descriptions?

Professor Dyson Hague says, "We do not gild gold. We do not put paint on rubies. We cannot brighten diamonds. And no artist can add any final touch to the finished Word of God. It stands as the sun in the sky. This proud age can add nothing to it. If the greatest Bible-lovers of our own or any other time had attempted to improve it, their work would have been a patch, a disfigurement. It has the glory of God."
(***The Wonder of the Book*** **by Dyson Hague.)**

It cannot be improved upon, and since it is perfect adding anything can only mar it. Not only that, but the truth would be disfigured and darkened, and thus God counts it a very serious matter to tamper at all with His truth in the Scriptures.

In addition to this, it should be observed that this warning is not restricted to the book of Revelation alone. Consider the following verses and note that while the first two warnings are from the second book of the Law, the last is from the book of wisdom.

- *Ye shall not add unto the word which I command you, neither shall ye diminish ought from it, that ye may keep the commandments of the LORD your God which I command you* (Deuteronomy 4:2).

- *What thing soever I command you, observe to do it: thou shalt not add thereto, nor diminish from it* (Deuteronomy 12:32).

- *Add thou not unto his words, lest he reprove thee, and thou be found a liar* (Proverbs 30:6).

The penalty for this is to be visited with the plagues written in this book. What a fearful prospect. How careful we must be with the Word of God will be evident in the following verse as well.

Rev 22:19 *And if any man shall take away from the words of the book of this prophecy, God shall take away his part out of the book of life, and out of the holy city, and from the things which are written in this book.*

To show just how far the Bible's completeness goes, I offer the following from that noted Bible scholar, Dr. A.T. Pierson. Dr. Pierson first asks us to consider the following five verses to make his point.

1. Hebrews 12:27 *And this word, <u>Yet once more</u>, signifieth the removing of those things that are shaken, as of things that are made, that those things which cannot be shaken may remain.*

2. Galatians 4:19 *My little children, of whom I travail in birth again until Christ<u> be formed</u> in you.*

3. John 8:58 *Jesus said unto them, Verily, verily, I say unto you, Before Abraham was, <u>I am</u>.*

4. John 10:34 - 36 *Jesus answered them, Is it not written in your law, <u>I said, Ye are gods</u>? If he called them gods, unto whom the word of God came, and the scripture cannot be broken; Say ye of him, whom the Father hath sanctified, and sent into the world, Thou blasphemest; because I said, I am the Son of God?* (See: Psalm 82:1-8)

5. Galatians 3:16 *Now to Abraham and <u>his seed</u> were the promises made. He saith not, And to seeds, as of many; but as of one, And to <u>thy seed</u>, which is Christ.*

"If these passages are examined, it will be seen that: in the first instance the argument turns on one phrase *yet once more;* in the second, on the passive voice rather than on the active voice of the verb; in the third, on the present rather than on the past tense; in the fourth, on the inviolability of a single word; and in the fifth, on the retention of a singular number of a noun rather than the plural. Taking the five passages together, they teach us that to alter or omit a phrase, change the voice or mood or tense, change a single word or even the number of a noun is to break the Scriptures."
(As quoted from WWBI course on Biblical Inspiration)

There is a three-fold penalty for removing, denying or diminishing the "words of this book." Before we look at the penalty itself, note that it is the "words" that are the central subject.

The Bible affirms what is called, verbal, plenary inspiration. What that means is that the <u>words</u> themselves are inspired and that <u>all</u> the words of <u>all</u> the canonical Scriptures are inspired.

Lewis Sperry Chafer, past president of Dallas Theological Seminary, defined inspiration like this: "God so superintended human authors that without destroying their individuality, literary style, or personal interests, His complete and connected thought toward man was recorded."

Therefore, God has attached a most severe penalty for the one who would tamper with His eternal truth. *God shall take away his part out of the book of life, and out of the holy city, and from the things which are written in this book.*

Thus the somber warning is that he shall forever be barred from the blessings and glories set forth here, from the holy city itself, and from having any part in the book of life – serious penalty for tampering with the Word of God! It is a warning this generation needs to hear clearly, when there seems to be a serious lack of reverence toward the Bible.

Finally, the penalty is stated as, *God shall take away his part out of the book of life.* Does this mean God strikes out a name from the book of life that once was there?

Albert Barnes thinks not. As noted previously; "the meaning is not that his name had been written in that book, but that he would take away the part which he might have had, or which he professed to have in that book.

Such corruption of the divine oracles would show that they had no true religion, and would be excluded from heaven" (Albert Barnes; Notes on the Scriptures).

Rev 22:20 *He which testifieth these things saith, Surely I come quickly. Amen. Even so, come, Lord Jesus.*

How seriously should these words be taken? Jesus Christ Himself is the Testamentary – He has given His testimony. That should settle the matter forever.

John rested what he said on the testimony of God. Remember his words in the last chapter of his first epistle.

> *If we receive the witness of men, the witness of God is greater: for this is the witness of God which he hath testified of his Son. He that believeth on the Son of God hath the witness in himself: he that believeth not God hath made him a liar; because he believeth not the record that God gave of his Son. And this is the record, that God hath given to us eternal life, and this life is in his Son. He that hath the Son hath life; and he that hath not the Son of God hath not life* (1 John 5:9-12).

Furthermore, not only is His testimony inviolable, but He Himself is coming and his coming will be sudden and soon. To that promise John cries with greatest enthusiasm, "*even so come, Lord Jesus.*" And we should be ready to echo that prayer and answer with another hardy, "AMEN!"

Rev 22:21 *The grace of our Lord Jesus Christ be with you all. Amen.*

Finally, we are reminded that it is all of Grace. From beginning to end we have deserved nothing but Divine wrath and judgment.

But God, who is rich in mercy, for his great love wherewith he loved us, Even when we were dead in sins, hath quickened us together with Christ, (by grace ye are saved;) And hath raised us up together, and made us sit together in heavenly places in Christ Jesus: That in the ages to come he might shew the exceeding riches of his grace in his kindness toward us through Christ Jesus (Ephesians 2:4-7).

"Marvelous Grace of our loving LORD,
Grace that exceeds our sin and our guilt.
Yonder, on Calvary's mount outpoured,
There, where the blood of the Lamb was spilt.
Grace, Grace, God's Grace,
Grace that will pardon and cleanse within.
Grace, Grace, God's Grace,
Grace that is greater than all our sin."
Julia H. Johnston (1911)

BIBLIOGRPHY

Barnes, Albert, *Albert Barnes Notes on the Bible*, Public Domain, 1885.

Carroll, J. M., Trail of Blood, The Bible Nation Society, 1931, republished 2017

Clark, Adam, *Adam Clarks Commentary on the Bible*; Public Domain, 1826.

Darby, John; *John Darby's Synopsis of the Bible*, Public Domain, 1862.

Gaebelein, Arno C. *The Revelation*. Neptune, New Jersey: Loizeaux Brothers, 1915.

Henry, Matthew, *Matthew Henry's Commentary on the Whole Bible*, Public Domain, 1714.

Hislop, Alexander, The Two Babylons, A & C BLACK LTD. 1916, republished Loizeaux Brothers, Neptune, New Jersey, 1943

Hunt, David, The Woman Rides the Beast, Harvest house Publishers, 1994.

Inter-Varsity Press Bible Background Commentary, IVPBBC, 2000.

Ironside, H. A. *Lectures on the Book of Revelation*. Neptune, New Jersey: Loizeaux Brothers, 1960.

Jamieson – Faucett and Brown; *Jamieson – Faucett and Brown Commentary*, Public Domain, 1871.

Keil & Delitzsch; *Keil & Delitzsch Commentary on the Old Testament*; Public Domain, 1891

McGee, J. Vernon. *Reveling Through Revelation*. 2 vols. Pasadena, California: Thru the Bible Books, 1962.

Morris, Henry M. *The Revelation Record*, Tyndale House, 1983.

Newell, William R. *The Book of Revelation*. Chicago, Illinois: Moody Press, 1935.

Ryrie, Charles C. *Revelation*. Chicago, Illinois: Moody Press, 1968.

Seiss, J. A. *The Apocalypse, Lectures on the Book of Revelation*. Grand Rapids, Michigan: Zondervan Publishing House, 1957.

Strauss, Lehman. *The Book of Revelation*. Neptune, New Jersey: Loizeaux Brothers, 1964.

Tenney, Merrill C.; Interpreting Revelation, Wm. B. Eerdmans Publishing Co. 1980.

Walvoord, John F. *The Revelation of Jesus Christ*. Chicago, Illinois: Moody Press, 1966. (Excellent comprehensive treatment.)

Walvoord, John F. and Zuck, Roy B., *The Bible Knowledge Commentary*, Cook Communication Ministries, 2004.

Williams, Gene M. *From Now To Eternity*, Gene Williams Evangelistic Assoc. 2004.

Wuest, Kennth S., *Wuest's Word Studies*, Wm. B. Eerdmans Publishing Co. 1955

ABOUT THE AUTHOR:

Born in Altoona, Pennsylvania, Dr. Shade completed studies at Philadelphia Bible Institute and Wheaton College. He began serving in faith missionary work in 1956 with **Scripture Memory Mountain Mission** in Southeastern Kentucky, where he regularly ministered to 10,000 teenagers in seven counties through the high school ministry. During the same time, he became pastor of McRoberts Missionary Baptist Church where he served for eight years.

In 1964, Dr. Shade moved to York, Pennsylvania, where he founded and directed the **Grace and Truth Evangelistic Association** which was active in radio and television ministry, evangelistic campaigns, and camp/conference ministries. He was the founder and director of **Teen Encounter**, **Camp of the Nations** and **Wayside Maternity Home** for unwed mothers. He also directed the project of preparing curriculum for **World-Wide Bible Institutes**, which organizes Bible institutes in local churches and mission stations around the world. During this time he received his Doctorate, from Toledo Bible College & Seminary.

Dr Shade has served for over twenty years with **Source of Light Ministries International**, eight years as General Director. He now serves as Director Emeritus and Minister-at-Large. The Shades continue actively serving with SLM in Bible teaching, evangelism and conference ministry both in this country and abroad.

BOOKS BY THE SAME AUTHOR

* * * * *

Amazed by Grace, the book that tells of God's marvelous faithfulness and miraculous acts in the life and ministry of Dr. Bill & Ruby Shade, is available now.

The Prophetic Destiny of Israel & The Islamic Nations could hardly be more timely. How is the present conflict going to end? This book finds the biblical answers to that question and more.

Dispensationalism in a Post-Modern World challenges the Post-Modern belief that History has no metanarrative. This book lays out God's plan worked out through the Ages and presents a bright hope for tomorrow.

Suicide Unmasked: behind every suicide spiritual Powers are at work. When recognized and confronted they can be overcome.

Dispensational Chart:

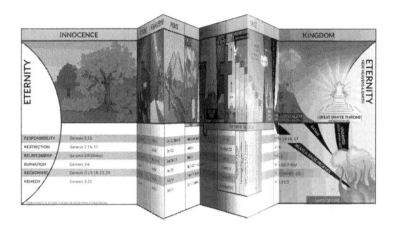

This beautifully illustrated, full-color Dispensational Chart makes an excellent reference or study aid to accompany the book *Dispensationalism in a Post-Modern World*. The Dispensational Chart is available in several formats that will make a valuable addition to any study library.

Order any of these materials at:
BillShade.org

Made in the USA
Middletown, DE
18 August 2019